15,00

D0564154

Communist
China's Agriculture

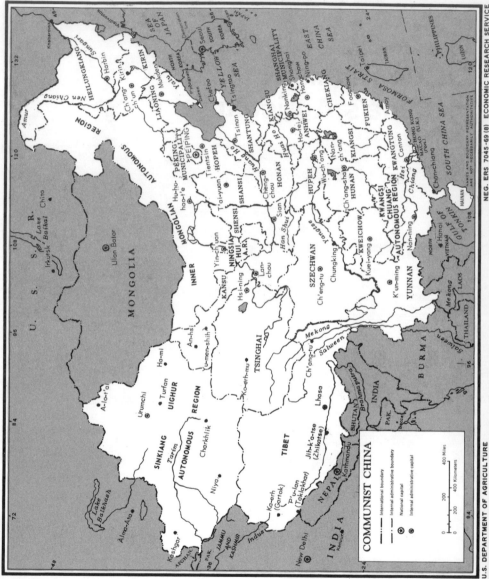

COMMUNIST CHINA

—·—·— International boundary
——— Internal administrative boundary
⊗ National capital
⊙ Internal administrative capital

0   200   400 Miles
0 200 400 Kilometers

NAMES AND BOUNDARY REPRESENTATION
ARE NOT NECESSARILY AUTHORITATIVE

NEG. ERS 7045-69 (8) ECONOMIC RESEARCH SERVICE

U.S. DEPARTMENT OF AGRICULTURE

PRAEGER SPECIAL STUDIES IN
INTERNATIONAL ECONOMICS AND DEVELOPMENT

Communist China's Agriculture

ITS DEVELOPMENT AND FUTURE POTENTIAL

Owen L. Dawson

PRAEGER PUBLISHERS
New York • Washington • London

The purpose of Praeger Special Studies is to make specialized research in U.S. and international economics and politics available to the academic, business, and government communities. For further information, write to the Special Projects Division, Praeger Publishers, Inc., 111 Fourth Avenue, New York, N.Y. 10003.

PRAEGER PUBLISHERS
111 Fourth Avenue, New York, N.Y. 10003, U.S.A.
5, Cromwell Place, London S.W.7, England

Published in the United States of America in 1970
by Praeger Publishers, Inc.

Library of Congress Catalog Card Number: 77-94249

Printed in the United States of America

PREFACE

Agriculture is recognized as the core of Communist China's economy and therefore its ups and downs measure the pulse of the country's welfare. Technical developments in that sector are prerequisite to Communist China's basic strength and her posture as a threat to the Free World.

This study brings together newly researched data on basic agricultural resources and agricultural trends. Several books and papers have appraised these developments in varied extent and scope in the last twenty years. Recent examples include Food and Agriculture in Communist China by J. L. Buck, O. L. Dawson, and Yuan-li Wu and works by Liu Jeh-hsing and Yeh Kung-chia, Walter Galenson, Dwight Perkins, and others.

But at this important stage in Communist China's plans and policy, it seems timely to appraise developments broader in scope and depth, in order to measure better China's strengths in the next decade.

This particular study has gone further than previous studies in using available provincial data, which, though scattered, have been very helpful in presenting a fuller picture of the national economy. With its deep analysis of productive factors, the study provides a firmer base of estimating production requirements and making projections. Besides providing a better factual and analytical base for estimating potential supply for home consumption and exports, it is also a vital tool in the analysis of political prospects as a most important element in the assessment of the degree to which the personal needs of the Chinese people can be realized.

Communist China has not presented consistent national figures on food grain production since 1957, but a vast amount of information has been available provincially and for the country as a whole, which we have collated and evaluated.

As U.S. Agricultural Attaché to China for seventeen years, the author was charged with reporting on current agricultural developments affecting trade and internal economy. Since leaving China in 1949, he has made several studies on developments there and has kept up tables of estimates on annual food grain and cotton crop production that comprise some 85 per cent of the total crop production. He is presently consultant to the Economic Research Service of the U.S. Department of Agriculture.

This study follows up a study begun in 1966 by the Strategic Studies Center of Stanford University for the Department of State, Office of External Affairs. The help of Mr. Frank Hoeber of Stanford Research Institute in initiating the study in 1966 is much appreciated, as is the support given the project by the Department of State. From the response to the present study, there is no doubt that it will serve a useful purpose.

I am greatly indebted to my associate in the study, Mr. C. L. Tung, former Vice Minister of Economics in prewar Nationalist China. The usefulness of this study is due in large part to the indefatigable research of Mr. Tung in Chinese sources that have not before been extensively cited.

The study was prepared in consultation with Mr. Edwin Jones of the Bureau of Intelligence and Research, Department of State, whose substantive suggestions were very helpful. Mr. E. Raymond Platig, Director of the Office of External Research, has encouraged the publication of this study, which is based on a report of the same title prepared by the author with the support of the Department of State. It is understood that the author is solely responsible for its contents, including the accuracy of statements of fact and interpretative comments.

Others taking part in the study were the staff of Asia Science Research Associates, Palo Alto, California. They prepared the section on special crops, which is attracting much interest. Daniel and Lois Tretiak of the University Research Center, Kowloon, Hong Kong, made an extensive survey of livestock developments.

I am especially indebted to Miss Roberta Armbrister, who gave generously of her able services in editing and shaping the report.

Besides those working closely on the project, I am indebted to Mr. Tung Yueh of the Hong Kong Consulate General and the different agricultural officers who in the last twenty years have provided comments and special information. (However, their food grain crop estimates are much lower than mine.)

On my two trips to the Far East in 1966 and 1968, I had useful conferences with Prof. Shigaru Ishikawa at the Institute of Asian Affairs, Tokyo, and in Taiwan with Dr. C. T. Wu, Institute of East Asian Affairs. J.C.R.R. (Joint Commission on Rural Reconstruction) officials, especially Dr. T. H. Shen, director, were most helpful. Numerous contacts in Hong Kong included the Union Research Institute and University Service Center.

The advice and encouragement of Dr. J. Lossing Buck and Dr. Y. L. Wu in the preliminary work has been most helpful. Contacts in Washington with Dr. John S. Aird of the Foreign Manpower Section of the Bureau of Census have helped my approach to the study of population and food. The Office of Area Research in the U.S. Department of Agriculture promoted the study from its outset and helped me to prepare the first-draft proposal.

Because of the vast amount of information that had to be sifted and appraised, some technical errors have occurred. We have tried to correct these, so far as they have been brought to our attention.

The study is incomplete and should be carried further as circumstances permit. Much information on provincial conditions has been collected, and should be tied together in a projected study of the strategic importance of agriculture in its potential economic constraints upon China's freedom of action.

CONTENTS

Chapter   Page

LIST OF TABLES AND CHART

CHINESE MEASUREMENTS

For the convenience of the reader, some of the Chinese measurements commonly used in Mainland China follow below:

1 ounce	=	1/10 catty
1 catty	=	1/2 kilogram
1 picul	=	100 catties or 50 kilograms
1 mow	=	1/15 hectare

Communist
China's Agriculture

CHAPTER **1** INTRODUCTION

The importance of agriculture to Communist
China's economy hardly needs restatement. Some
80 per cent of China's population is engaged in
agriculture, and low farm-labor productivity limits
China to a meager standard of living. Major changes
in agriculture are an essential prerequisite if
China is to succeed in economic development and in
modernizing its society.

In the coming decades China must greatly increase gross farm output to provide for increasingly
high living standards and for the inevitable sharp
population growth that ensues from a doubling of
life expectancies, even if this growth can be somewhat modified by an early adoption of fertility controls.

China must also secure a significant increase
in farm-labor productivity so that a larger share
of its population can be employed off farms to support an expanding industry and commerce. If Chinese
agriculture cannot meet these twin requirements, one
quarter of the world's population will be condemned
to recurring hardships and political instability,
with serious implications for peace in Asia and the
world.

The problem is not a new one. While the land
and population records of the past three centuries
do not have high reliability, the broad trend they
show is undoubtedly valid. China's population

1

increased roughly eightfold, from about 70 million
in 1650 to 583 million in 1953. In the same period,
cultivated land expanded two to three times with
the opening of new lands in the northeast and southwest, the drainage of swamps, the terracing of hill-
sides, and the extension of irrigation.

Per capita cultivated land fell from over .5
hectares to under .2 hectares, implying a marked increase in the intensity of cropping. The farmer undoubtedly became harder-working over this period,
spending an increasing number of labor days per year
in agriculture with the spread of multiple cropping
and the necessity of maintaining the extensive land
modifications that expanded the number and productivity of his cultivated areas.

From 1850 to 1953, this process of growth
slowed sharply. Political and social upheavals and
rural ills multiplied, and population growth declined markedly. China appeared to be running out
of land that could be newly brought into cultivation.
Its crop yields and intensity of cropping and the
diligence of its farmers were unrivaled in other
premodern rural societies and seemed susceptible to
little further improvement. Dr. J. L. Buck, analyzing the land resources and farm practices in the
mid-1930s, estimated the maximum potential increase
in Chinese farm output at one quarter, with only
marginal possibilities envisaged for increasing
cultivated land or the intensity and efficiency of
farm labor.

Subsequent development of farm technology, particularly the experience of Japan in raising farm
productivity, suggests a considerably greater potential for raising China's farm output. The adoption
of this technology, however, will require considerable change in China's rural society--including the
rise of institutions to develop, test, and dissemi-
nate the new technology, the provision of such industrial inputs as fertilizer and mechanical power,
and the improvement of transport and marketing facilities to link the rural and urban areas.

Significant agricultural research and development began in China in the 1930s and, although interrupted by warfare, were renewed after 1949 by the Chinese Communists. However, a scarcity of funds, technical personnel, and industrial inputs limited the impact on agriculture until the 1960s. Nevertheless, in recent years successful implementation and coordination of various programs appear to have been achieved and to have begun to secure a steady growth in farm output.

This book reviews recent changes and the current situation of China's farm resources and farm practices. It attempts to ascertain the basis for the present level and growth in farm output, and to project over the next decade the requirements and prospects for sustaining a satisfactory growth in farm output.

THE SETTING

Combined influences of geography and history developed in China a unique pattern of agricultural economy in which the unchecked growth of population was constantly pressing upon a limited area of arable land. Continuous interaction of these two factors in the past created the well-known "war cycles" in Chinese history, each with its damaging effects upon the whole social structure. The cumulative results through long ages of convulsion inevitably led to the following steps:

1. Gradual disintegration of the rural economy, as manifested in farm fragmentation, capital scarcity, increase of tenancy and rural indebtedness, high rate of interest and low standard of living, etc.

2. Gradual deterioration of agricultural resources, as manifested in soil erosion, deforestation, crop degeneration, and negligence in water conservation and land utilization.

3. Gradual degradation of rural livelihood with its final drop to a subsistence level, as symbolized by the following special features in China's farm structure around the 1930s:

a. Microbic farm structure (a median-size farm covers 3.31 acres of cultivated area, compared with India's five acres or Egypt's 6.3 acres).

b. Fragmentary crop fields (there were generally six or more parcels to a farm, all scattered, about 1/3 to 1-1/2 miles from the farmstead).

c. Labor intensive in operation (a median-size farm was usually operated by two units of man-equivalent and less than one unit of animal power, one third of the farms having no labor animals).

d. Absence of livestock industry (with the exception of scavenging hogs and poultry, a farm ordinarily could not afford more than one unit of labor animals. It takes seven acres of grazing land to support a horse and ten acres to support a steer, while the same areas, if planted with grain and potatoes, could respectively support two or three families, together with their domestic animals, and also supply by-products for other uses).

The "subsistence" nature of China's rural economy is generally recognized, and most farm studies in the prewar period listed similar conclusions about the precarious situation. From his comprehensive study on China's rural standards of living, Dr. D. K. Lieu suggested that "over three mow of crop land per capita, or two acres for a family of five, is absolutely necessary to meet the requirements of food alone." If this area is augmented with one acre for nonfood uses, a total of 3.25 acres would closely approximate D. J. L. Buck's median farm of 3.31 acres as a national average. This is far from Prof. Raymond East's minimum requirement of ten acres for a Western family, or from Dr. Josiah Stamp's one acre per capita for the British middle-class household.

Fundamental measures to promote general agriculture in China received little support from the Chinese Government prior to 1928. As soon as the Nationalist Government had organized, it began moderately to plan for rural reconstruction.

The general conditions of rural progress in China and application of remedies available were recognized by the National Congress on Agricultural Economics held in December, 1929. A Ministry of Agriculture and Mines was formed in January, 1930, and a comprehensive program was laid out during the year in agreement with the ministries of Communications, Railways and Education and the National Reconstruction Commission.

Significant progress was made in certain lines, especially in the improvement of cotton and wheat, the expansion of experiment stations, granaries, and cooperatives, and the building of dikes for flood prevention and canals for irrigation. Statistical surveys relating to agricultural production as well as agricultural education and research were pushed. Exorbitant rates of credit were reduced.

There were two other very important developments: Dr. J. L. Buck supervised a survey of land utilization in China that presented the historical development and future potential of agricultural resources, and the University of Nanking organized a modern College of Agriculture, stressing crop improvement, particularly for cotton.

By 1936 the largest agricultural yield in recent years was achieved. This was promoted by political stability and general measures to improve agriculture. When it is considered that only a start had been made in many lines of agricultural improvement, results were very encouraging. This was especially true of technical improvement, compared with a frontal attack on the basic problems of land tenure, debt, and taxes.

Although much of this progress was notable, the Nationalist Government really contributed only

a minute part of its budget to agricultural improvement (something less than 1 per cent). The Agricultural Attaché from the United States had close
contact with the Ministers of Agriculture from 1931
to 1949. During the prewar period, more than ten
ministers served in this post. These officers included admirals, generals, educators, youth leaders,
and others, some well-meaning, but all having only
a pittance with which to work.

After the survey of the Sino-American Agricultural Mission, more attention was directed toward
the basic problems of agriculture, but it came too
late to build appreciable resistance against Communist incursion.

The years between 1937 and 1949 were violently
convulsive. After eight years of war with Japan
and three years of civil strife, it is hardly surprising to find the nation's economy in very bad
shape. It was estimated on the eve of the Communist
takeover that about 9 million people had been lost
and 15 per cent to 20 per cent of crop land had been
devastated. Food grain production had dropped
25 per cent from the prewar level; cotton had dropped
by 48 per cent; other industrial crops suffered yet
heavier losses.

Thus the Communists did not inherit a bountiful estate ready for easy exploitation, but a war-
torn, impoverished land economy that needed careful nursing and substantial replenishment in both
human and material resources. The Peking regime
has never stopped boasting about the "quick recovery" in the early years under its rule, and a
"steady progress" from 1953 onward. But this is
not true, if "recovery" and "progress" are measured
by per capita food supply as calculated from their
official or semiofficial statistical reports.

PREWAR AGRICULTURAL PROBLEMS: WORK OF THE
UNITED STATES AGRICULTURAL MISSION

The fundamental rural problems of China, long
recognized in prewar China, were due to many natural
and inherited causes.   The following causes are frequently mentioned:

1.   Density of population in relation to soil
resources depleted by cropping and erosion.

2.   Periodic floods and droughts.

3.   Poor communications.

4.   Uneconomic systems of land tenure.

5.   High cost of credit facilities.

6.   Inequitable taxes.

7.   Lack of improved varieties of plants and
breeds of stock.

8.   Ravages of plant and animal pests.

9.   Lack of sufficient implements and fertilizer.

10.   Unsystematic state and local administrations and exactions of middlemen.

11.   Poor health and education facilities.

The Nationalist Government, following its inception in 1927, took moderate steps to improve
these conditions.   It made many surveys and consult-
ed foreign specialists.   During the Sino-Japanese
War such measures were much disrupted, and efforts
were necessarily concentrated on emergency problems.

China had made some notable progress on her
agricultural problems from 1931 to 1937.   But with

the outbreak of hostilities with Japan in 1937,
some accomplishments already realized were lost.
Production of crops and trade were seriously affected; recovery had only partly been made by 1948,
with notable help by the United Nations Rehabilita-
tion Section.

To review the whole situation, a joint China-
United States Agricultural Mission was set up, composed of eminent specialists from both countries.
It traveled some weeks through important regions of
China to survey production firsthand, and reported
on the problems and methods of dealing with them.
This guide, showing also demographical relationships, was valuable to the Ministry of Agriculture
and international agencies dealing with China.

The Ministry of Agriculture activated comprehensive measures to implement the recommendations
of the mission. It held a conference for reviewing
progress in twenty-four subjects, and filed a résumé of the papers. The projects of the Ministry
based on this conference were approved by the Exec-
utive Yuan, but had barely got underway when the
Communists took over. It is therefore clear that
while the Communist regime inherited manifold problems in agriculture, it profited from examination
of the basic problems by eminent specialists with
concrete recommendations for their gradual solution.

CHAPTER **2** CROP DEVELOPMENT

IN PREWAR CHINA

FOOD SUPPLY AND REQUIREMENTS
IN PREWAR CHINA

Since food requirements are the greatest demand on agricultural production, it is important to
estimate a prewar figure as a basis for computing
requirements under the Communist regime.

Different sets of data are available, based on
production per capita and food consumption surveys.

Using National Agricultural Research Bureau
(NARB) 1931-37 averages as representing a typical stable period, the following calculation presents itself:

Average of 170 million metric tons corrected
for nonreported land is used as explained by Food
and Agriculture in Communist China.[1]

An average prewar population figure of 530 million is used. The writer based this calculation on
assumed population increases by period, figuring
backward from the 1953 census of 583 million. Many
students of China's developments think the figure
is possibly high, if the 1953 census figure is ac-
cepted.

Using the figure of 170 million metric tons
and 530 million population, the following obtains:

Calculation 1.   170 M MT ÷ 530 M = 321 kg. gross
                 X .653 = 210 kg. for food use = 574
                 gr. daily = 1,980 calories ÷ 86 for
                 all food = 2,290 calories

The food balance sheet given by Shen[2] is .653.

A special NARB survey, "Amount of Staple
Foods Consumed Annually Per Capita in Rural Areas,"[3]
gives the following:

Calculation 2.*
    Food Gr.** & potatoes ÷ 4) = 298.5 kg. gross p.c.
    ÷ 108 for average year   = 276.4 kg.[4]
    X .80 food net   = 221.1 kg.***
    ÷ 365 days   = 606 gr. daily
    X 345 calories per
          100 grams   = 2,091 calories
    ÷ .86 other sources   = 2,431 calories

Even with the correction for an average year,
it is some 10 per cent higher than that calculated
from production per capita shown above.

If a deduction is not made for the average year,
it gives 2,625 calories per capita, or 14.5 per cent
above that calculated from revised production.

But if the assumed 1931-37 population is taken
as only 500 million, the result would be 2,438
calories per capita based on an average production
of 170 million metric tons, or about the same as
shown in Calculation 2.

----

    *1936 is assumed to be 108 per cent of the
average.

    **Respective abbreviations: grain, kilogram,
and per capita.

    ***Ratio of food use (excluding feed, seed, and
waste) to food net (i.e., after processing).

Calculation 3. From the land utilization nutrition survey in <u>Land Utilization in China</u>, p. 407,
Table 4, the following are obtained: For 17,351
families, grain and potatoes consumption per capita
equals 2,379 calories, or 2,730 all food equivalent.

H. L. Hu's study of working families of Shanghai
including information on waterworks, power companies,
and police showed an average food consumption of
2,280 calories per adult male unit,* or approximately 2,000 per capita.

Sydney Gamble's study, <u>How Families Live in
Peiping</u>,[5] shows consumption of grain and flour and
potatoes at 200 kilograms per capita, or about
2,200 calories per capita, which compares closely
with the Shanghai study. Mrs. William Drummond's
surveys of food consumption in certain North China
institutions made by the Rockefeller Institute also
indicate a per capita daily intake of about 2,200
calories.

A review of all the above suggests a possible
average daily caloric availability of 2,300 to
2,400 per capita, assuming urban consumption is
somewhat less than rural by the few surveys available.

Food Adequacy

Although over-all average caloric availability
in prewar China seems to have been nearly sufficient,
it varied greatly between extremes. During periods
of poor crops in certain provinces, severe under-
nutrition and even famine conditions prevailed,
while overconsumption prevailed in other areas.

It is also noted that carbohydrates from vegetable sources are less digestible than carbohydrates
from processed grain. Buck[6] states that in all

---

*Adult male unit x .83 = average per capita.

eight agricultural areas where the average intake of
calories is above standard, there are localities of
inadequate supply. Since these averages reflect the
food consumption in farms of every size and degree
of prosperity, the proportion of the rural population that has not enough to eat may still be considerable and, indeed, in some cases is very high.

The Chinese farmer is so close to the poverty
line that he reflects a poor harvest immediately by
eating less, and a good harvest by eating more.
Thus the land utilization survey found that 29 of
the 136 localities had insufficient food, while almost a fourth of the localities consumed an average
of 5,000 calories. While the figures are extreme
for a given locality, they give a picture that is
believed to be substantially correct for the area
as a whole, because in any year, unusual situations
must be expected in some localities.

It is therefore evident that in the pre-
Communist era, there was often widespread caloric
deficiency.

Not only was the diet often deficient in quantity but also in nutritional balance. Shen summarized the components.

Protein: Dietary surveys indicate that the
amount of protein usually taken by the adult in
China is probably adequate. The average daily intake is somewhere between 60 and 90 grams. Based
on the weight of the average Chinese as 55 kilograms,
this intake is more than sufficient to meet the
Western standard of 1 gram per kilogram of weight.
However, more than 92 per cent of the protein was
derived from vegetable sources, and in general,
such proteins are less digestible and have a low
biological value.

It is evident that the protein factor may be
critical for children, whose requirements for protein per unit of bodily weight are two or three
times that of the adult, while their ability to

consume and digest rough foods is especially limited.

Fat: The intake is very low. Fats provide
less than 10 per cent of the caloric intake in the
Chinese diet for optimum nutrition.   In Western
countries, an intake of 25 per cent calories is generally considered desirable.

Minerals: In the land utilization study[7] it
was found that calcium intakes were markedly low,
the average being a little more than one half the
standard of 0.8 gram for an adult weighing 70 kilograms.   Only 1 of the 136 localities had an intake
above the standard, while 5 localities had an intake below 0.2 gram.   Again the problem is most
critical with children, whose need per unit of bodily
weight is much higher than adults'.   The same is true
for pregnant or nursing women.

The reason for the calcium deficiency is clear
from the nature of the diet, as grains which make
up such a large proportion of the caloric intake are
low in this element.   Leafy vegetables, certain
roots, and to a lesser degree some fruits are high
in calcium content but make up a very small part of
the diet.

Phosphorus: The intake ranged from one to
three grains per capita per day.   In the land utilization survey the intakes were above the standard
in all but 7 of the 136 localities.   The diet,
based largely on seeds, is rich in phosphorus.

However, this ample supply of phosphorus is of
little value in view of the severe calcium deficiency.   These two elements are interdependent in
their metabolism, notably in bone formation, and
one is of little value without the other.

It is generally held that the best utilization
of these two elements occurs when they appear at
the ratio of 1:1 to 5:1.   The calcium-phosphorus
ratios in all areas are clearly unfavorable for the
best assimilation.   They range from 0.44:1 to 0.11:1

for 136 localities. Seeds that are primarily rich
in phosphorus must be supplemented by foods primarily rich in calcium, of which leafy vegetables best
meet the purpose.

Iron: The land utilization survey showed that
iron intake was above standard for every area of the
region and for the country as a whole, and there was
a marked surplus.[8] Yet in twenty-seven localities,
or approximately one fifth of the whole, the diet
did not contain enough foods rich in iron despite
the satisfactory situation shown by regional and
countryside averages. These localities were in the
rice region, and rice contains much less iron than
most other grains.

Vitamins: It is difficult to determine the
adequacy of vitamins, except in very general terms,
in the absence of chemical tests. Several foods
making up an important part of the diet have not
been analyzed, and neither has the effect of milling, preservation, and cooking processes. Buck's
tables show that only one third of the consumption
is drawn from good vitamins, and another quarter
from sources having an appreciable amount of vitamins. This is inadequate, yet not seriously deficient. While it was deemed unsafe to conclude that
this represented an adequate intake for the country
as a whole, there was no serious deficiency. Intakes in the rice region were markedly lower than
those in the wheat region, where they were twice as
high as the former.

The data showed that there were some situations
where the intake of vitamin A was low. It showed
many localities where a more liberal intake would
seem desirable for the healthy growth of children.

Vitamin B: Vitamins of the B group such as
thiamine, riboflavin, and niacin presented no serious problem in North China nor in most of the rural
sections of South China, since generally lightly
milled cereals are consumed. In the big cities
where polished rice was consumed, beriberi was

known to be prevalent and was often severe and occurred in epidemic form. Pellagra was reported in
various parts of the country. Vitamin G seems less
prevalent than Vitamin B.

Vitamin C: Deficient in many areas, provision
for a larger supply, distributed throughout the year,
is imperative.

Vitamin D: Of all the data shown in the survey,[9] Vitamin D makes the poorest showing. It was
clear according to the analysis that for all areas,
the diet was inadequate in this factor, particularly in terms of intake commonly specified for the
growing child.

While there were reports showing considerable
occurrence of rickets, attention was called to the
evidence of faulty calcium and phosphorus metabolism
in which Vitamin D in the diet is desirable.

Osteomalacia, a disease attributed to Vitamin D
deficiency as well as to faulty calcium and phosphorus metabolism, was a relatively common disease
in prewar China. In certain parts of Shansi,
Shensi, Kansu, and Manchuria, its incidence was estimated to be 1 to 5 per cent in all women over the
age of puberty. Other vitamin deficiency diseases,
such as scurvy and nutritional edema, were by no
means rare. It is possible that many of the deficiency diseases occurred in mild forms that did not
come to the attention of the clinician, but were
sufficient to undermine the general health and efficiency of the people.

Cotton

Cotton is China's most important nonfood crop.
Together with food grain it comprises 85 per cent
of the planted area. It provides some 90 per cent
of the nation's fabric requirement and is a major
source of foreign exchange.

For centuries, China has been producing cotton,

for which it is well adapted by soil and climate.
A Chinese classic, written about 2205 B.C., mentions
cotton in the manufacture of clothes, and as a trib-
ute paid to the rulers of the Middle Kingdom. By
the latter half of the eighteenth century, China
was exporting cotton piece goods to Europe and
America, according to records of shipping companies.
However, as early as 1800, imports may have already
begun offsetting exports. Estimates by the United
States Department of Agriculture indicate China
then must have been producing around 1.5 million
bales of cotton.

     According to estimates drawn from the National
Agricultural Research Bureau, adjusted for incomplete coverage, cotton output increased in 1931-37
as follows:

Acres (in millions)	Yield (lbs. acre)	Production (1,000 bales of 480 lb.)
9,348	191	4,322

Beginning with 1932, production expanded to reach a
record in 1936 of 4,739,000 bales. Following the
Sino-Japanese War the acreage dropped, but reached
a second high point in 1958, producing 8,700,000
bales. Another drop in 1965 to 5,800,000 is again
on the upward trend.

     China was a large importer of raw cotton in
1931-35, importing some 567,000 bales, and is today
a still heavier importer, as explained later.

Oil Seeds

     Next to food grains and cotton, oil-seed pro-
duction is of greatest importance in China.

     The prewar production of eleven oils in China
(including Manchuria), 1934-35 to 1938-39, amounted
to 3,883,000 metric tons. Of these, 238,000 tons
represented six industrial oils, and 3,650,000 represented five edible oils. The sum of these two
groups was about a third of the world output.

During the war, production decreased 15 per cent, mostly in the industrial group. Edible vegetable oils were in great demand, and the production revived considerably, with rapeseed exceeding prewar levels.

Despite these declines China still remained potentially one of the world's greatest suppliers of vegetable oil and seeds. Revival under the Communists is discussed later.

Livestock

Phillips, Johnson, and Moyer[10] present estimates, corrected for underestimate of farms, as follows:

(in millions)	
Large Animals	66
Hogs	85
Sheep and Goats	66

The ratio of animals per farm is small, but for cultivated area larger than in the United States. The year 1957 shows a notable increase in numbers and in ratio to cultivated area. It is also related to feed and pasturage, as stated in the section on developments in the Communist regime.

Fisheries

Before the Sino-Japanese War in 1937, writes T. H. Shen,[11] the annual production was estimated at 1,361,000 metric tons. Of this, two thirds was marine and one third freshwater. This production was one fourth of world production, resulting from the vastness of China's fishing grounds and the high development of freshwater fisheries. It can be seen that the available supply per capita was very low, only two to three kilograms.

Later developments are discussed under the Communist regime.

Forestry

In the past, China had a vast area of natural forests that was gradually denuded, due to the needs of an increasing population. Accordingly, the watersheds of the Yellow and Yangtze rivers have experienced serious soil erosion and floods. China, therefore, imported much lumber and processed goods. The annual imports of lumber, paper, and rayon during the decade 1927-37 averaged 2,722,000 cubic meters.

Fruit

China is rich in fruit of excellent quality, including peaches, apricots, and sweet oranges. A survey conducted (1944-45) in nine provinces revealed a surprising variety of fruit. The annual production of fruit in twenty provinces in China was estimated by Dr. T. H. Shen of NARB in 1947 as 3,214,912 tons. It is estimated that the statistical mode for China per capita would be about 14 kilograms, compared with 70-80 kilograms in the United States. The required fruit per capita for a balanced diet, according to the Food and Agriculture Organization, is near the United States figure. It can thus be seen that the production in prewar China was woefully below requirements. The possibility of increased production is recognized as great. Progress under the Communists is discussed in Chapter 3.

Vegetables

There are more kinds and varieties of vegetables in China than in any other country of the world. The office of the Agricultural Attaché in Shanghai, making a survey of the vegetables on the market during 1947, found some seventy kinds.

Buck estimated the area devoted to vegetable production in eight agricultural regions at 1.1 per cent of the cultivated land. To meet a satisfactory dietetic standard, the vegetable-growing area should be at least doubled.

Under the Communist regime, vegetable production increased greatly, especially in the private
plots.

Other special products of importance include
such various animal products as wool, hides and
skins, eggs, and some meat. Among hard fibers are
ramie and jute. These, along with silk, sugar, and
tobacco, are discussed in the Appendix.

NOTES

1. John Lossing Buck, Owen L. Dawson, and
Yuan-li Wu, Food and Agriculture in Communist China
Published for the Hoover Institution on War, Revo-
lution and Peace, Stanford University (New York
and London: Frederick A. Praeger, 1966), p. 57,
Note 4.

2. T. H. Shen, Agricultural Resources of
China (Ithaca, N.Y.: Cornell University Press,
1951), p. 378.

3. "A Calculation of the Rural Dietary from
Crop Reports of Tung and Chang, 1939," Chinese
Journal of Physiology, Vol. XIV, No. 4.

4. Estimated by Dawson.

5. Sydney David Gamble, How Families Live in
Peiping (New York and London: Funk, 1933), pp. 88-
106.

6. J. L. Buck, Land Utilization in China
(Shanghai, China: Commercial Press, 1937), p. 409.

7. Ibid., p. 167.

8. Ibid., p. 427.

9. Ibid., Table IX.

10. Ralph Wesley Phillips and Others, <u>Live-stock of China</u>, U.S. Department of State Publication No. 2249, Far Eastern Series No. 9 (Washington: Government Printing Office, 1945), 174 pp.

11. <u>Lu in China</u>, p. 300. See Lu Kao Hui, West China Union University, 1943, unpublished data; citation translated from the Chinese.

CHAPTER **3** AGRICULTURAL
ECONOMY UNDER THE
COMMUNIST REGIME

HISTORY

The eight years of war with Japan (1937-45),
and subsequent civil strife up to the eve of the
Communist takeover, greatly depressed China's rural
economy. Severe losses occurred in both human and
material resources. The production of food grain,
cotton, and other technical crops considerably declined. So did most agricultural exports.

Confusion reigned from 1950 to 1952. People
constantly moved between cities and villages, and
redistribution of land further disturbed rural
society. The Communists' information on land,
crops, and population during these years was largely drawn from the former incomplete Nationalist
data and was not reliable enough to be used as a
basis for statistical study. The figures for 1949
were seriously underestimated. It seems that a
statistical correction was made on some of the figures up to 1953, when a population census was taken.

The first Five-Year Plan was then set in operation. A fairly stable period ensued when production
increased following increased inputs into agriculture. The first Five-Year Plan saw a period of
normal growth in agriculture, which followed some
of the well-made plans of the Nationalist Government just preceding the Communist take-over. This
is especially true of cotton production. The peasants were freed from some of their traditionally
oppressive taxes, rent, and high interest rates.
Scarce as fertilizer was by 1957, it was becoming

21

more available. Use of tractors and power pumps increased. The irrigated area was extended. (See the
section on irrigation in Chapter 5.) Food grain
production increased from 170 million metric tons in
1952 to 185 million in 1957, and 205 million in 1966.

The Communists, in their urge toward rapid
progress, made prodigious mistakes during the years
from 1956 to 1959. Their efforts to socialize agriculture disregarded individual initiative and popular sentiment among the rural masses. The transformation of the Elementary Producers' Cooperative to
the Advanced Producers' Cooperative, and later to
the communes, is described by numerous writers.

The "Great Leap Forward" was launched primarily
to create more jobs for rural employment. But the
movement was stretched too far at the expense of
regular farm work, and the repeated failures of
these mass projects added to the disillusion and
disgust with the Communist leadership.

All forms of private property (including private lots, draft animals, and farm equipment) were
taken over.

One of the worst features was the undermining
of the family system, in the course of relieving
women from their home chores for communal services.

These misconceived policies and projects, added
to poor weather for crops, contributed to the disastrous years of 1959 to 1961.

A change in official thinking was registered
during 1960 in the announcement of "agriculture as
the foundation" and in the new priority for China's
national development, followed by light industry
and heavy industry. This change reversed the 1953-
57 objectives, which placed heavy industry first.

PRODUCTION FACTORS

Emphasis on four production factors to improve agriculture were stated as:

1. Chemicalization, including chemical fertilizers and drugs, such as insecticides.

2. Mechanization to produce and use more machinery, adapting it to the terrain. Heavy tractors serviced the great plains of North China; light tractors, the gentle slopes of Central and southwestern China; and garden tractors, the vegetable gardens and dried rice fields.

3. Promotion of rural electrification wherever demand was urgent and water power available.

4. Selective water utilization. Large-scale projects for irrigation and drainage were primarily regarded as state enterprises, for the joint endeavors between the state and the provinces. No mass enterprise was to be encouraged without special financial and technical backing from the state. All conservation projects stressed "consolidation," "coordination," and "improvement" of projects that had already been started or completed.

These policies were well disseminated and showed the rethinking of Communist China on economic development. Effects on agricultural production began to show in 1963, and were quite apparent in 1967, a year when favorable weather produced a record crop.

There was a moderation in the organization of the rural communes, the "basic ownership" of lands, which fell first upon the production brigades and then upon the smaller production teams. The production team was a close-knit organization of twenty to thirty households, which gained the ownership of draft animals, farm tools, and other means of production. It had become the basic production unit as well as the income and expenditure distribution

unit.   Although the commune retained its formal feature as an overseer organization, it was only a
paper facade of the brigades and production teams.

Individual households of these teams were allowed to cultivate private garden plots, raise oxen,
pigs, and poultry, and grow bamboo, fruit trees, and
other economic plants. Products from these subsidi-
ary occupations were allowed to be sold in the local
free market as private earnings. This resulted in
the peasants putting more effort, fertilizer, and
other productive elements into the private plots.
We have not attempted to assess the results quantitatively. There was some attempt by the Peking
regime to restrict and reduce the private plots, but
this has not been pushed very far.

                          DYNAMICS

These conditions probably saved the Communist
structure from total collapse in the early 1960s,
and also served as a great impetus for China's economic revival in the recent past few years. Con-
troversy over these very concessions seems to have
germinated the seeds of an internal strife among
Communist leaders which, after several years of
undercover brewing, recently burst into an open
clash under the name of "Cultural Revolution." According to analysts, the real issue involved represents struggle between utopianism and pragmatism
among the leadership of the Chinese Communists. So
far as agricultural policy is concerned, the utopian
faction, led by Mao Tse-tung and his group, would
immediately cut short the period of relaxation and
start a second "Great Leap" campaign under command
of the Puritan type of rural communes. On the other
hand, the pragmatic Communists, led by Liu Shao-chi
and most of the "old comrades," would prolong the
period of relaxation. This would afford more opportunity for individual incentive among the rural
masses and prepare a stronger farm economy as the
foundation for a gradual program of industrial development.

Whatever the outcome of this factional strife on China's official agricultural policy, an important reaction of the Chinese peasantry resulted. No official policy can again win their full support unless it can be reconciled with local interest and local aspirations for well-being. It should be remembered that the Chinese peasants of today are no longer the "sand-loose" and tame individuals of the old society. It seems true that there has been a change in the spirit of the Chinese peasantry, although it cannot just be asserted without reasons. The following section is suggestive.

PEASANTRY

The egalitarian leveling of rural society, as a result of land reform and socialism, has produced a new village unity from the doctrine that "everyone eats and works alike." Schooling, development propaganda, and the local evidence of the effectiveness of many new production measures have replaced the old "mei fa-tzu" fatalism with a new hope for material improvement. This improved morale, together with indoctrination praising the worker and the peasant, has increased the peasant's sense of his own social worth and of his right to share in the benefits of the new society. The peasant's attitude can be described as follows:

1. Being generally law-abiding, the Chinese peasants will never try to evade the burden of agricultural or other taxes. Yet they will be very reluctant to meet state purchases in full measure whenever pressed by their own needs for livelihood or for means of production.

2. Harboring disillusion and distrust toward the Communist leadership, the peasants will not hesitate to refuse involvement in any further adventures or fantastic schemes as those imposed upon them during the "Great Leap" years.

3. They show an interest in policies and

programs, but an indifference to and distrust in ideological campaigns. Their general attitude toward all Party campaigns and public policies may be interpreted as superficial conformity, reserved antipathy, and limited cooperation whenever possible-- enwrapped in a "cold front" of indifference.

The peasant's objectives can also be summed up in three areas:

1. The primary objective of peasants under collectivization would naturally focus upon retaining, as private property, their own house with furniture and fixtures, their private lot with vegetable garden, fruit trees, fish ponds, etc., and their own farm tools, working animals, and vehicles for travel and transportation.

2. Collectivized peasants want to improve their livelihood through increasing incomes from the sources of wage payments for collective marks; sale of products from the private plot; occasional earnings from sideline occupations; and bonuses, prizes, special rewards, and other permissible incomes.

3. Collectivized peasants want to improve their physical, economical, and cultural surroundings in the locality through the dispensing of reserve funds accumulated from farm surpluses. The power of disposal lies with the brigade and team committees, which can hardly refuse the popular demand on any project for local development.

POLITICS

In conclusion, we may advance the following points in connection with this brief survey of Chinese agriculture:

1. Despite its impressive facade, the Peking regime discredited itself through a long series of "Leap" follies, and antagonized the whole rural populace with its communal control over all aspects of individual thought and life.

2.   The Communist power structure began to dis-
integrate and decentralize in 1958, when both the
Peking elite and the local cadres chose fantastic
schemes for political prestige at the expense of
human and material resources that could have been
wisely used for real productive purposes.

3.   The "economic center of gravity" has
dropped to the local level, and has stayed in the
hands of production brigades and teams. These have
provided the nation with food and raw materials for
industry and for export in return for capital goods.

4.   Party cadres at the local level, utterly
disillusioned and disheartened with the Peking
elite, have gradually turned "realistic" and "under-
standing" in their relations with the rural masses.
This process of "soul transformation" seems to have
worked upward through all levels of the Party apparatus, until a split of leadership at the apex was
brought into the open with the advent of the Cultural Revolution.

5.   While opposing factions in the Communist
Party are fighting over the issue of "relaxation"
or "reinstitution" of strict Party control, the
Chinese peasantry as a class will never hesitate to
stand firmly on their own ground either to attain
or to retain the minimum amount of their basic objectives.

6.   There is no doubt that the peasants are
determined to protect their own interests, no mat-
ter which of the contending factions wins as the
dictator of future policies. These peasants can
carry on passive resistance for some time on their
own resources, while making use of such outside
agricultural requisites as are available--such as
chemical fertilizer, when it can be obtained on
reasonable terms.

4

LAND RESOURCES AND CULTIVATED AREA

INTRODUCTION AND SUMMARY

The proportion of cultivated land resources is of first importance in assessing potentials of China's farm development. Data on this subject vary as to sources and interpretation. An attempt is made to arrive at reasonable estimates of present arable but uncultivated land, that which could be developed with feasible economic outlays.

Mainland China ranks as the world's third largest country. It has a geographical area of 9,561,000 square kilometers (956,100,000 hectares), including Tibet but excluding Taiwan and Outer Mongolia. As a basis of agricultural potential, however, the nation is found to have an arable land area of only 146,600,000 hectares. This is a mere 15 per cent of its total area, including Tibet, or 18 per cent if Tibet is excluded.

In spite of mass movement for land expansion over the ages, China's cultivated area probably has never extended beyond 113,000,000 hectares. For the last thirty to forty years, the figure hovers at around 111,000,000 hectares.

ESTIMATES OF CULTIVATED LAND

The first realistic estimate of China's cultivated area was made by Dr. J. L. Buck in his Land Utilization Surveys, 1929-33. With the data of

border regions supplementing his findings of twenty-
two provinces, the cultivated area for that period
is 107,400,000 hectares, or 11.24 per cent of the
nation's geographical area. This figure is quite
close to the Communist official data of 1952
(107,910,000 hectares), which signifies that China's
farm economy practically regained its prewar level
in the early 1950s.

Under a new definition set forth by the Communists in 1958, a cultivated area must be "utiliz-
able for the current year," by means of which the
1958 cultivated area was reduced to 107,780,000
hectares (1,616,800,000 mow), dropping almost 4 million hectares from the 1957 figure. Taking this
realistic figure as a starting point, the estimation
of China's cultivated area for recent years is made
by applying two annual average rates of reclamation
for two successive periods. The rate for 1959-63
is 233,000 hectares (3,500,000 mow), and that for
1964-67 is 260,000 hectares (4 million mow). Thus
by the end of 1967 or the beginning of 1968, Mainland China would possess a cultivated area of
110,300,000 hectares, including Tibet.

Although China could manage to have two thirds
of its arable land under cultivation, one should
not be too optimistic about the outcome without
closely scrutinizing the diverse quality of cultivated fields. The People's Daily, October 25, 1959,
has stated that "29 per cent of China's total cultivated area was low-yielding; 40 per cent was of
medium productivity; and only 31 per cent should be
considered as fertile soil." The Chinese Agricultural Journal, No. 8-10, 1958, has listed twenty-
four provinces in which the percentage of "low-
yielding" lands ranges from 26 per cent (Honan) to
50 per cent (Kwangsi)*. Again, the Red Flag, on
August 1, 1962, reported that "there were in China
about 300 million mow of alkali and saline soils in

---

*Now Kwangsi-Chuang Autonomous Region.

northwest, northeast, northern China, and the coastal areas of North Kiangsu. Of this total, about
100 million mow were in the cultivated areas, occupying 10 per cent in North China's cultivated area,
and 20 per cent in its irrigated area." This shows
that while extension of cultivated area is extremely important for China's farm development, the enhancement and preservation of its soil productivity
perhaps is just as essential and urgent in the developmental scheme, especially in consideration of
the nation's limited amount of arable potentials.

ESTIMATES OF ARABLE LAND

As shown in the Progress Report of April 5,
1968, Tung and Dawson have estimated China's uncultivated arable areas for 1967 in four separate
regions. They total 36,500,000 hectares.

China proper	87,000,000 mow)	
Manchuria	240,000,000 mow)	15.52% of geograph-
Sinkiang	215,000,000 mow)	ical area
Tibet	6,000,000 mow)	

In terms of physical area, Manchuria and
Sinkiang seem to offer the greatest hope for China's
farm expansion. But each of these regions presents
a number of obstacles that must be overcome before
any reclamation program can be carried out effectively.

1. Manchuria: Most arable lands in this region are in the northern section, especially on the
"Three-River Plain" of Heilungkiang. Here precipitation is high and evaporation is low; the low-
lying marshy areas are almost constantly waterlogged. A coordinated system of flood control and
drainage must be established in response to the
need of reclamation enterprises.

2. Sinkiang: This is arid desert land where
surface flows are constantly suffering from a high
rate of evaporation and infiltration. Irrigation
water must depend upon underground "cellars" for

storage and underground piping for transportation,
very expensive in installation and maintenance. Undoubtedly reclamation projects in such regions could
be undertaken only by army corps state farms, or by
combined collective units with ample state aid in
finance and mechanical equipment.

RECLAIMABLE WASTELANDS

Under a decree of the Peking regime, a total of
51,500,000 hectares of "wastelands" from twenty-four
provinces or regions* was reported. Of this,
35,400,000 hectares had been surveyed up to 1958,
with 20,500,000 hectares labeled as "fit for agriculture" and the remaining 14,900,000 hectares as
"usable" for pasture, forestry, and other productive purposes.

The 20,500,000 hectares of agricultural wastelands belong to ten of the twenty-four reporting
provinces. These were resurveyed and divided into
four classes. The first three classes (a,b,c,) are
arable lands, which could be used for farming with
various degrees of soil reconditioning. The total
of the a+b+c classes from the ten provinces is
14,400,000 hectares. We have made comparable estimates of the a+b+c classes from the remaining fourteen provinces; the total amount is 3,700,000 hectares.

When the two sets of a+b+c data are combined
to make a total of 18,000,000 hectares, it represents the reclaimable wastelands for agricultural
purposes. (See Table 4, Note 1 for definition.)
If a reclamation rate is set at 350,000 hectares
per year, this amount could last fifty years.

It should be noted that the estimated 3,700,000
hectares from the fourteen provinces are mostly

_____

*
  Twenty-one provinces, five autonomous regions,
and three administrative cities.

arid saline soils from the interior provinces or
coastal saline soils bordering on Po-hai, the Yellow
Sea, and the Eastern Sea. The ground is level, the
communication is easy, manpower is plentiful, and
mechanical power is generally available. The main
task of "reclamation" here is drainage and irrigation. Under a well-financed and well-managed project, the work could be done much more efficiently
in the interior and coastal provinces than in the
border areas of the Northwest and the Northeast.

REGIONAL CONDITIONS

The first step in assessing China's farm development potentials is an examination of the scale
and utilization of its land resources. China ranks
third largest among the world's nations, with a
geographical area of 9,561,000 square kilometers
(956,100,000 hectares, or 14,341,500,000 mow), including 300 million mow or 200,000 square kilometers of
water surface. Being situated in eastern Asia and
encircled by a "magic ring" of jungle, mountain,
desert, and oceans, her teeming millions are destined to depend upon "Mother Earth" as the vital
source of life. As a basis of agricultural potentials, however, topography has given China only
14 per cent of land that is below 500 meters of elevation, and climate has afforded her 35 per cent of
land that is above 500 millimeters of annual precipitation. After meshing through further limitations from other decisive factors such as temperature, growing season, soil fertility, water supply,
and so forth, China has found to her dismay an
arable land area of 146,000,600,000 hectares. As
previously mentioned, this is a mere 15 per cent of
her total area, including Tibet; a mere 18 per cent
if Tibet is excluded.

China's noted geographer Dr. Hu Huan-Yun has
suggested that if a diagonal line is drawn from
Aigun in northern Heilungkiang to the border of
Tenchung in southern Yünnan, it will divide the
Chinese domain into two broad regions, each with

highly distinctive characteristics. The region lying northwest of this line contains 64 per cent of
the nation's geographical area with 4 per cent of
her population, while the region lying southeast of
this line contains 36 per cent of her area, with
96 per cent of her population. Professor T. H. Shen
has further amplified Hu's contrasts by filling in
more particulars of China's agricultural resources
to show the striking differences between these two
regions.

Agricultural Resources	Northwestern Region (%)	Southwestern Region (%)
Cultivated areas	6	94
Rice production	1	99
Wheat production	7	93
Soybean production	14	86
Corn production	3	97
Cotton production	1	99
Hemp production	17	83
Wool production	42	58
Silk production	0	100
Tung oil production	0	100
Tea production	0	100

It is noteworthy that northwest of Hu's line,
the terrain is chiefly composed of high plateaus
and rugged mountains, with altitudes mostly ranging
from 1,000 meters to 4,000 meters. On the other
hand the main features southeast of this line consist of broad plains, low hills, lake basins, and
river deltas, very few of which are more than 1,000
meters in elevation.

According to the classification of Prof. Chi-
Yi Chang, China's "agricultural belts" should follow a general division of her broad domain according
to elevation.

1. Elevation at 200 meters or below, which
covers nearly all of China's alluvial plains, may
be devoted entirely to agriculture, with choice of
crops according to ecological factors.

2. Elevations between 200 and 500 meters are partially suitable for agriculture. Careful choice of crops should be made according to their adaptability to specific surroundings.

3. Elevations between 500 and 1,000 meters are fit only for special varieties of crops, because of aridity, frigidity, poor soil quality, and brief growing season in many places.

4. Elevations between 1,000 and 2,000 meters are generally considered as "grass belts," mostly suitable as pastures for animal husbandry.

5. Elevations between 2,000 and 3,000 meters are naturally the "tree belts," where only forests should be developed, with scattered sunny gentle slopes allocated for pasture.

Estimates of Arable Land

Five authorities have recorded more acceptable estimates of China's arable land within the past three or four decades.

Dr. Wong Wenhow made his estimate in 1932, mostly based on his general survey and research on China's land forms. Although much improved upon O. E. Baker's estimate of 29 per cent (of total area), Dr. Wong Wenhow's estimate of 23 per cent is still too high, as estimated by other authorities of a later date.

Chen Chang-heng tried to improve upon Wong's estimate with two alternative assessments. His lower estimate of 17.60 per cent seems to be more realistic, though still too high.

Dr. J. L. Buck's estimate is perhaps the closest to China's true arable situation, as evidenced by other estimates in the last decade. This estimate is composed of two parts:

1. Buck's own data on cultivated area (highest estimate) plus his own estimate of uncultivated

arable land in twenty-two provinces* (35 million acres).

2. Tung's and Dawson's supplement of arable estimates for the borderlands in the 1930s (500 million mow for Manchuria, 250 million for Sinkiang, and 10 million for Tibet).

Chiao Chi-Ming's arable estimate is only the borderland's supplement, and it corresponds to Tung's and Dawson's.

The fifth source, the Communist estimate, consists of two parts for 1957:

1. The official Communist figure of cultivated area for 1957, which covers all Mainland except Tibet.

2. Tung's and Dawson's supplement of uncultivated arable areas for China proper, Manchuria, Sinkiang, and Tibet. (See detailed figures in the Notes attached to Table 4.)

The Communist estimate for 1958 also consists of two parts:

1. The 1958 Communist figures of cultivated areas.

2. Tung's and Dawson's supplement of uncultivated arable areas in China proper and the borderlands.

The percentages are lower than in 1957 because the Communist figures of cultivated area are lower.

China Project's estimate for 1967 is Tung's and Dawson's estimate for the Mainland and also consists of two parts:

_____

*The number of provinces later changed.

1. Tung's and Dawson's estimate of cultivated area in 1967. (See figures and explanation in section on cultivated area.)

2. Tung's and Dawson's estimate of uncultivated arable areas for China proper and borderlands. (See Notes to Table 4.)

The striking feature in the later estimates, from Buck down to the present, is that the nation's arable lands have shown a strong tendency to center around 16 per cent. This estimate uses China's geographical area as a basis of calculation, and Professor Buck is responsible for the main part of this estimate. This means that his highest estimate of cultivated area in the early 1930s, plus his 11 per cent estimate of uncultivated area (in twenty-two provinces) for the same period, was probably closest to the real situation at that date. Tung's and Dawson's estimates of uncultivated arable lands in China proper in 1957-58, as well as in 1967, are all based on Buck's initial 11 per cent, with reduced amounts, excluding the cultivated portions, for each year under investigation.

Estimates of Reclaimable Wastelands

The term "wastelands," as used in Chinese official reports and private publications, has never been clearly defined. Perhaps nobody has any definite idea as to its limits and contents, and no two land experts can agree on the exact boundaries of the same piece of "wasteland." In practice, however, there is a general notion to regard as wastelands any portion of land that could be made useful through human efforts. This would include all productive lands for farming, pasture, fisheries, and forestry. Whenever such a piece of land is touched by the application of labor, it is called "ripe waste," while the untouched but prospectively useful lands are called "raw wastes." (See Note 1 to Table 4.) Yet even this general notion of "productiveness" and "usefulness" is very vague and uncertain, and all official records of wastelands in

the past have almost always shown great disparities,
year after year and place after place, without explanation.

The Communists require reports and surveys of
wastelands. In great efforts to extend reclamation,
since the early 1950s the Peking regime has requested
all provinces to make "realistic" reports on their
wastelands--independent of the "old wild records."
Judging from the reduced figures of the reported
areas, these preliminary new data seem to be more
tangible and useful as a basis for surveying plans.
Many surveys had been made on the reported regions
in various provinces, with a total surveyed area of
35,400,000 hectares out of a total reported area of
54,760,000 hectares up to 1958. The wastelands in
ten provinces had been resurveyed and classified
into five categories, with four categories labeled
as "fit for agriculture." The fifth category is
labeled "fit for pasture, forestry, and other purposes." Among the four agricultural categories, the
fourth category, designated as "not ready for present utilization," amounted to 6,101,000 hectares for
the ten provinces. The first of the "agricultural
categories" are respectively designated as follows:

(1)	(2)	(3)
Usable with no need of recon- ditioning	Usable with slight recondi- tioning	Usable with much recondi- tioning
2,850,000 hec- tares	3,400,000 hec- tares	8,000,000 hec- tares

The total of the three categories is 14,300,000
hectares for the ten provinces whose reported wastelands had been surveyed and classified. This constitutes about 36 per cent of the total reported
area from these provinces. This was the situation
up to 1958, as reported in the book China's State
Farms in Galloping Progress (1958), published by
the Ministry of Reclamation and State Farms. But
there were fourteen other provinces whose reported
wastelands were not yet resurveyed and classified

by 1958. Although there is no news about their
status since that date, it may be assumed that a
comparable amount of wastelands in these provinces
must have been similarly classified "fit for agriculture," as in the first ten provinces. Once can
then proceed to make a supplemental estimate of
wastelands for these fourteen provinces in the first
three classes given above. The total result for the
fourteen provinces is 3,700,000 hectares, amounting
to about 30 per cent of their reported areas, comparable with the 36 per cent of the first ten
provinces. (See Table 6.)

Then these estimated figures for twenty-four
provinces (no report from Ningsia* and Tibet) are
put together. This totals about 8,500,000 hectares
of agricultural wastelands, which are regarded as
reclaimable in the immediate future with varied degrees of requirements for reconditioning.

China's reclamation rate during the period of
the first Five-Year Plan is estimated at 1,500,000
hectares oer year. Tung's and Dawson's estimated
annual rate for 1959-63 is 250,000 hectares, considering the depressive conditions for that period.
For the period of recovery and development, 1964-67,
Tung and Dawson have set a higher rate of 270,000
hectares per year. In view of the availability of
quantities of arable lands, as shown in Table 4,
there should be opportunity for agricultural expansion to the limits of organizational efforts and
technical equipment matched with tasks. If the annual reclamation rate is raised to the high figure
of 350,000 hectares a year, this, with the estimated 18 million hectares of arable land of the
first three classes, would take fifty years. This
estimate may be a bit high.

---

* Now Ningh-Hui Autonomous Region.

China's Arable Potentials in the
Borderlands

So far as suggested by existing sources of information, China's great hopes for arable potentials are confined to two main regions of its
borderlands--northern Manchuria and the interior
basins of Sinkiang.

Manchuria

There are several diversified estimates regarding arable lands in Manchuria, all of which
seem to agree on the great prospect of Heilungkiang's
great northern waste in the confluent delta region
of the "Three-River Plain." Two important estimates
may be mentioned.

1. The Japan-Manchoukuo Yearbook of 1939 gives
a 1936 figure of 61,400,000 hectares of arable area
for the whole of Manchuria, with about 38 per cent
already under cultivation.

2. China's Northeastern Regional Administration cites another figure, based on information
from the Northeastern Association of Science and
Technology. This estimates (1946) that there exist
about 43,500,000 hectares of arable land in Manchuria. Approximately 50 per cent of this arable
total was already under cultivation in the 1940s,
and the remaining 20 million hectares is still
available for later development. This is the figure Tung and Dawson have adopted in connection with
arable estimates in that region.

Sinkiang

Aside from several prewar estimates giving uncertain low figures for arable potentials here,
there are two recent assessments based upon the
supply of water, which seem to reveal the key to
Sinkiang's agricultural development in the coming
decades.

1. In Tsao Cheh-Yen's estimate, Sinkiang possesses 62,800 million cubic meters annual flow of
water from melting snow and ice, about 70 per cent of
which is wasted through the desert basins. Proper
conservation projects could save a high percentage
from this waste to supply a minimum of 6,500,000
hectares of croplands in the near future. (China
Reclamation, May, 1957).

2. A 1953 estimate by the Ministry of Reclamation and State Farms reports that Sinkiang is endowed
with more than 60,000 million cubic meters of surface flow. At the rate of 400 cubic meters per mow
for irrigation, it could supply 10 million hectares
of farmland. At a reduced rate of 200 cubic meters
per mow, by using underground pipes for irrigation,
it could supply at least 20 million hectares of
farmland. And the state farms run by corps have
already made a record in using 175 cubic meters per
mow (1955) in their cotton fields with great success. But owing to great difficulties and expense,
total reclaimable area may be no more than 10 million hectares.

CULTIVATED AREA

Discussion of cultivated area requires definition of "operative fields" and "prospective fields"
and information on the registration of 1950.

The cultivated areas of a country can never
remain static for any length of time. They will
slowly fluctuate in response to the counterplay of
contending factors such as bumper harvests or crop
failures, land rushes or farm abandonment, high
rents or low rents, war or peace in the country,
advances or retreats at the frontiers, and a host
of other contradictory influences. This may be applied to the cultivated areas of a region, a community, or an individual farm in a small way.

In the case of traditional China, a farmer always tried to expand his business in good years by

purchasing or leasing additional fields, or by
opening up some marginal lands or hill slopes,
banks of lakes, or even sandbars along the rivers.
The contrary would be true if fate was working
against him. He would probably pledge the house,
sell the cattle, and abandon a portion of his tilled
lands for a few seasons or a few years. The lands
that are under actual cultivation may be called
"operative fields," and the lands that are temporarily abandoned may be called "prospective fields."
During periods of frequent natural disasters or
prolonged social disturbances, there would always
come into existence a marginal belt of prospective
lands in the community. These might be called
upon to serve as "spare parts" for the bulk of
operative fields. Yet as soon as peace was re-
stored and prosperity began, this belt of prospective fields would tend to shrink or disappear.
Then all farms attempted to expand activities up
to or even beyond the belt's limits.

Moreover, these prospective fields could serve
the owners otherwise. Whenever it was to the ad-
vantage of an owner, his prospective fields would
either be "covered up," as in the case of tax assessment, or "opened up," as in the case of loan
negotiations that might give him better terms with
a larger acreage as security. As noted later,
these prospective fields also enable their owners
to earn more dividends from the elementary type of
agricultural production cooperatives, when these
are registered as stock shares by right of membership.

New definitions of "cultivated area" were evident in Communist statistics of 1958. In the confusion of land reporting and land registration of
the late 1950s, there were issued three official
and semiofficial documents with direct bearing on
a new definition of "cultivated areas":

1. Simple Explanation of Terms Used in the
First Five-Year Plan (Peking, 1955).

    2. <u>Agricultural Handbook of Statistical Works</u>
(Peking, 1956).

    3. "Tabular Forms for Agricultural Planning"
(by Liao Hsien-hao, <u>Planned Economy</u>, No. 4, April,
1957).

According to separate references on the definition of "cultivated areas" from these documents, a
piece of cultivated land must be usable during the
current year; the statistical category of cultivated
areas should include:

    1. Well-developed fields under active opera-
tion.

    2. Newly reclaimed fields ready for productive
use.

    3. Developed fields left uncultivated for less
than three consecutive years.

    4. Land lying fallow in the current year.

    5. Lands primarily devoted to cropping on
which fruit, mulberry, or other "economic" trees are
also planted.

Lands devoted to fruit orchards, mulberry gardens, prairies, or grazing grounds, though specialized in nature, are not regarded as cultivated areas.

Presumably due to these limitations, the
1958 statistic of cultivated area was fixed at
107,800,000 hectares. This showed a sharp drop of
4 million hectares, which was first formally ac-
cepted in 1957 and then dropped in 1958, without any
explicit explanation.

Land Registration and Land Surveys

China's cadastral system had collapsed long
before the Republic and the Nationalist program of
land registration had a chance to prevent it. In

pre-Communist days, any official inquiry on the land
status of a person or a community would invariably
result in a high percentage of underreporting.
Therefore, the much adulterated files of the localities had too often been used as the basis for too
many unrealistic estimates. Professor Buck's land
utilization survey (1929-33) was really the fact-
finding attempt that disclosed the sad truth.
China's cultivated lands had been, for ages, one
third underreported at least. Several other inves-
tigators found an even higher percentage of underreporting, based upon some incomplete data from the
Nationalist land registration programs.

During the land redistribution program of the
Communists, 1950-52, landlords were liquidated. It
was the simple practice of China's former tiller-
owners and tiller-tenants to follow the old ways of
evasion or concealment whenever possible. Perhaps
they "omitted" from reports not only all their
prospective fields but also a portion of their operative fields during the confused onrush of land redistribution.

Hence the Communist writer Hsiao Yu frankly ad-
mitted in 1958 that of the so-called People's
Reclamation of 3,320,000 hectares, reported as
achieved by members of the agricultural cooperatives
since 1953, at least 2 million hectares were actually "omissions" in reporting old fields already under
cultivation, and the remaining 1,300,000 hectares
may be ascribed to elimination of roads, boundaries,
and graves in the process of collectivization.

In our opinion, however, probably the whole
amount of 3,300,000 hectares of "People's Reclamation"
should be regarded as cultivated areas omitted from
reporting in the process of land redistribution.
This represented a mixture of prospective fields (in
larger proportion) and operative fields (in smaller
proportion) under their management.

It should be remembered that immediately after
completion of land redistribution in 1952, China's

"independent farmers" were called upon to join the
agricultural cooperatives "voluntarily," and were
promised "generous" terms of land dividend. All
prospective members were told that they could retain
ownership of their original land holdings. These
would be registered in the Cooperative Book as stock
shares, from which they could draw annual dividends
according to size and productivity of the land.
Naturally, new members would make a full or even inflated report of their original holdings, including
both operative fields and prospective fields; and
they would label them "newly reclaimed lands," recovered since the days of land redistribution. This
is clearly reflected by the trends of acreage increase in China's cultivated areas from 1952 to 1957
in 1 million mow:

1952	1953	1954	1955	1956	1957
1,618.78	1,627.93	1,640.32	1,652.34	1,677.37	1,677.45

The rate of increase was very small from 1952 to
1955; but from that year on, it suddenly jumped
10.15 per cent from 1952 in 1956 and 1957. Let us
compare these trends with the trends of cooperativi-
zation in the same period. Farm households became
members of the cooperatives, at a similar wave of
fluctuation:

	1952	1953	1954	1955	1956	1957
(%)	0.1	0.2	2.0	14.0	96.0	96.0

The increases of acreage and membership proceed
in almost parallel lines. They both proceed slowly
from 1952; both showed a big jump in 1956, then remained on a level in 1956 and 1957. This clearly
indicates the following:

1. The cultivated areas increased slowly from
1952 to 1955 and suddenly jumped in 1956 and 1957,
because these area figures embraced the land regis-
trations inflated from the agricultural cooperatives.

2. The cooperative land registers were inflated because the members had counted in undue

amounts of land, including all their prospective
fields, and perhaps a small portion of operative
fields formerly omitted from reporting during the
land redistribution.

Re-examination of Communist Statistics on Cultivated Area, 1957-58

1. The 1957 cultivated area of 112,000,000
hectares showed an increase of 3,900,000 hectares
over that of 1952 with 107,860,000 hectares. It
was the highest record ever achieved under Communist
rule, if taken at its face value.

2. But according to the reclamation records,
77,560,000 mow accumulated during the plan period.
If there was an addition of 5,170,000 hectares from
reclamation, why should the 1957 cultivated area
have shown an increase of only 3,900,000 hectares?

3. While no direct public explanation has
ever been given on this point, there are indicative
reports that help to answer this puzzling question.

Tao Hsi-Chin, Deputy Secretary General of the
State Council, disclosed in People's Daily of January 7, 1958, that "in the course of eight years
or more, the State had requisitioned more than
1,330,000 hectares of land for construction purposes."
Chou En-lai also told Edgar Snow in 1960 that requi-
sition of farmland for construction purposes amounted
to nearly 2 million hectares from 1955 to 1958. Taking these figures at face value on both sides of the
balance sheet, it may be assumed that the above-
mentioned deficit of 1,260,000 hectares in "lost
reclamations" was more than offset by the construction requisitions.

4. The nature of "People's Reclamation" in the
plan period.

Communist Hsiao Yu, previously cited, writes
that of the 3,667,000 hectares of the "People's
Reclamation," at least 2 million hectares were due

to omitted reports of private holdings, and only
1,300,000 hectares could be regarded as their real
contribution. Tung and Dawson think, however, that
this 3,320,000 hectares was actually a sort of con-
cealed land holding, practically all belonging to
the category of marginal prospective fields. It
was mainly for this reason that the Communist statistics of 1958 on cultivated area discarded the
whole lot, according to their new definition of
"cultivated areas."

    5. Discrepancy between the 1947 and 1958 sta-
tistics on cultivated area.

    The 1957 cultivated area consisted of 112 mil-
lion hectares; that for 1958 was 107,700,000 hectares, showing a sudden drop of 4,043,000 hectares.
What caused this great discrepancy in Communist reports for these two years? After carefully scrutinizing Communist land problems during these years,
Tung and Dawson suggest that this discrepancy falls
into two areas:

    1. The 3,300,000 hectares of "People's Recla-
mation," being mostly prospective marginal lands,
should be excluded from cultivated area for 1958
under the new definitions.

    2. Hsiao Yu revealed that "approximately
1,330,000 hectares of cultivated areas in the borderlands of the northeast, northwest, and Inner Mongolia
were annually reported as being abandoned, fallowed,
or left unused for various reasons." He thought that
about 660,000 hectares should be regarded as actually
fallow, while the other 660,000 hectares were forced
out of use primarily on account of shortages in
fertilizer, water supply, and manpower.

    This means there existed a chronic tendency of
land abandonment at an annual rate of 660,000 hectares among the borderlands. If this amount is added
to the 3,600,000 hectares of fancied "reclamation"
by the agricultural cooperatives, the great discrepancy between 1957 and 1958 (4,043,000 hectares) can
easily be accounted for.

Estimates of China's Cultivated Areas,
1929-67

1. D. K. Lieu's and C. M. Chen's estimates
were largely based upon the original reports of the
Ministry of Agriculture and Commerce (1914), with
liberal adjustments on provincial figures. Coincidentally, this estimate has approximated the Communist estimate of 1957.

2. C. C. Chang's estimate was low, probably
due to underreporting in the early 1930s, which
Professor Buck was then disclosing.

3. G. B. Cressey's estimate summarized its
national total from local data with much overlapping
and omission. The total figure seems to be too
small in comparison with other estimates.

4. J. L. Buck's estimate based upon his highest estimate of twenty-two provinces seems closest
to the real situation. It was reflected in the
Communist estimates of 1957 and 1958.

5. Communist estimate for 1957. (See Notes
to Table 1.)

6. Communist estimate for 1958. (See Notes
to Table 1.)

7. The China Project's estimate for 1967.

a. The estimated figure of 1,110,300,000
hectares (Table 1) represents a summation of the
provincial estimates.

b. Three other estimates are used as
"guide" references in the provincial assessments.
These are the Economic Geography estimates for
1957, the People's Daily estimates of 1958, and
Taiwan's Atlas of Mainland China estimates for 1965.
(See Table 2.)

3.   Criteria references are drawn from up-to-date Communist as well as non-Communist sources, including the 1967 Yearbook on Chinese Communism (Taiwan) and Agricultural Notes, 1964-68, U.S. Consulate General's Office, Hong Kong.

4.   Tung and Dawson have also made another estimate by the central approach, based on the principle of gradual advancement, keeping pace with the trends of recovery and development from post-"Leap" years down to present.

5.   For the period 1959-63, they set an annual increase of cultivated area through reclamation on the basis of 107,700,000 hectares in 1958.   With an accumulated addition of 1,160,000 hectares, the cultivated area in 1963 would be about 109 million hectares.

6.   For the period 1964-67, the annual rate of increase in cultivated area is set conservatively at 260,000 hectares on the basis of 109 million hectares in 1963.   With an accumulated area of 1,066,000 hectares in four years, the total area in 1967 would be about 110 million hectares, not including Tibet.   It would be about 110,300,000 if Tibet is included.

7.   In view of the quick recovery in agricultural production from 1963 onward, and gradual expansion of grain acreage in most provinces, we feel strongly that an annual increase of 233,000 to 266,000 hectares in cultivated area for the last nine years (1959-67) seems to be quite plausible and rather moderate.

TABLE 1

Comparative Estimates of Cultivated Area in Mainland China
1928-67

Authority	Date of Estimate	Estimated Cultivated Area (1,000 ha.)	Cultivation Index (%)	Remarks
D. K. Lieu and Chun-ming Chen	1928	114,000	11.92	With Chinghai, Ningsia, Sikang, and Tibet added to original estimate of 112,100,000 ha.
C. C. Chang	1932	87,000	9.09	With Kwangsi, Chinghai, Sikang, and Tibet added to original estimate of 83,212,000 ha.
George B. Cressey	1944	85,500	8.94	With Sikang and Tibet added to original estimate of 85,050,000 ha.
J. L. Buck (including Tibet) (A)	1929-33	107,400	11.23	Original highest estimate of 22 provinces (93 million ha.) supplemented with Buck's data of Sikang, Sinkiang, and Manchuria, adding 200,000 ha. for Tibet

(Cont.)

TABLE 1 (Cont.)

Authority	Date of Estimate	Estimated Cultivated Area (1,000 ha.)	Cultivation Index (%)	Remarks
J. L. Buck (including Tibet) (B)	1929-33	101,600	10.62	Original second highest estimate for 22 provinces (87 million ha.), supplemented with Buck's data of the same borderlands, adding 200,000 ha. for Tibet.
Communist data	1957	112,000	11.71	Official data of 111,800,000 ha. supplemented with an estimated 200,000 ha. for Tibet.
Communist data	1958	108,000	11.29	Official data of 107,800,000 ha. supplemented with estimated 200,000 ha. for Tibet.
Communist data	1967	110,300	11.53	Our estimated cultivated area of the mainland, including 266,000 for Tibet.

50

NOTES TO TABLE 1

Comparative Estimates of Cultivated Area
in Mainland China
1928-67

a.   In order to make the above estimates comparable, their diverse basis of calculation, geographical area, has been converted into officially
recognized figures: 9,561,000 square kilometers,
of 956 million hectares, excluding Taiwan and Outer
Mongolia.

b.   The incomplete coverage of cultivated areas
in these estimates is supplemented either with the
authority's own data or with the author's estimated
data for the missing areas.

c.   The data for D. K. Lieu and C M. Chen,
C. C. Chang, and G. B. Cressey are all cited in
C. M Chao's Social Economics of China's Rural Areas,
published in Shanghai, 1947. Professor Buck's data
are presented in his book Food and Agriculture in
Communist China, jointly written by J. L. Buck,
Owen L. Dawson, and Y. L. Wu., 1966   The Communist
data for 1957 are given in Ten Great Years, Peking,
1959, and data for 1967 are from the author's
Progress Report for 1968.

d.   Sources for Tibet: Tseng Shih-Yin's General Atlas of China, by Provinces, 1932; and People's
Handbook, 1959.

TABLE 2

Comparative Estimates of Cultivated Area in Mainland China
1965 and 1967

Area	Province	"Atlas of Mainland China" (Taiwan) Estimate for 1965 (1,000 mow)	Index	Tung and Dawson Preliminary Estimate for 1967 (1,000 mow)	Index
Northeast	Liaoning	73,000	32.0	70,500	31.12
	Kirin	71,000	25.0	71,250	25.40
	Heilungkiang	105,000	15.0	73,200	10 52
subtotal	1,000 ha.	249,000 16,600		214,950 14,300	
North	Hopeh (including Peking)	136,500	42.4	125,500	38.06
	Shansi	56,560	24.0	70,850	30.06
	Shantung	139,000	60.0	138,200	60.10
	Honan	134,000	53.5	136,700	54.31
	Inner Mongolia	85,000	4.8	86,000	4.87
subtotal	1,000 ha.	551,060 36,700		557,250 37,100	
Northwest	Sinkiang	41,000	1.6	32,500	1.31
	Kansu	60,000	11.0	59,300	10.78
	Shensi	58,700	20.0	68,500	23.32

	Chinghai	7,500	0.7	9,200	0.85
	Ningsia	14,000	14.0	14,700	14.75
subtotal	1,000 ha.	181,200		184,200	
		12,100		12,300	
East	Kiangsu (including Shanghai)	98,100	60.5	95,200	62.10
	Chekiang	33,700	22.1	34,500	22.59
	Anhwei	73,000	34.8	89,400	42.60
subtotal	1,000 ha.	204,800		219,100	
		13,600		14,600	
Central	Hupeh	64,000	22.7	65,200	23.14
	Hunan	57,000	18.0	58,350	15.31
	Kiangsi	41,400	16.7	43,400	17.55
subtotal	1,000 ha.	162,400		166,950	
		10,800		11,100	
South	Kwangtung	45,000	12.9	55,450	13.09
	Kwangsi	37,000	11.2	38,220	11.56
	Fukien	22,200	12.0	22,500	12.18
subtotal	1,000 ha.	104,200		116,170	
		6,700		7,800	

(Cont.)

53

TABLE 2 (Cont.)

Area	Province	"Atlas of Mainland China" (Taiwan) Estimate for 1965		Tung and Dawson Preliminary Estimate for 1967	
		(1,000 mow)	Index	(1,000 mow)	Index
Southwest	Szechwan	115,000	13.5	115,900	13.57
	Kweichow	31,300	12.0	32,500	12.45
	Yünnan	42,000	6.4	44,460	6.79
subtotal	1,000 ha	188,300		192,860	
		12,600		12,800	
Tibet		(4,000)		(4,000)	
Grand total	1,000 ha.	190,600	11.5	110,300	11.53
	1,000 mow	1,644,960		1,654,480	

a Now Kwangsi-Chuang Autonomous Region.

54

TABLE 3

Comparative Estimates of Arable Lands in Mainland China
1932-67

Authority	Date of Estimate	Estimated Arable Lands (1,000 ha.)	Percentage of Geographical Area	Remarks
Wong Wenhow	1932	222,000	23.21	Note c.
Chen Chang-heng	1935			Note d.
(a)		168,000	17.60	
(b)		227,000	19.92	
J. L. Buck	1929-33	157,000	16.40	Note e.
C. M. Chiao	1934	152,000	15.87	Note f.
Communist data	1957	151,000	15.77	Note g.
Communist data	1958	146,700	15.35	Note h.
Communist data	1967	146,800	15.35	Note i.

(Cont.)

NOTES TO TABLE 3

Comparative Estimates of Arable Lands
in Mainland China
1932-67

a. "Arable land" is defined as the land that
is fit for agriculture and susceptible to tillage.
While subject to physical limitations such as temperature, rainfall, topography, soil, productivity,
growing season, etc., the arable area of a country
is by no means static in nature, and can be modified
from time to time in two ways:

1. It can be extended with the advancement of technology, as by irrigation, drainage, fertilization, choice of crops, improvement of soils,
etc.

2. It can be reduced on account of sudden
calamities such as earthquake, landslide, change of
course in rivers, etc., or through a slow process of
deterioration, such as deforestation, erosion, soil
salinization and alkalinization, etc.

Owing to the diversified evaluation of
these factors, geographers and agriculturists have
differed widely in their estimation of China's
arable lands. But estimates of the last thirty
years range, from 15 to 19 per cent with the lower
percentages prevailing, except in the earliest estimate by Wong Wenhow. This probably means that the
later estimates are gradually approaching the real
situation of the nation's arable lands under the
existing circumstances of physical limitation and
technical attainment.

b. To make the above estimates comparable, two
procedures of adjustment may be adopted:

1. Fix the nation's geographical area, as
officially recognized by both pre-Communist and
Communist administrations, at 9,561,000 square

(Cont.)

NOTES TO TABLE 3 (Cont.)

kilometers (or 956,100,000 hectares), excluding Outer Mongolia and Taiwan.

     2. Supplement the incomplete coverages of arable lands in these estimates with their own data or with estimated data of the missing regions.

     c. Wong Wenhow's[*] arable figures were based upon his crude estimate of China's topographic regions.

A.
    (Hai-ho Basin   )
    (Hwang-ho Basin   )
    (Huai-ho Basin   )
    (Yangtze River Basin,   (Delta regions)   ) 700,000 sq. miles
    (middle & lower reaches - (Lake areas)   )
    (Szechwan Red Basin   (Hilly lands)   )
    (Southeastern coastal region   )
    (Pearl River Basin   )

B. Sungari-Liao-ho Basin in the Northeast) 120,000
                                   sq. miles

C. Northwestern region: Wei-ho Basin   )
                        Sui-yuan Plain   )
                        Ho-tao Plain   ) 47,000 sq. miles
                        Ningsia Plain   )
                        Kansu Corridor   )
                        Chinghai Lake Basin)
                        Sinkiang Inland   )
                        River Basins   )

     d. Chen Chang-heng's[**] territorial coverage

---

     [*]Independent Critique Weekly, No. 3-4, 1932.

     [**]Chen Chang-heng, "A Preliminary Study of China's Land and Population in Relation to its National Policy for Economic Reconstruction," Geographical Journal, Vol. II, No. 4 (1935).

                                          (Cont.)

NOTES TO TABLE 3 (Cont.)

primarily embraced Wong's areas, with certain adjustments on the border regions. He had made two
estimates of the maximum and minimum areas of the
nation's arable lands.

    e. Buck's land utilization survey[*] revealed
11 per cent of arable land in China not now cultivated, nearly 35 million acres, or 14 million hectares, in twenty-two provinces. With this added to
his highest estimate of cultivated areas at 93 million hectares, China proper would then possess an
arable potential of 106,300,000 hectares not considering Sikang, Manchuria, Sinkiang, and Tibet. As
a supplement to Buck, the following estimates of the
arable borderlands are presented

    1. Manchuria: 33,300,000 hectares. Ja-
panese estimate gives about half under cultivation,
as cited by the Northeastern Association of Science
and Technology in 1946.

    2. Sinkiang: 16,600,000 hectares. The
Communist Ministry of Reclamation and State Farms
claimed in 1958 that Sinkiang has an arable potential of 20 million hectares based upon calculation
of water supply. The figure might be set at 10 million hectares.

    3. Tibet: 66,000 hectares. (Includes
Chang-tu, which is a part of Sinkiang.) Dawson's
estimate is based upon prewar data.

    Supplemented with these 43,660,000 hec-
tares in the border regions, Buck's arable total for
that period would amount to 151,420,000 hectares,
which is 15.8 per cent on the basis of a geographical area of 956 million hectares.

----

    [*] John Lossing Buck, Land Utilization in China
(Shanghai: Commonwealth Press, 1937), p. 169.

                                        (Cont.)

NOTES TO TABLE 3 (Cont.)

f.   Chiao's method of survey was similar to
that of Buck's, but findings turned out to be
6.36 per cent instead of 11 per cent. Computing
from this lower percentage, supplemented with the
same amount of potential areas from border regions,
his arable total amounted to 145,400,000 hectares
and resulted in a lower percentage of 15.6 per cent.

g.   The arable potential under the Communist
regime in 1957 is estimated in the following steps.

1.   To the official figure of 11,830,000
hectares, as the main body of China's arable land
that has already been cultivated, 112,000 hectares
from Tibet should be added.

2.   The uncultivated arable area in China
proper is estimated at 6,670,000 hectares, which is
a little less than 50 per cent of Buck's figure at
14 million hectares in the early 1930s, or 5 per
cent as compared with Buck's 11 per cent and Chiao's
6.36 per cent.

3.   The uncultivated arable total for Manchuria, Sinkiang, and Tibet, including Chang-tu, is
estimated at a reduced figure of 32,133,000 hectares, because the cultivated portion is already included in the national total of cultivated areas.
This figure of 32,133,000 hectares includes
16,667,000 hectares for Manchuria, 15 million hectares for Sinkiang, and 267,000 hectares for Tibet
(including Chang-tu).

4.   With the uncultivated arable lands of
(2) and (3) added to the 1957 cultivated total area
of 1,680,450,000 mow, the result is an arable total
of 2,262,450,000 mow.

h.   The 1958 official cultivated area is
1,616,800,000 mow. C. L. Tung and O. L. Dawson
estimated uncultivated arable area for China proper,
Manchuria, Sinkiang, and Tibet as being the same

(Cont.)

NOTES TO TABLE 3 (Cont.)

as the 1957 figure. This is a total of 582 million
mow, with the same distribution among different sectors of the mainland.

i. 1. The Tung and Dawson estimate of cultivated area for the mainland as a whole in 1967 is
1,654,480,000 mow. (The process of estimation is
explained in another section of this book.) For
this year the uncultivated arable land in China
proper is estimated at 87 million mow; that for Manchuria, 240 million mow; that for Sinkiang, 150 million mow; that for Tibet 6 million mow--a total of
483 million mow.

2. Adding the cultivated total of
1,654,480,000 mow to the uncultivated arable total
of 483 million mow, there is an arable total of
2,137 million mow, with a ratio of 14.9 per cent.

TABLE 4

Reclaimable Wastelands, 1958-67

Provinces	Wastelands Reported by Provinces (1,000 mow)	Reported Areas Surveyed (1,000 mow)	Wastelands Reclaimable for Agricultural Use				Communist Estimated Total of (a)+(b)+(c) (1,000 mow for 10 provinces)	Cur. Estimated Total (a)+(b)+(c) (1,000 mow for 14 provinces)
			Lands Usable with No Reconditioning (a) (1,000 mow)	Lands Usable with Slight Reconditioning (b) (1,000 mow)	Lands Usable with Much Reconditioning (c) (1,000 mow)	Lands Not Ready for Current Utilization (d) (1,000 mow)		
Arid saline wastelands in northwestern regions (Sinkiang	180,000	105,770	8,000	17,120	46,170	32,810	71,290	
(Chinghai	32,000	6,320	3,080	1,030	1,180	1,030	5,290	
(Kansu	50,000	26,750	4,250	5,400	9,360	2,430	19,010	
(Shensi	8,110	4,310						3,600
(Shansi	6,000	1,400						3,200
(Honan	7,470							4,200
Marshy wastelands in northeastern regions (Heilungkiang	131,160	131,160	10,840	19,560	54,630	46,130	85,030	
(Kirin	42,910	42,910	1,300	250	3,020	2,060	4,570	
(Inner Mongolia	94,500	54,080	11,080	2,980	1,390	2,460	15,450	
Saline wastelands in coastal regions (Liaoning	4,650							2,400
(Hopeh	15,730							4,500
(Shantung	4,270	4,270						3,400
(Kiangsu	4,650	4,690						3,500
(Chekiang	1,840	600						1,200

(Cont.)

TABLE 4 (Cont.)

Provinces	Wastelands Reported by Provinces (1,000 mow)	Reported Areas Surveyed (1,000 mow)	Wastelands Reclaimable for Agricultural Use				Communist Estimated Total of (a)+(b)+(c) (1,000 mow for 10 provinces)	Cur. Estimated Total (a)+(b)+(c) (1,000 mow for 14 provinces)
			Lands Usable with No Reconditioning (a) (1,000 mow)	Lands Usable with Slight Reconditioning (b) (1,000 mow)	Lands Usable with Much Reconditioning (c) (1,000 mow)	Lands Not Ready for Current Utilization (d) (1,000 mow)		
Lake Basin wastelands in interior provinces (Anhwei	8,000	6,580	2,560	1,330	2,690		6,580	4,800
(Kiangsi	15,000	1,860						6,500
(Hupeh	39,100	13,030						3,400
(Hunan	5,370	860						
Hilly red-soil waste lands in southern China (Kwangtung	58,010	58,010	1,140	1,280	1,850	3,510	4,270	7,600
(Kwangsi	42,000	24,610						
(Fukien	5,230		250	1,600	280	1,280	2,130	2,800
(Yünnan	40,730	30,440						
Plateau wastelands in south-west China (Szechwan	14,600	11,930	270	1,000	1,230	130	2,500	4,300
(Kweichow	10,000	1,550						
Total:	821,370	531,130	42,770	51,550	121,800	91,840	216,120	55,400
Grand Total: (1,000 ha.)	54,760	35,400	2,850	3,437	8,120	6,123	271,520,000 mow 18,000,000 ha.*	3,700,000 ha.*

* Seems low

Source: Estimated by C. L. Tung and O. L. Dawson.

62

NOTES TO TABLE 4

Reclaimable Wastelands, 1958-67

a.   "Reclaimable wastelands," in China's traditional usage of the term, practically means the
wastelands that could be reclaimed for agricultural
purposes in varied degrees of utilization. Such
lands that have never been touched by a plow are
called "raw wastes," while those once tilled and
then abandoned are called "ripe wastes," which correspond to the "marginal lands" as used in farm
economics literature in Western countries.

b.   The data in Table 4 (with the exception of
last column under the heading of "Current Estimated
Total [a+b+c]") are transcribed from the book
China's State Farms in Galloping Progress, published
by the Communist Ministry of Reclamation and State
Farms, Peking, 1958. It presents a general picture
of the nation's wasteland.

1.   The reported wastelands from all provinces or regions, excepting Ningsia and Tibet,
amount to a total of 54,700,000 hectares. This is
a little less than the 73,700,000 hectares reported
by twenty-one provinces under the Nationalist Government in 1929.

2.   The Communist regime has carried out a
partial survey of 35,400,000 hectares among the reported areas.

3.   From the surveyed areas about three
fifths, a little over 20 million hectares are classified and reported as fit for agriculture; the remaining portion is regarded as potential pasture or
forest lands.

4.   The areas fit for agriculture are
divided into four classes according to their readi-
ness for reclamation and cultivation:

(Cont.)

NOTES TO TABLE 4 (Cont.)

a. Lands usable without any reconditioning.

b. Lands usable with slight reconditioning.

c. Lands usable with much reconditioning.

d. Lands not ready for current utilization.

5. Probably only the first three classes
(a+b+c, comprising 14,400,000 hectares) are really
reclaimable for agricultural uses, because the
fourth class (d) is branded as "not ready for current utilization."

c. As shown in Table 4, the survey is not yet
complete for all provinces and regions, and only
ten provinces have their surveyed areas classified
up to 1958. Presumably further survey and classification followed after that year. Since no information of such further steps is available at present, researchers have to gauge the possible usabil-
ity of the reported but unclassified wasteland areas
in the remaining fourteen provinces and regions.

d. Tung and Dawson have found that the first
three classes (a+b+c) of the ten provinces under
classification total about 36 per cent of their
reported areas.

e. The Tung and Dawson estimate of the first
three classes (a+b+c) of usable wastelands in the
remaining provinces is 3,700,000 hectares. Comparing this with the total reported area of 12,330,000
hectares in these provinces, the resulting 30 per
cent seems to be quite realistic and realizable.

(Cont.)

NOTES TO TABLE 4 (Cont.)

f. Including the first three classes (a+b+c) of usable wastelands of all provinces and regions (excepting Ningsia and Tibet) yields a total of 18 million hectares. This may be regarded as the available potential lands for China's agricultural development in the coming half century.

5

WATER RESOURCES
AND IRRIGATED
AREA, 1967

WATER RESOURCES

Water may be called the lifeblood of an agrarian community; irrigation may be called a process of transfusion, which serves to replenish and to revitalize its farm economy through three forms of water resources: (a) rainfall ("sky water"); (b) streams (surface water); and (c) "hidden springs" (ground water). However, it is not so much the magnitude of these resources but rather their geographical distribution and periodic variability that are destined to play a decisive role in the agricultural development of a country.

In spite of its rich domain and skillful "Farmers of Forty Centuries," China has never been able to free itself from the ill fate of three dominant calamities: drought, flood, and waterlogging. These are brought about by the variability of precipitation, the uneven distribution of surface flow, and the uncertain supply of groundwater. Not only did traditional China fail to find any basic remedy for these "water maladies," but even the Communist regime has stumbled time and again over its wavering policy and fickle programs for water conservation in the past seventeen years.

It is surprising that during the 3,703 years in Chinese history up to 1937, the nation had suffered 1,074 droughts (an average of one every three years and four months) and 1,058 floods, including waterlogging (on the average of once every three years and five months).[1] It would be more surprising

to read the calamity reports of Mainland China under the Communist rule, which may be summarized in
a brief table as follows:[2]

(A) Flood (including waterlogging)

Period	Frequency of occurrence	Estimated damage on farmland average for each occurrence (mow)
1949–58	5 times in 10 years	128,000,000
1959–61	2 times in 3 years	60,000,000
1962–66 (est.)	3 times in 5 years	130,000,000

(B) Drought

Period	Frequency of occurrence	Estimated damage on farmland average for each occurrence (mow)
1949–58	10 times in 10 years	178,000,000
1959–61	3 times in 3 years	817,000,000
1962–66	4 times in 5 years	300,000,000

In order to understand these failures in this
struggle for water control, a brief review of some
fundamental facts underlying China's conservation
problems is set forth below.

Rainfall

China's rainfall distribution is largely determined by the seesaw confrontations of two mon-
soon systems, mingled with seasonal westerly cy-
clones moving toward the Pacific and the summer
typhoons sweeping northward along the southeastern
coast. It's the counterplay of these air masses
over China proper, as a battleground, that has created a particular scheme of rainfall distribution

with two distinctive features:

    1. An isohyet of 750 millimeters stretching
along the Tsingling mountain range and the Huai
River valley that divides agricultural China into
north and south sectors, each with its special crop
pattern corresponding to the distribution of annual
precipitation.

    2. Concentration of annual precipitation in
the summer season with a higher percentage (60-70
per cent) in the north and a moderate percentage
(30-55 per cent) in the south. While bountiful
rainfall is beneficial for all crops in the growing
season, overconcentration in the summer months has
frequently resulted in flood and waterlogging.
Scanty rainfall in other seasons often produces dry
spells harmful to winter crops all over the country.

    The following table represents a general pat-
tern of China's seasonal distribution of precipitation in relation to its geographical regions.

Geographical regions	Distribution of precipitation (%)			
	Spring	Summer	Autumn	Winter
South China	16	54	25	5
Hilly lands south of Nanling	30	46	15	9
Coastal lands of eastern Chekiang	30	30	24	16
Hilly lands south of Yangtze Valley	39	32	14	15
Basin areas in middle reaches of Yangtze	34	38	17	11
Eastern China plain	19	52	18	11
Hilly lands of Szechwan and Kweichow	26	43	26	5
North China plain and Inner Mongolia	10	65-70	10-15	5
Northwestern mountain lands	25	15	30	30
Sinkiang	(over 50% in May and June)			
Southwestern plateau	(over 77% May-September)			

As plainly shown in the above pattern of seasonal distribution, North China is frequently affected by excessive rainfall in summer months, which
invariably results in flooding over the shallow
beds of its rivers. Winter or spring drought then
follow, which raises the rate of surface evaporation
and reduces soil moisture with damaging effects on
the winter crops. To a lesser degree the same is
true for the south and northeastern provinces, although their occasional drought would be much miti-
gated by a higher annual supply and less uneven
distribution of rainwaters.

Surface Flow

China is endowed with over 1,600 rivers of
various sizes, providing an annual total of about
2,680 billion cubic meters (M^3) of surface water.
This is more than enough for all agricultural, industrial, and civil uses in spite of the growing
population of 750 million. Unfortunately the geographical distribution of this huge body of water
is highly uneven in relation to the nation's cultivated and cultivable areas between the south and
north.

The Yangtze Valley and regions to the south,
sharing only 33 per cent of the nation's cultivated
area, is generously provided with a surface flow of
76 per cent. North China and the northwest, occupying 51 per cent of the nation's cultivated area,
on the other hand receive a bare 7 per cent of the
surface waters. There are only about 30,000 to
40,000 M^3 of surface water for every square kilometer in the northwest, but every square kilometer
in Central and South China is equipped with the
huge quantity of 520,000 M^3.

The Huai River basin possesses a cultivated
area of 12,700,000 hectares, with an annual surface
flow of 36,600 million M^3, yet a Communist development plan proposed to "borrow" 25 per cent of the
area's water supply from the Yellow River and the
Han River. The Communist plan for permanent control

of the Yellow River assumed only 65 per cent of the
basin's 44,300,000 hectares of farmland could be
irrigated by its own resources of water, and 35 per
cent had to be "diverted" from the Yangtze River in
a future project. Although no definite plan for
the Hai Ho basin system development has been drawn
up, its 8,700,000 hectares of cultivated lands will
most likely require a supplement of 15 per cent in
surface water from other river systems.

Professor Richard Tawney, commenting on China's
farm problem in the 1930s, shrewdly observed that
"there is too much water in the South and too little water in the North." When the Communist leadership announced their new conservation policy in
1956, they seemed to believe that a magic formula
had been formed on the three-pronged principles of
a "storage priority-small project-collective enterprise." Unfortunately, they overlooked the most
fundamental fact in China's conservation problems.
Wherever water is in chronic shortage over a vast
area, as in China's northern and northwestern provinces, no concerted efforts could create something
out of nothing. There also still remains a constantly decreasing amount for storage if these so-
called projects prove to be incomplete, defective,
and uncoordinated as created by the frenzied campaigns in the fateful years from 1957 to 1959.

This probably prompted the Soviet expert B. M.
Korniev to criticize China's new conservation as
"upsetting the equilibrium of water quantity." He
continues:

> . . . taking the individual basins,
> almost all the water resources of
> Yellow River, the Huai River and the
> Hai River systems have already been
> harnessed. Further irrigation is not
> promising. . . . Hence it is neces-
> sary not to build seasonally regula-
> tory reservoirs (small projects) . . .
> but to pass over to perennially regu-
> latory reservoirs (large projects)

> that could store up all the water
> during any year of abundant discharge.

Quite a number of Chinese "rightist" experts had
also offered the same opinion.

It should be noted that the soundness of these
arguments has been borne out by actual developments
of recent years. The Yellow River has been pre-
vented from flooding, since the completion (excepting power installations) of the Sanmen Gorge Project*
in 1960 and partial completion of two other projects,
with a total reservoir capacity of 70,600 million M^3
for the three. Even the Huai River is controlled
against high flood of fifty years' frequency, having a total reservoir capacity from ten large and
medium projects in Honan and Anhwei, of 8,178 million M^3. Hai-ho has failed (there was a serious
flood in 1963) in this respect, because it has only
one large reservoir (Mi-Yun), with a capacity of
4,100 million M^3. Its Kwan-ting reservoir, with a
capacity of 2,270 million M^3, has been 7.7 per cent
silted. But drought and waterlogging are still
serious, large-scale problems in North China.

Groundwater

Groundwater has always been an unknown quantity
in China's conservation plans.[3] This suggests that
a huge stratum of groundwater must have underlain
the thick alluvial plain of North China. The Yellow River with its annual flow of 46,500 million M^3
has been meandering over this vast plain of sandy
sediments for millions of years. While the bulk of
its flow annually enters the sea with heavy loads
of silt, a considerable portion of water must have
filtered through the porous strata of its bed and
accumulated underneath into an immense "subterranean
sea." This is the source of groundwater that has

----

*Gates have not been installed, says James
Jordan, possibly for fear of silting.

supported millions of people, furnishing about 10
million wells (8 million reported in 1958) with irrigation water for an estimated 6,600,000 hectares
of farmland.

This subject has been discussed at length in
the section on irrigation by O. L. Dawson in Food
and Agriculture in Communist China.[4]

According to Lo Kno-Yu, "a vast subterranean
sea," about 200,000 square kilometers in extent,
has been recently (1960) discovered under the East
China plain. It is a water-bearing formation, or
aquifer, deep down under the surface of the earth.
It stretches beneath most of Kiangsu Province,
parts of northern Anhwei and eastern Honan, and a
small section of southwest Shantung. The hydrological workers estimate that it holds reserves of
several billion tons of water, together with the
groundwater lying under the 300-kilometer stretch
of territory that once formed the bed of the
Yangtze River.

Here the geologists found that the water-
bearing formation 60 meters below the ground is
still connected with the present Yangtze River.
When the river rises, its water seeps through the
old gravel floor and causes a rise in the body of
groundwater.

IRRIGATED AREAS

Definitions[5]

"Irrigated area" in Communist statistics has
been defined as "the cultivated area that is supplied with water, according to the needs of crops,
by irrigation facilities. Examples are channels,
ponds and dams, reservoirs, wells, water wheels and
pumps." Irrigated areas include:

1. The "wet fields," or rice paddies, that
are provided with facilities to regulate water
supply.

2.   The "dry fields" that are provided with
facilities for the same purpose.

All official data of irrigated areas before
1957 were collected and presented on this basis,
until drastic revisions were made in 1958 and finalized as published in the Ten Great Years of 1959.
Thus the irrigated area in its revised version,
published by People's Daily, May 3, 1958, was no
longer the sum of a portion of wet fields plus a
portion of dry fields, with the presumption that
all wet fields were provided irrigation facilities.

Assuming no change in its definition since
then, Dawson and Tung have estimated irrigated area
in terms of the Mainland total as well as the com-
ponent figures from the provinces.

But a land provided irrigation facilities is
not always effectively irrigated nor completely
irrigated nor, in most cases, immediately irrigated.
These complexities forced the Communist statisti-
cians to set up a standard of assessment, and to
give a clear-cut definition of "effectiveness,"
with regard to price of irrigation installation.
Although no official proclamation has been made on
this subject, general practice has set a minimum
requirement of effectiveness as "the capacity of
drought resistance for a duration of 30, 50, or 70
days" depending upon varied conditions of different
localities. Of course, this is still a hypothetical yardstick for technical fitness, against which
few projects could have a real chance to be tested
in the stated time limits. For practical purposes
in our process of evaluation, there is no choice
but to adopt the Communist definitions in the original phraseology.

1.   "Irrigated area" is the cultivated area
provided with facilities for irrigation, including
all wet fields and a portion of dry fields that are
so provided for the needs of crops.

2.   "Effective irrigated area" is the irrigated area under operation of a completed project that

currently possesses the drought-resistance capacity
for a duration of 30, 50, or 70 days, depending
upon specific requirement of the locality.

Review of China's Conservation
Situation

Before proceeding with estimations, we should
briefly review the reported Communist achievements
on irrigation from 1957 to 1967, with the official
figure of 35 million hectares as the final product
of the first Five-Year Plan. There is no need to
enumerate the wild claims of 1958 and 1959, which
the Communists themselves have had to discount under various "interpretations."

1. The tabulated 1958 data released by the
People's Daily, May 3, 1958, set the national total
of effective irrigated area at 43 million hectares,
which amounted to 74 per cent of its gross irrigated area (58 million hectares) and 38 per cent of
its cultivated area (112 million hectares).

2. The tabulated 1957 data, drawn from the
separate volumes of Economic Geography of China by
Provinces (a semiofficial publication of the Chinese
Academy of Science, Peking, 1958 to 1960), give a
national total of irrigated area (presumably being
"effective") of 43 million hectares with a ratio of
39.2 per cent against its cultivated area for 1957
(112 million hectares).

3. The People's Daily again reported on December 30 that China's effective irrigated area was
around 529,950,000 mow, which was only about 32 per
cent on the basis of cultivated area (1,616,800,000
mow) for 1958. The percentage would be even lower
if calculated against the increased cultivation of
the early 1960s.

Process of Estimation

In the Progress Report of October, 1967, Dawson and Tung took the above-mentioned 530 million

mow (35,300,000 hectares) of irrigated ("effective")
area for 1963 as a starting point, which may be low.

While Communists repeatedly claimed an annual
increase of 1,400,000 hectares in irrigated area
for the mid-1960s, Dawson and Tung hesitated to ac-
cept this figure on its face value. They had conservatively estimated 36 million hectares for 1964,
which represented a moderate increase of 700,000
hectares over that of 1963.

A careful examination of current material from
various sources, including the 1967 Yearbook on
Chinese Communism from Taiwan and the Agricultural
Notes from Hong Kong, Dawson and Tung have now decided to give a more liberal estimate on China's
irrigated areas from 1964 to 1967, primarily in
consideration of the following factors:

1.   Recent Communist achievements on a number
of large-scale conservation works such as the
Heilungkiang and Tzeyaho projects of Hopeh, the
Tukai and Malkai project of Shantung, the Ting-ting
Lake project of Hunan, the Po-Yang Lake project of
Kiangsi, and the Su Hsien project of Anhwei.

2.   The numerous electric and mechanical pumping stations with their estimated 7 to 8 million
horsepower in the central and southern provinces;
the speedy increase of mechanized wells on the
North China plain; the widespread terraced slopes
on the southwestern hilly lands; and the large
stretches of leveled grounds, drained marshes, and
improved soils over the coastal regions.

3.   All these new developments in the last few
years will decidedly afford fine opportunities for
irrigation expansion, which is at the same time the
cause and effect of a long series of agrarian advancement.

[Text continues on p. 83.]

TABLE 5

Estimated Effective Irrigated Areas by Province, 1967

Province	(a) Cultivated Area (1,000 mow)	(b) Effective Irrigated Area (1,000 mow)	Ratio of (b) to (a) %
Northeast: Liaoning	70,500	11,280	16
Kirin	71,250	10,687.5	15
Heilungkiang	73,200	8,784	12
Subtotal	214,950	30,751.5	14.30
1,000 ha.	14,300	2,050	
North: Hopeh (including Peking)	125,500	42,670	30
Shansi	70,850	12,753	18
Shantung	138,200	45,606	32
Honan	136,700	43,744	31
Inner Mongolia	86,000	11,180	13
Subtotal	556,250	148,184	26.64
1,000 ha.	37,100	10,000	
Northwest: Sinkiang	32,500	32,500	100
Kansu	59,300	9,488	16
Shensi	68,500	12,330	18
Chianghai	9,200	1,012	11
Ningsia	14,700	2,058	14
Subtotal	184,200	57,386	31.15
1,000 ha.	12,300	3,800	

Region			
East:	Kiangsu (including Shanghai)	95,200	57,120	60
	Chekiang	34,500	23,640	68
	Anhwei	89,400	58,100	65
Subtotal	1,000 ha.	219,100	138,670	63.24
		14,600	9,200	
Central:	Hupeh	65,200	24,124	37
	Hunan	58,350	31,509	54
	Kiangsi	43,400	19,530	45
Subtotal	1,000 ha.	166,950	75,163	45.02
		11,100	5,000	
South:	Kwangtung	55,450	38,815	70
	Kwangsi	38,220	14,523.5	38
	Fukien	22,500	10,125	45
Subtotal	1,000 ha.	116,170	63,463.5	54.63
		7,700	4,200	
Southwest:	Szechwan	115,900	48,678	42
	Kweichow	32,500	9,750	30
	Yünnan	44,460	14,227	32
Subtotal	1,000 ha.	192,860	72,655	37.67
		12,800	4,800	
(Tibet excluded)				
Grand Total:	1,000 ha.	1,650,480	586,273	35.52
		110,000	39,000	

Source: C. L. Turg and O. L. Dawson.

(Cont.)

77

NOTES TO TABLE 5

Estimated Effective Irrigated Areas
by Province, 1967

a. Definition: "Irrigated area is the cultivated area that is supplied with water, according
to the needs of crops, by irrigation facilities,
such as channels, ponds and dams, reservoirs, wells,
waterwheels and pumps." This is the definition
given in an article "Brief Explanations of the Ter-
minologies used in the Draft of the Second Five-
Year Plan," as cited in Planned Economy, No. 10,
October, 1956.

It is also designated as "the area of farmland
which could be effectively irrigated following the
completion of repairs to irrigation works." If
"owing to certain reasons such as lack of rainfall,
however, irrigation were not carried out," this
project would not be regarded as "effective."

Irrigated area is always computed on the basis
of cultivated area, but not on the sown area. The
increase of irrigated acreage should be only the
area of nonirrigated land (dry land) turned into
irrigated fields, not including the field for
single-crop rice that is turned into a field of
double-crop rice.

In the article cited above, the definition of
irrigated area up to 1957 did not include all the
wet fields (rice paddies), but was composed of two
categories of land:

1. Those wet fields equipped with fixed
or permanent irrigation facilities, known as "irrigated wet fields."

2. Those dry fields equipped with such
facilities, known as "watered fields."

(Cont.)

NOTES TO TABLE 5 (Cont.)

Beginning with the latter half of 1957, however, the statistics of irrigated acreage were revised several times, until all of them were finalized by the State Statistical Bureau as issued in
Ten Great Years. As was made public in May, 1958,
irrigated acreage was defined as the sum of all wet
fields (rice paddies) and a part of watered fields
(dry lands irrigated with water).

It should be noted that not all irrigated areas were effective. Of the "mass achievements" in
irrigation work during 1957-58, only about three
fourths of the irrigated acreage was regarded as
"operative." Again, out of a 550 million mow of
increased irrigated land claimed for 1958-59, only
300 million mow were pronounced "effective" during
the three years from 1958 to 1960. ("Ninth" Plenary Session of the Eighth Central Committee of the
Chinese Communist Party," China Pictorial, No. 3,
March, 1961.)

Although no definition of "effectiveness" had
ever been stated regarding irrigated areas, Communist publications in mainland China had often
called for a minimum standard of "drought resistance for 30, 50, or 70 days." Perhaps this was
what they tried to apply as a yardstick for measur-
ing effectiveness in China's irrigation works. It
is quite plain from analyzing numerous Communist
reports on their achievements of irrigation that:

1. An "irrigated area" is meant to denote
a "cultivated area" that has been equipped with irrigation facilities such as reservoirs, ponds,
canals, wells, waterwheels, waterpumps, and so
forth.

2. The "effectiveness" of these facilities is measured by their capacity of "drought resistance for 30, 50, or 70 days," depending upon

(Cont.)

NOTES TO TABLE 5 (Cont.)

the need of the locality. This definition has never
been publicly announced.

b. Methodology: As in the case of "cultivated area," we have several other authoritative estimates on China's irrigation for our "standard reference":

1. The official Communist "Estimate of
Cultivated Area and Irrigated Area in 1958," released by People's Daily, May 3, 1958, provides a
detailed distribution of China's irrigated areas by
provinces.

2. "Economic Geography of China" (published by the Chinese Academy of Science, Peking,
1958-60) also gives irrigated areas for most provinces, presumably based on local reports without
adjustments.

3. The Taiwan publications Atlas of Mainland China and the 1967 Yearbook on Chinese Communism both have made some critical studies of Communist national figures on irrigation, but supply no
information on the conservation situation in individual provinces.

In estimating China's irrigated areas for recent years, the records of old projects, as reported and finalized by Peking authorities, have been
carefully examined. The nation's local developments have also been considered in relation to population, distribution, and land and water resources.

In getting location information on China's
conservation works, use has been made of relevant
materials that may be collected from various Communist or non-Communist papers, periodicals, and
monographs that are obtainable in Hong Kong, Taiwan,
Japan, or this country. The weekly Agricultural

(Cont.)

Notes issued by the U.S. Consulate General in Hong Kong are especially useful in providing local data on this subject as announced from time to time by local broadcasts from different provincial capitals.

     c. Criteria: The criteria used to evaluate the achievements or failures of China's conservation programs are primarily the same as those used to scrutinize the changes in its cultivation performances and cultivated areas. The same set of factors (physical-technical or economic-political) that tend to promote farm production would logically call for a corresponding expansion of its land basis. The same set of factors that tend to expand cultivation would also logically call for a corresponding construction of conservation projects. It is natural that cultivation and conservation activities of the country advance hand in hand, in the course of normal agricultural development, except that conservation usually proceeds at a higher speed than cultivation.

     In view of the recent conservation policy adopted by Peking, however, there are some particular problems that may frustrate China's urgent programs for water utilization:

     1. The fundamental deficiency of water supply in North China and northwestern China, which would render all irrigation projects "ineffective" regardless of their type, size, or technical quality in structure and function.

     2. The basic character of soil structure in China's northern and coastal provinces, which is constantly susceptible to salinization and alkalinization at the slightest mismanagement in carrying out various programs for irrigation and drainage.

     3. The principle of "small projects" to be realized by commune members or county authorities

(Cont.)

NOTES TO TABLE 5 (Cont.)

sounds very easy and simple. Could these "self-
made" schemes dovetail into each other, whenever
and wherever there is some urgent need of large-
area coordination in order to meet certain emergen-
cies or to push through certain common programs for
the benefit of all adjacent localities?

        4. The spirit of "self-reliance" in water
conservation as well as in other tasks of rural construction also raises questions as to its sincerity
and feasibility. The Chinese peasantry has not yet
risen high above the line of bare subsistence, and
the rural production teams are always overburdened
by public requests (from state, province, or locality) for labor, food, and materials of one kind
or another. Even if they want to build their own
conservation works in the spirit of "self-reliance,"
could they actually push through such schemes without plunging into great financial and technical
difficulties?

        In consideration of these knotty problems con-
fronting China's public policies as well as private
efforts relative to their conservation development,
we have questions on their reported achievements.
In any given year or any given season, the nation
may proclaim an "irrigated area" that is unprece-
dentedly extensive, a range of "irrigation facilities" that is overwhelmingly multitudinous. So
their "effectiveness" may prove to be exceptionally
illusory and disheartening.

In view of these improvements, Dawson and Tung
have hypothetically set an accelerating schedule
for irrigation advancement in the three years from
1964 to 1967. Starting with an effective irrigated
area of 36 million hectares for 1964, they allow an
increase of 800,000 hectares in 1965, 1 million
hectares in 1966, and 1,260,000 hectares in 1967.
The final result for 1967 is an effective irrigated
area of 39 million hectares, which is 35.5 per cent
of our estimated cultivated area for that year, or
110 million hectares excluding Tibet. This still
seems low, and further study of the data may be
useful.

Regarding the estimates of irrigated areas for
the provinces, we have considered two earlier Communist estimates: the Economic Geography estimate
for 1957, and the People's Daily estimate of 1958.
But these old data of the 1950s are used only as
general references against which Dawson and Tung
check their own materials, make their observations,
and draw their conclusions. These two sets of
Communist data have shown wide discrepancies in
many provinces. Apparently the compilers of the
Economic Geography depended mostly upon original
reports from the provinces, while the People's
Daily tried to "redress" their data for public consumption. Dawson and Tung are obliged to differ
with either or both of them in many instances.
While realizing close approach to the realities of
China's local conditions is difficult, they tried
objectively to present a realistic picture of the
nation's conservation situation in its latest development.

TABLE 6

Hydrological Balance in the River Systems

River Systems	River Basin (sq km)	Precipitation (mm)	Depth of Flow (m)	Surface Evaporation (mm)	Coefficient of Surface Flow (%)
Sungari River	523,580	512	141	371	27.6
Liao River	219,000	465	74	391	15.9
Hwong-ho River	745,100	415	65	350	15.7
Upper Reach (Lanchow)	216,190	427	148	279	35.0
Feng River (Ho-Ching)	38,650	471	49.7	321.3	11.0
Lo River (Chun-tao)	62,700	436	28.1	407.9	6.5
Ching-ho (Chang-Chia-Shan)	41,800	462	46.5	415.5	10.1
Wei-ho (Hua-hsien)	63,550	573	142	431	25.0
Huan River	164,560	840	148	642	23.6
Yangtze River	1,808,500	1,050	565	482	54.1
Ching-Sha Chiang	502,050	662	329	333	50.0
Ning Chiang	133,570	1,100	722	378	65.6
Chia-ling Chiang	159,810	892	408	484	46.0
Wu Chiang	88,220	1,135	586	549	52.0
Tung-ting Tributaries	261,100	1,445	852	593	59.0
Han Shui River	174,350	900	356	544	40.0
Po-yang Tributaries	158,670	1,670	971	699	58.2
Chien-Tang River	49,930	1,650	940	710	57.0
Nin River	69,800	1,710	1,074	636	62.8
Han Chiang	29,700	1,655	982	673	59.0
Pearl River	437,230	1,480	890	590	60.2
Tung Chiang	26,300	1,758	1,203	555	68.4
Pei Chiang	45,600	1,885	1,370	515	73.0
Hsi Chieng (Wu Chow)	328,000	1,370	773	603	56.0
Hu Chiang (Naning)	74,310	1,340	646	694	48.0

Source: Kuo Ching-hwei, "Physiographical Causes in the Formation of China's River

84

TABLE 7

Conservation Projects, 1950-60

Projects	Reservoir Capacity (100 million M³)	Work Started	Work Completed
Honan:			
Sanmen Gorge	647.00	1954 (Apr.)	1960 (Dec.)
Shi-men-tan	0.47	1955 (Apr.)	1955 (July)
Pan-chao	4.18	1952	1957 (Aug.)
Pai-Sha	2.74	1951	1957 (Aug.)
Po-Shan	2.92	1952	1954 (Dec.)
Nan-Wan	9.32	1953	
Chao-ping	6.80	1958 (May)	1960 (June)
Lung-Shan	2.90		
Ta-po-ling	2.60		
Shen-Chia-Tien	1.70		
Chan-yu-Shan	0.70		
Tu-Shu-Cheng	1.50		
Chi-lo-Shan	4.70		
Anhwei:			
Fu-tze-ling	5.82	1952	1954 (Oct.)
Mei-shan	22.75	1953	1956 (Apr.)
Tung-ho kon	5.70	1959 (Aug.)	
Hsiang-hung-tien	23.42		1958 (Dec.)
Mutze-tan	3.36		1958 (Dec.)
Lin-huai-Kuan	(?)		
Shantung:			
Tung-pin-hu	40.00		1958 (Oct.)
Tai-hang-ti	12.30		1958 (Aug.)
Wei-Shan	(?)	1958 (June)	
Hsia-Shan	10.85	1958	
Lung-Wan-tao	1.00	1958 (Nov.)	

(Cont.)

TABLE 7 (Cont.)

Projects	Reservoir Capacity (100 million M³)	Work Started	Work Completed
Hopei:			
Kwan-ting	22.70	1951 (Oct.)	1955 (May)
(Peking) Min-ling	0.82	1958 (Jan.)	1958 (July)
(Peking) Mi-Yun	41.00	1958 (Sept.)	1960
(Peking) Huae-Juo	0.90		1958 (July)
(Peking) Tou-ho	1.34		1956 (Dec.)
Shansi:			
Ta-fu-Shih	15.80	1960 (Jan.)	
San-Kan-ho	7.20	1958	
Feng-ho	7.00	1958 (July)	1959 (Dec.)
Kuan-ho	1.00	1958 (Mar.)	
Kuay-ho	0.75	1958	1959 (June)
Liaoning:			
Ta-ho-fang	19.70	1954	1958 (Sept.)
Hsin-li-tun	(?)	1959	
Huan-jen	83.00	1958 (May)	
Ching-ho	9.57	1958 (May)	
Kirin:			
Yun-feng	35.00	1958	
Hsiao-feng-men	125.00	1953	1957 (Nov.)
Kansu:			
Yen-Kuo Gorge	2.00	1958	
Liu-Chai Gorge	57.00	1958	
Hsi-ma-hu	0.13		1957
Sinkiang:			
Ma-Ku-hu	1.58		1958 (Dec.)
Yi-Kan-Chi	0.62	1955 (Aug.)	1956 (Nov.)

Projects	Reservoir Capacity (100 million M³)	Work Started	Work Completed
Hupeh:			
Tan-Chiang-Kuo	283.00	1958 (Sept.)	
Shih-men	1.23		1957 (July)
Min-shan	1.30	1957	1959 (May)
Chekiang:			
Hsin-an-Chiang	178.00	1957 (Apr.)	1960 (Apr.)
Fukien:			
Chai-Chang	1.86	1957 (May)	1958 (Nov.)
Ku-tien	5.74		1956 (Nov.)
Ting Chiang	21.80	1959	
Kwangtung:			
Hsin-feng-Chiang	115.00	1958 (June)	
Liang-teh	6.30	1958	
Lui-Chi-ho	3.26	1956 (June)	1958 (Aug.)
(Hainan) Sung-tao	28.90	1958	1959
Kwangsi:			
Shan-yu	7.00	1955 (Mar.)	
Wan-an	11.00	1958	

Source: Figures transcribed from the Atlas of
Mainland China, by province (Chinese), published in
Taipeh, Taiwan, 1966.

SUMMARY AND OUTLOOK

A brief sketch of China's conservation policy is expected to show the following tendencies of development in the coming decades.

Flood Prevention

Timely completion (excepting power installations) of the Sanmen Gorge Dam on the Yellow River in 1960 has temporarily protected the North China plain from serious flooding in the past seven years. The ten reservoirs completed on the Huai River in 1959 have also been claimed as capable of preventing floods with fifty-year frequency. The Ching-Chiang flood-diversion basin in the middle Yangtze Valley, together with several small projects on the Han River, seems to have saved the Chiang-Han plain from innundation in recent years. Flood control in both Manchuria and South China have also achieved partial success through a large number of small and medium projects along the main river courses and their tributaries.

However, owing to decentralization of financial-economic powers since the late 1950s, and the decline of Peking authority since post-"Leap" years, extra-large and multiple-purpose projects (such as the unfinished "staircase dams" on the Yellow River, the giant structure blueprinted for the Yangtze Gorge, and the ambitious plan to transfer surface water from the south to the north) probably could never be realized in the next one or two decades. On the other hand, moderate projects for conservation could be carried out by joint efforts of several provinces, or within a province, by the joint efforts of several counties with the support of communal labor and grain reserves. At the same time, many small projects could be developed by collective units in the spirit of "self-reliance," chiefly as a palliative measure to be integrated later with larger projects on a regional basis.

Irrigation: Types of Facilities

Along with the partial success of flood-prevention in recent years, irrigation systems have gradually been extended in the nation's main river basins. According to Communist estimate in 1964 (Economic Reporter, November 16, 1964), of China's 500 million odd mow of effective irrigated areas, about 58 per cent draw their water either directly from river flows or indirectly from river dams through the connection of irrigation canals. Wherever such sources are not available, water is drawn from lakes, reservoirs, ponds, or other storage facilities (about 35 per cent). A small portion (7 per cent) of irrigation water is drawn from traditional wells, machine wells, or other sources of groundwater.

The current tendencies in China's irrigation programs seem to converge along three lines of development:

1. In delta and lake basins and along river banks, channel irrigation is prevalent and power pumps have been widely adopted in recent years. Yangtze delta, Pearl River delta, the Lung-ting and Po-Yang Lake regions, and the plain areas along Yellow River, Yangtze River, Huai River, and Han River are illustrative examples in this category.

2. Among rugged regions with hilly slopes, where rainfall is plentiful and evaporation low, ponds, ditches, and mountain barrages are usually constructed to store water for irrigation and to be recharged from seasonal precipitation. Power pumps are also gradually adopted wherever power is available. Irrigation facilities installed in the mountainous regions of Manchuria borderlands, the middle Yangtze Valley, the Si-Kiang River basin, and in the southwestern provinces belong to this type.

3. In the plain and plateau regions of North China and the Northwest, where rainfall is scanty and surface flow is irregular and unstable, well

irrigation has rapidly increased since the 1960s to
supplement channel irrigation, which has often
failed to produce sufficient water supply to meet
the increasing demands of crop areas. The current
tendency is to open up a great number of machine
wells with larger size, greater depth, and a mechanical outfit for water operation.

Irrigated Area

Irrigated area can be extended at a much
greater speed in the coming decades for the following reasons:

1. Improvement of flood control will protect
vast tracts of surrounding farmland that have formerly suffered from periodic flooding.

2. Large flood-control projects, often
multiple-purpose in function, usually provide ample
water storage in reservoirs for the use of irrigation.

3. Irrigation pumps, motivated either by
electricity or other forms of power, installed either in plain regions or hilly areas, have been extended rapidly in recent years.

Our estimated effective irrigated area for
1964 is 36 million hectares, and that for 1967 is
39 million hectares, an increase of about 1 million
hectares per year on the average. In view of the
favorable factors stated above, we expect a greater
annual increase in the next two decades; probably
1,200,000 hectares of annual increase for the period 1968-77, and 1,500,000 hectares for the period
1978-87.

Drainage

Negligence of drainage in China's pre-1960
conservation programs resulted in an annual average
of about 7 million hectares of waterlogged areas,
which in turn quickly contributed to the extension

of soil salinization and alkalinization in the nation's low-lying croplands along the coast or in the interior. The Communists have attempted to remedy this precarious situation through a series of large and medium drainage schemes since the early 1960s, as illustrated by the Heilungkiang project and Tzeyaho project of Hopeh, the Tuhai and Machai projects of Shantung, the "Red Banner" project of Honan, the Su Hsien project of Anhwei, the Tungting project of Hunan, the Po-Yang project of Kiangsi, and a number of lesser projects in other parts of the country.

The continuous promotion of drainage along with irrigation projects would not only reduce waterlogging and expedite desalinization, but would also contribute to the extension of cultivated areas and improvement of deteriorated soils. This would especially bring great benefits to depression areas along the coast of Liaoning, Hopeh, Shantung, and Kiangsu, and also in the beach areas around Tung-ting Po-Yang, and Hung-tze lakes.

NOTES

1. Teng Yun-teh, <u>History of China's Farmers and Relief</u> (Shanghai: [n.p.], 1952), pp. 55-56.

2. Data drawn from the 1967 <u>Yearbook on Chinese Communism</u> (Taiwan, 1967), and <u>Agricultural Notes</u> (Hong Kong, 1964-66).

3. John Lossing Buck, Owen L. Dawson, and Yuan-li Wu, <u>Food and Agriculture in Communist China</u> Published for the Hoover Institution on War, Revolution and Peace, Stanford University (New York and London: Frederick A. Praeger, 1966), pp. 149-67.

4. <u>Ibid</u>.

5. <u>Ibid</u>., pp. 151-54.

CHAPTER **6** AGRICULTURAL
RESEARCH AND
DEVELOPMENT

INTRODUCTION

The pertinent chapters on land, water, and fertilizer resources make way for this chapter on scientific research through extension and demonstration projects. The program is of basic importance in promoting the agricultural potential of Communist China.

This subject has been covered at length by Professor Tien-hsi Cheng of the University of Pennsylvania, who spent a year in Hong Kong studying the Chinese documents.[1] He is co-author with Ralph Nash of two 1965 articles on this subject. Mrs. Grace Wu and Roland Y. M. Wu of Stanford gave a paper on this subject at the Inaugural Meeting of the Asian Studies Group on the Pacific Coast, June 16-18, 1966. The reports of the Consulate General, Hong Kong, in the past two years contain varied references to the subject. Scattered news writings from the Survey of China Mainland Press further refer to the subject.

This report aims to: (1) summarize organization developments and chief lines of research and significant achievements under the Communists, based on the above sources; and (2) cite specific developments in seed variety improvement.

Pre-Communist China Developments

During the late 1940s, the Nationalist Government of China tried vigorously to strengthen

92

agricultural research as support for long-range production planning. This is well set forth in the
report of the China-American Agricultural Mission
of 1948. T. H. Shen's <u>Agricultural Resources of
China</u>[2] explains the organization. The most compre-
hensively organized agency of the government was
the National Agricultural Research Bureau. Four
other bureaus were established up to 1947. The gov-
ernmental organization was well designed but much
too small, and did not have time to work long on
the multifarious problems of agriculture before the
incursion of the Communists. Quite a bit had been
accomplished on seed variety improvement at the University of Nanking. Many economic surveys were made
through the Agricultural Economic Division of the
University of Nanking, including the monumental <u>Land
Utilization Survey</u> by Buck.

At the provincial level there was a great array
of agricultural research institutes, improvement
bureaus, experiment stations, seed and animal breed
increase stations, demonstration farms, and other
centers; but these were in general understaffed,
poorly equipped, and inadequately supported.

There were at that time, according to Shen,
over one hundred agricultural experiment stations,
branches, and field stations, both national and provincial; but there was a great need for coordination
and closer cooperation in experimental and demonstration work between the national and provincial stations. Such a recommendation was made by the China-
United States Agricultural Mission in 1948.

This brief résumé of agricultural research in
pre-Communist China shows well-organized and coordinated planning. There were a number of Western-
trained scientists in universities and agricultural
colleges that chiefly emphasized teaching. Research
began expanding shortly before the Communists took
over, and many basic plans for future production
were set forth.

When the Communists took over, they began to

organize and establish agricultural research institutes, colleges, laboratories, and bureaus. Much of the effort was negated because of restrictions placed on activities of Western-trained scientists, and some erroneous and untested agricultural practices resulted from placing pseudo-scientists from the Party in important positions.

The present Communist Chinese policy, espoused by Mao Tse-tung, calls for a national agricultural transformation within twenty to twenty-five years. This broad goal seems to be a very visionary one. According to Professors Cheng and Nash,[3] "qualified agricultural scientists, many of them Western-trained, have now been given positions of greater responsibility and have been provided with support and facilities necessary to develop technology to increase agricultural production. All agricultural research is oriented to increase agricultural production." Yet only moderate increases of food grain are evident in the last ten years. Progress in the next five years will be watched with interest.

ORGANIZATION

Scientific agricultural research activity is mainly under the jurisdiction of the Chinese Academy of Agricultural Sciences, established in 1957. This is subordinate to the Ministry of Agriculture, which is under the Staff Office of Agriculture and Forestry and subordinate to the State Council. This academy, with its well-equipped headquarters in Peiping, supervises the work of twenty-six specialized research institutes and laboratories, which cover agricultural problems all over the country. Certain sections of the Chinese Academy of Sciences overlap; but it concentrates on basic research, whereas the Academy of Agricultural Science emphasizes applied research.

In addition to the Chinese Academy of Agricultural Sciences, many of the twenty-eight provinces and autonomous regions have their own academies of

agriculture; each province and autonomous region
also has its own agricultural research institute,
as do the municipalities of Peiping and Shanghai.
Specialized agricultural science institutes are
found also in most of the provinces and in a number
of counties and cities. For example, the newly
opened farm areas or grasslands of Heilunkiang Province and, in Sinkiang and the autonomous regions,
Sinkiang and Inner Mongolia have their own agricultural research centers.

It is thus evident that Communist China has developed a vast network of experiment stations and
demonstration farms. The organizational concept of
agricultural research has been closely adhered to,
an asset in getting and providing information for
improvement of agricultural production. The best
agricultural research pertaining to China's food resources is conducted by several institutes within
the Chinese Academy of Science, where there are several outstanding agricultural scientists.

With a vast organization comprised of many research agencies, greater progress in agricultural
production should be expected; but over-all direction and coordination of the projects have been disrupted by personnel changes and China People's Republic policy changes.

Part of the agricultural research in Communist
China is conducted by the thirty or more agricultural colleges. It is coordinated with the Chinese
Academy of Agricultural Sciences in a pattern similar to that of the U.S. land grant college system.
Research in some of the colleges is particularly
good, as in Peiping and Nanking.

A program for the future development of Chinese
agricultural science and technology was defined, and
the major research tasks were specified, by a Conference of Agricultural Science and Technology during February and March, 1963. This conference was
sponsored by the Tenth Plenary Session of the Eighth
Central Committee of the Chinese Communist Party,

and was the largest gathering of its kind ever held
in China.

Major research tasks set forth were as follows:[4]

(a) Extensive investigation of the
    natural resources in the country
    and their use, and the study of
    efficient tapping of new resources.

(b) Application of China's traditional
    experience in intensive farming, and
    of the latest science technology,
    to raise substantially the level of
    production.

(c) The overall study of the better
    utilization of land and water
    area and the extension of culti-
    vated lands, including reclama-
    tion of alkali and other poor
    soils. (This is commented on
    under the sections on land and
    water resources.)

(d) Strengthening of theoretical re-
    search in economy and development
    of new branches of agricultural
    sciences. The chief point in
    priority stressed was the increas-
    ing of the per-hectare yield of
    the present farm land. Ten large
    comprehensive experimental and
    research centers were to be estab-
    lished throughout the country.

Procedure and schedule are lacking in this
statement of tasks and priorities. No detailed
national or regional plans are stated, but these
are eagerly awaited. Production increases are
slow; food falls behind population increases. (See
section on food and fertilizer.)

The conference was attended by more than 1,200

scientists and other specialists relating to agriculture. More than 3,000 topics were proposed to achieve goals set by the National Program of Agricultural Development.

For propaganda purposes the National People's Congress in 1960 announced the forty-point National Program. Mao Tse-tung's Eight Point Charter is included within the forty-point program. Reiterated platitudes are again put forth, "to make the fullest and most efficient use of the country's land and water surface," etc.

The present policy seems to contradict that seen in the "Leap Forward" and has some elements of a step-by-step approach toward realistic goals. The poor planning and unrealistic goals of the old program hampered the best use of agricultural resources.

The present program of placing Chinese agriculture on a modern technical basis is a considerable improvement over the past. Communist ideology and the extreme pressure from the Communist leaders for greater agricultural production will continue to negate some scientific efforts. For example, political leaders continually encourage agricultural scientists to go among the peasants, endeavor to set up laboratories on the first line of production, size up the experience of the peasants, popularize the results of scientific research, and take part in the mass revolutionary movements of class struggle and scientific experimentation. No doubt the scientists can learn some practical agriculture from outstanding peasants, and can make on-the-spot improvements in practice. But these are short-term achievements only, and systematic research and experimentation cannot be done on peasant farms. It appears that China hopes to lift the technical knowledge of Chinese peasants by lowering that of the agricultural scientists.[5]

DEMONSTRATION AND MODEL FARMS

Experimental and demonstration farms have been established throughout China as noted above, but in many cases sufficient time and control have not been devoted to finding the best techniques. Therefore the value of these experimental farms is much less than would appear on paper.

One of the outstanding efforts in this field was the establishing of the ten model fields as decided at the Conference of Agricultural Science and Technology during February and March, 1963, earlier cited. These fields were to be set up in typical areas such as Kiangsu, Chekiang, Peking, northeastern China, northwestern China, Pearl River delta, Szechewan, and Hainan.

Mao boosted the program in his "three revolutionary drives," and it was actively introduced more widely in rural areas. The "model field" has three attributes: It unites scientific workers, party cadres, and the peasantry; combines testing with demonstration and extension; and unites the laboratory, the experimental station, and the farm.

In general there are three different types of model fields: the test field, the laboratory field, and the "nucleus model field." The latter is for demonstration to benefit the communes.

At present there are model fields for crops such as soybean, peanuts, and tobacco. There are also fields for experiment with and demonstration of fertilizer and its use, disease prevention, pest control, etc.

A report in 1965 indicated that 25 per cent of the total number of agricultural and scientific workers had assisted in setting up more than 1,000 model fields. The area of model fields reportedly had risen to 6,667,000 hectares distributed over important provinces, with Kiangsu first, having 866,000 hectares. The output of these model fields

is much propagandized, where yields have been reported from 20 to 30 per cent higher than in the
peasants' fields.

The value of the model field experiments is
questioned in many cases, since the input is high,
and more fertilizer and irrigation are applied.
Many peasants say that the expense prohibits them
from adopting the model. Communes will probably be
pressured to devote their quality inputs to the
model fields. The cost and quality of results can
be seriously questioned. The cost and returns will
also tend to upset the plans of operation of total
farm land. It will be especially interesting to
watch any experiments on fertilizer use.

BREEDING AND SEED SELECTION

Goals

Relatively speaking, seed improvement is a
quick and inexpensive way of increasing agricultural
production, particularly for a country of China's
size. Scientists in Communist China think agricultural production can generally be increased by 10
to 15 per cent through seed improvement.[6] Peking
started to tackle the seed problem early after the
political take-over. Lack of facilities for research, breeding, and extension plus the regime's
subjective desire to rush ahead without adequate
preparations show that progress in this direction
was slow. Many mistakes, some involving big losses
to crops, were incurred by introducing new strains
of seed. These were either not tested in areas of
adoption, or the peasants had little knowledge of
their requirements. This situation is partially reflected by the regime's own claims of unit yield in
the 1950s.

Despite weather conditions, claims of increased
fertilizer supply, and improvements in irrigation
and cultivation methods, etc., the officially claimed
unit-yield for all grain crops in 1957 was only 11

per cent higher than 1952. Cotton was 21 per cent
higher, but rapeseed lower by 23 per cent, soybean
lower by 3 per cent, and peanuts lower by 16 per
cent.[7] During the same period, it was claimed that
extension of "improved seeds" increased from
8,445,000 hectares, or 6 per cent of the total crop
acreage in 1952, to 84 million hectares, or 55 per
cent of the total crop acreage in 1957.[8]

The regime's policy on seed improvement in the
early years was one of "farm selection and actively
extending existing improved strains." This policy
of stressing local resources changed little except
for some improvement in both the number of new seed
strains and the extension facilities. The policy
slogan in 1962 was "self-propagation, self-selection,
self-retention, and self-use." Further improvement
appeared in 1963,* when the regime decided to supplement the mass movement with the establishment of
seed-breeding centers, seed farms, and demonstration
farms, etc., at the county, commune, and even production team levels. By 1965, it was claimed that
of the 2,064 counties in China, approximately 1,780
counties (or 86 per cent) had seed-breeding or
propagation farms providing annually 165 million
kilograms of fine seeds. About 10,000 communes and
production brigades in China also set up their own
seed farms, and about half of the production teams
had their own seed plots.[9] These farms and plots
are manned mainly by educated city youths, who are
sent to work in rural areas together with selected
local peasants and a few trained persons.

While strict uniformity is lacking, this is
how the system works in areas where it has been
well established. When a new seed strain is introduced to the area for extension, it is first tried
out at the brigade's experimental farms. If it is

_____

*This was the year when Mao Tse-tung introduced
the "Three Revolutionary Movements," of which scientific experiment was one.

found to be satisfactory under local conditions,
the new seed strain is released to production teams,
where it is further tested. Satisfactory strains
are propagated on the team's seed plots for its
use.[10] In Kwangtung, the guiding rule is to have
one mow of seed plot for every thirty mow of rice.[11]
To prevent seeds from being eaten, they are accorded
a higher rate of food grain equivalent and a higher
rate of remuneration for those engaged in seed production. At a brigade in Hupeh, 100 units of seeds
are set to equal 110 units of food grain.

Despite all these improvements and claims of
extension success, the seed problem in China has
been only slightly scratched in terms of quality
seeds and extension services. Against a total seed
requirement for the whole country of about 10 billion kilograms a year, the 1,300 state-operated centers for better seed demonstration and propagation
during 1963, were able to supply only 150 million
kilograms of seeds. This is 1.5 per cent of the
total requirements.[12] Even with those produced by
county, commune, brigade, and team-managed seed
farms (which apparently produce much-inferior seeds)
the total supply in 1965 was only a little over 3
per cent of the total need. In other words, for all
the seed needs in the country at present, the over-
whelming part comes from "field selection" or seeds
retained or "selected" by state companies through
their procurement of farm products. The State Food
Company is a big supplier of grain seeds. The high
rate of impurity has been a constant complaint in
all these years.

Undoubtedly the mass movement to improve seed
had its advantages, one of which is the speed with
which new seed strains could be extended. According
to official claims, during the first Five-Year Plan,
ending in 1957, the area sown with "fine seeds" had
increased by ten times over that in 1952; or from
6.2 per cent of the total crop area to 55 per cent.
By crops, the area under "fine" rice seeds increased by 13 times, wheat by 15 times, miscellaneous grains by 7.4 times, and potatoes by 156.7 times.[13]

This point was also illustrated by recent extension
for short-stem strains of early rice, a highly lodge-
resistant variety extended to the coast of East and
South China, an area often subject to typhoons.
After success for two or three years, the area
planted with four such strains in 1965 reportedly
reached 3,330,000 hectares.[14] During the same year,
about 50 per cent of the total rice acreage was
sown with "fine" seed strains of all kinds.[15] Since
the regime came to power in 1949, it was claimed,
cotton seeds had been renewed and regenerated on a
large scale three times.[16] The acreage under double-
crossed hybrid corn in 1966 was reportedly three
times that of 1965. These Chinese claims seem very
extravagant.

On the other hand, the regime's impatience for
normal experimental procedures and overemphasis on
political ideology, etc., have backfired and generally slowed down real progress. Many of the new
seed strains now used for extension have not been
properly tested and stabilized. Even for the greatly reduced period of testing and stabilization, a
good deal of the work is carried out by unqualified
persons. A few of the new seed strains were produced by so-called peasant breeders who hardly follow the scientific approach. The complex technique
of producing double-crossed hybrid corn seeds is
allowed to be carried out by the peasants. In the
candid words of the National Chinese News Agency
(NCNA), November 27, 1965, this was the only way to
obtain a large amount of such seeds to economically
and quickly meet the demand. Since the movement
began in 1962, a large number of scientists and technicians have been sent to rural areas from time to
time, sometimes for an extended period, disrupting
and weakening their normal work in laboratories and
experimental farms. In 1965, about 10,000 agricultural scientists, comprising about 40 to 60 per cent
of all personnel in agricultural scientific institutions and government, were sent to work in rural
areas.[17]

However, some progress has been made. Cotton,

for instance, has made a few improvements by building on the Nationalist foundation. As early as 1937,
it was claimed that 95 per cent of the total cotton
acreage was sown with improved seeds.[18]

According to the Chinese Academy of Agricultural Science, in two large-scale renewals of cotton
seeds, the average length of cotton staple in China
increased by 22 per cent by 1950, and 26.7 per cent
by 1957.[19] These were in addition to the claimed
unit-yield improvements, which were 15 per cent during the first renewal, and 10 to 30 per cent during
the second renewal. Admittedly there is some exag-
geration in these claims of improvement. Each year,
over 1 million hectares of early and late rice in
Kwangtung were damaged by typhoon, which also men-
aces the crops in coastal areas from Fukien to
Kiangsu in East China. The loss to rice in Kwangtung
alone was estimated at several hundred tons a year.[20]
The extension of short-stem varieties has made a
good start in solving this problem. Similar cita-
tions for other crops show that steady improvements
are being made.

TABLE 8

Claimed Extension of Improved Seeds
(in million ha.)

	1952	% of Total	1957	% of Total	1965	% of Total
All crops	8.4[a]	6.2	84.0[b]	55	+13.3[c,d]	–
Rice	1.5[h]	3.3	21.5[h]	66.7		50[b]
Wheat	1.3[b]	5.2	21.0[b]	76.2	–	50[d]
Misc. grains	2.5[b]	5.0	21.2[b]	41.9	–	50[d]
Potatoes	–	–	6.1[b]	58.1	–	–
Cotton	2.7[b]	4.7	5.4[b]	95	–	–

[a]Chinese Agricultural Bulletin, No. 15, August
8, 1959.

[b]People's Daily, January 8, 1958.

[c]Rather than actual decline, the smaller percentages in 1965 reflect, on the part of the regime,
a more serious attitude to seed quality.

[d]Radio Peking, February 1, 1966; increase over
1964.

Results

According to Cheng and Nash, "Crop breeding research is probably the most advanced of all China's agricultural sciences." Notable success had been achieved, especially in cotton and wheat, before the Communist take-over, as before mentioned. A number of competent, trained geneticists and plant breeders were developed, and many who remained in Communist China now lead the Chinese Academy of Agricultural Sciences. Several newly introduced crop strains and hybrids have given significantly increased yields in many areas. Chen Shan-poo, Vice President of the Chinese Academy of Agricultural Sciences, has developed a winter wheat strain Nanta No. 2419 that is extensively grown.

Most of the Chinese crop breeding research is geared to practical purposes of increasing yields.

Four new sugar cane varieties have been introduced and are rapidly replacing both the old bamboo and the old reed cane that have been grown for centuries. Six new strains of soy beans have been developed that grow taller, have a strong stem, and are suitable for mechanical harvesting. One soy bean variety has an oil content of 23.2 per cent, the highest recorded in China. This is especially important for increasing the export to Japan, as discussed with Hiroshi Sera and his mission to China, who said that China's beans suffered in competition with beans of the United States owing to their lower oil content.

Among other varieties of grain improvement recorded was the so-called Pi-ma #1, a variety of stiff straw wheat highly resistant to rust. It is claimed to have a yield 20 to 30 per cent higher than the local varieties under ideal local conditions in Shansi. In addition, a new rice variety, Nan-to-hao, has been adopted for a large area. This is said to yield 10 to 20 per cent more than the local varieties, but its reaction to ample applications of chemical fertilizer is not stated.

During 1962, the three major wheat varieties, Pi-ma #1, Nanta 2419, and Kansu 96, were planted to a total of 11 million hectares. Some 8 million hectares of rice were devoted to five new varieties, and 3,500,000 hectares of cotton to Tai-tzu Mien No. 15, but its yield was reported to have decreased. This tendency of new varieties to degenerate has been noted in recent years. This has probably been due to overextension, as the strain may be suitable for a limited area only. Besides inadequate supply and resultant hybridization, they may also be susceptible to pests and diseases not previously tested.

In support of their crop breeding program, since 1955 the Chinese have collected over 200,000 specimens belonging to 53 crop groupings, and in 25 crops a total of 487 new strains have been introduced. In addition, several foreign strains have been imported. The Chinese claim that the new strains have increased yields from 10 to 40 per cent over common strains. Much of the research indicates that good methods and research have been used; but frequent mistakes have been made in rushing some of these strains into commercial use before adequate testing. Within the next few years many well-tested strains should replace old strains, and provide increased yields.

This will be an extremely important development, if adequate supplies of chemical fertilizer can be effectively applied at the farm. (See discussion in Chapter 7.)

Many experiments have been conducted to select and develop rice and wheat varieties that will tolerate China's extensive areas of cold, drought, and salty soils. So far only minimal gains have resulted.

CROP PROTECTION

Chinese entomologists have made great progress in implementing and adapting insect control practices

of the West and the Union of Soviet Socialist Repub-
lics to varied conditions on the Mainland.

The most noteworthy contribution is their work
on the migratory locust. This includes both applied
and basic studies on its biology, physiology, behavior, food habits, population, distribution, and
methods of control. (The economic importance of
locust control is now described in the Japan travel
notes of the author.)

Other food crop insects are being controlled
by chemical, physical, and biological means. In
chemical control a wide variety of formulated insecticides in the West have been tested. Many native plants have been found to have insecticidal
properties, such as derris and anabasis aphylla,
which contains nicotine.

DISEASE PREVENTION

The Communist regime from the beginning has
given first priority to control of diseases of food
crops, especially of rice and wheat, and second
priority to diseases of fiber crops. According to
estimates reported by plant protection agencies in
Communist China, annual losses due to plant diseases
and pests approximate 10 per cent in food crops and
30 per cent in fruits. Recent research findings on
etiology, epidemiology, and distribution of some
major plant diseases have paved the way for effective prevention and control of some of these plant
diseases. Progress in varying degrees has been
achieved in surveys of the distribution and extent
of damages incurred in affected localities, formula-
tion of a prevention and control program, breeding
of resistant varieties, and enactment of a plant in-
spection and quarantine system.

Chinese scientists have contributed few modern
techniques that are new to the Western world. Nevertheless, the methods they employ (seed treatment,
breeding of resistant varieties, use of biological

agents, and improvement of cultural practices) have
played a significant role in reducing crop damages.
They have suppressed some of the most devastating
diseases of cereal, potato, and vegetable crops.

Leading scientists in plant disease are few,
and it will take time to develop the less experienced researchers; but control programs for plant
disease should improve considerably in the next
decade. Many plant diseases are under investigation, such as blast, blight, smut, and wheat rust--
the most serious of all plant diseases. This causes
losses of up to 30 per cent in northern and northeastern provinces. Inadequacy of basic information
regarding plant diseases has hampered the development of an effective control program, but a considerable effort is being directed to a study of related environmental factors. Long-range forecasts
of epidemics are difficult. An important phase of
the research program is the breeding and propagating
of resistant varieties. So far only partial success
has been achieved; some varieties have undergone
"degeneration," as stated above.

CROP PHYSIOLOGY

Some research has been done to better adapt
rice and wheat, on plant-water relationships, and
on crop tolerance to cold, drought, and salt. The
tolerance of crops to adverse conditions is emphasized. It is hoped to expand the areas sown to
crops, as well as to increase production on existing cultivated areas. This task is big and will
require time. A winter wheat variety, Sao-Yang-Mai,
offers promise for introduction to cold regions of
the north. In this case, water is also an important
factor.

An effort is being made through scientific surveys to find new species of edible wild plants that
might provide oil or starch. Thus far over 400
species of plants have been found that are oil-
bearing, and more than 900 species have been found

that yield starch or starchy fruits. These have
been used to prepare alcoholic beverages, sugars,
and various other foodstuffs. Important research in
this field is being done at the Institute of Plant
Physiology.

AGRICULTURAL CHEMICALS (DRUGS)

The importance of agricultural drugs in cutting
down crop losses, and in controlling plant and animal diseases as well as insects and rodents, has
been strongly emphasized by T. H. Shen.[21]

The loss to growing crops and stored products
is very conservatively estimated at 12 million by
specialists; but since the loss in the United States
is put at 10 per cent under modern methods of control, China's must be considerably greater. Tung
and Dawson would put it at at least 25 to 30 million
prewar. The Communists' strong campaign to reduce
the losses from rodents, flies, and locusts is well-
known. The campaign against many plant diseases is
not so well-known, but has been pursued strongly
and consistently.

Regarding animal diseases, the prewar toll was
tremendous. T. H. Shen[22] summarizes the alarming
situation:

> It was estimated before World War II
> that about 12 to 15 per cent of the
> cattle and water buffaloes, 20 to 25
> per cent of the swine, and 60 per cent
> of the poultry died of infectious dis-
> eases annually. Losses due to para-
> sites and malnutrition are slower to
> appear but they are also severe.

The Communists have attacked these problems
vigorously; it is reported by Japanese survey trips
to China that the livestock sanitary situation has
tremendously improved, especially on foot-and-mouth
disease and other annual disease-control conditions.

It can be safely estimated that savings to crops under Communist protective measures have aggregated some 10 million tons for food grain, and that animal disease control has resulted in a 10 per cent saving of animals and poultry.

China's emphasis on agricultural drugs is second only to its production of chemical fertilizers. But owing to limitation of techniques and facilities, its efforts have been concentrated on only a few essential items that can be easily handled at the present stage of development. There were 190 items of agricultural drugs under research as of 1959; ten of them have been trial-produced with reasonable success. The main items along the line of insecticides are DDT and BHC, both of which are in great demand all over the country.

DDT was first successfully produced in 1951. The 1959 output of this item was reportedly 139 times that of 1952. BHC, which started production in 1952, was reported to be about 50 per cent of China's total agricultural drugs production in 1958, reaching a record amount of 40,000 tons. The prospect of this drug (BHC) is rather promising, because its main requirements of raw materials are benzene and chloride. Benzene can be obtained as a byproduct of coking coal, and chloride as a by-product from soda manufacture.

According to the National Agricultural Drugs Conference held in June, 1960, China's production of agricultural drugs had showed a rapid proportional increase with 137,000 tons in 1959, as compared with 61,000 tons in 1957 and 82,000 tons in 1958; but it is still small in view of requirements. Besides the general category of agricultural drugs, production had also expanded in range and variety since the late 1950s. It included 21 types of insecticides, 14 types of germicides, 3 types of maggot killers, 2 types of mouse poison, and 3 types of drugs functioning in weed-killing and plant acceleration. These 43 different types of drugs were as a rule manufactured in mass-production

systems at 90 different factories. More than half
of these 90 factories started production in the
1950s, most of them in 1957. The Chinese factories
along these lines are advancing toward the stage of
pursuing research and experimentation on inventions,
although they are still hampered by limitation of
raw materials and plant facilities in the broad
fields of chemical industry.

NOTES

(For Notes to Chapters 6, 7, 8, and 9, documen-
tations paged as "1 vol." or "unp.," sometimes cited
from clippings and offprints, were not currently
available for complete verification.)

1. Tien-hsi Cheng and Ralph Nash, "Research
and Development of Food in Communist China," 2 Pts.,
Bio Science, XV, Nos. 11-12 (Washington, D.C.:
American Institute of Biological Science, Nov.-Dec.,
1965), pp. 643-56, 703-10.

2. T. H. Shen, Agricultural Resources of
China (Ithaca, N.Y.: Cornell University Press,
1951), p. 352.

3. Tien-hsi Cheng, loc. cit.

4. Ibid.

5. Ibid.

6. People's Daily (Peking, June 12, 1962);
articles by the Research Institute of Crop Cultivation, Chinese Academy of Agricultural Science.
Other scientists placed the range of increase at
15 to 20 per cent.

7. Ten Great Years (Peking [n.p.] 1959), 1 vol.

8. Chinese Agricultural Bulletin No. 15
(Peking, Aug., 1959), and People's Daily (Jan. 8,
1959).

9. *People's Daily* (Aug. 3, 1963).

10. *Ibid.*, Sept. 21, 1962.

11. *China Youth Daily* (Peking, March 21, 1963).

12. *People's Daily* (Oct. 8, 1963).

13. *Ibid.*, Jan. 8, 1958.

14. *Chinese Agricultural Science* No. 2 ([n.p.] Feb. 15, 1965).

15. *Radio Peking* (Feb. 1, 1966).

16. National China News Agency (Peking, Oct. 18, 1964).

17. *Ibid.*, May 5 and Sept. 29, 1965.

18. *People's Daily* (Jan. 8, 1958).

19. *Ibid.*, June 12, 1965.

20. *Kwang Ming Jih Pao* (Dec. 18, 1965).

21. T. H. Shen, *op. cit*, Chaps. 7-8.

22. *Ibid.*, Chap. 6.

CHAPTER **7** CHEMICAL FERTILIZER REQUIRE-
MENTS TO MEET THE FOOD CROP
NEEDS OF THE EXPANDING
POPULATION TO 1975/76

THE PROBLEM

The problem has been restudied in this book
using a different assumption of population increase
and a slightly lower per capita requirement of food
than previously used.[1]   (See Table 9.)

The basic importance of chemical fertilizer in
increasing crop production is concisely set forth
in the section on fertilizer supply and food requirements by Dawson in <u>Food and Agriculture in
Communist China</u>:[2]

>   Since agriculture is the basis of the
> Chinese economy, much of Mainland
> China's future economic progress will
> depend upon the ability of the agri-
> cultural sector to produce enough for
> consumption and trade. In this re-
> spect the record shows that (1) Agri-
> cultural production was able to score
> only a moderate advance from the time
> of the Communist take-over in 1949 to
> 1958, and by dint of stringent and
> compulsory economies on the part of
> farmers agricultural exports were main-
> tained at a high enough level to pro-
> vide for the greater part of the coun-
> try's foreign exchange requirements.
> However, food grain production per
> capita remained at close to the mini-
> mum level, and from 1959-61 fell below

it. The problem of expanding production to meet the needs of the spiral-
ing population thus became urgent,
and the authorities took measures to
improve the situation especially by
expanding supplies of chemical fertilizer.

The report further explains the situation:

Because of the pressure exerted over
many centuries by a dense and growing
population on the limited land resources of China, yields of food
crops have tended toward a static
level despite the use of organic fertilizer. The sustained higher yields
needed to support population, as it
has become increasingly clear, can be
attained only through extensive use
of chemical fertilizer. Yet, Mainland China is still at the bottom of
the list of important countries in
the use of chemical fertilizer per
hectare of cultivated land, and has
only recently faced the colossal problem of setting up an adequate fertilizer industry.

The rapid expansion reported since, in chemical
fertilizer production, must be closely checked as
to its effectiveness and potential future development.

A wide range of estimates as to future chemical fertilizer requirements has been given out officially and semiofficially, but no logical method
of making such estimates has come to our attention.
Only rough estimates based on limited experimental
data are available for China.

Since organic fertilizer has been used so
widely and returns to the soil large amounts of
crop nutrients, it has seemed important to calculate

these amounts versus crop offtake of crop nutrients, principally N, P_2O_5, and K_2O, to determine as closely as possible what quantity of crop nutrients has to be supplied by chemical fertilizer to increase yields.

Taiwan and Japan have used organic fertilizer for many past years, and series of data on amounts used are available for several years. No such data are available for China. A recent study attempted to fill the gap by extended research on sources of organic fertilizer.[3]

It will suffice in this study only to mention here the main lines of analysis to support the need for definite amounts of increased supplies of chemical fertilizer in Communist China.

In the first study, returns from the application of gross chemical fertilizer were calculated roughly on the basis of three to one, assuming usual applications of organic fertilizer and improved techniques such as improved varieties, better methods of cultivation, control of pests and diseases, and better water irrigation.[4]

In the present study the methodology has been more direct.

THE METHOD

1. Future food grain production requirements of the chief crop nutrients N, P_2O_5, and K_2O have been calculated on the basis of what seems to be the most likely assumption of population increase to 1975-76, which is calculated to be 869 million.[5] This assumes a moderate improvement in agricultural techniques with no major upsets in general conditions.

2. Future supplies of the chief sources of organic fertilizer have been estimated on the different assumptions of human and animal population,

crop residues, and other items. The same crop nutrient content of the organic items was used as in
the original study with minor changes. Further
study may suggest revisions of such factors.[6]

   3. Results in calculations of N, P_2O_5, and
K_2O to come from fertilizer minus organic sources
are assumed to equal required amounts of the chief
crop nutrients to come from chemical fertilizer or
soil reserves (especially for K_2O). The results
are divided by .85 to include nonfood grain requirements.

   Tables 9 and 10 set forth crop production requirements of N, P_2O_5, and K_2O and amounts of these
crop nutrients calculated as supplied by organic
fertilizer. That the residual requirements must
eventually be supplied by chemical fertilizer has
been the experience of Japan and especially Taiwan.

   The wartime experience of Taiwan amply illus-
trates the point. In 1945/46, with the fullest use
of organic fertilizer but with little chemical fertilizer, yield of paddy rice had dropped to 1,661
kg/ha. From then on, the use of chemical fertilizer to 677 kg/ha in 1961 gave yields increasing to
3,376 kg/ha. For 1966, application increased to
853 kg/ha and yields to 4,000 kg/ha. (This dramat-
ic effect of chemical fertilizer application is illustrated in Chart A, page 113, of the study on
Food and Agriculture in Communist China.[7]

   The advance in agricultural production has
been a key factor in economic improvement in Japan
and Taiwan, due to application of large amounts of
chemical fertilizer. In a like manner needed improvement in China's economy is now recognized to
depend basically on advances in agricultural production due to ample supplies of chemical fertilizer along with improved techniques.

   The large increase in yield of paddy rice and
other dry land crops in Communist China, where
chemical fertilizer can be effectively applied but

now is used on only a small scale, can be envisioned. (This may be calculated in a later supplementary study.)

Sources of chemical fertilizer in Communist China are discussed at length, along with technical difficulties of factory expansion and effective application to the land, in the following notes. The capacity and production of chemical fertilizer plants in China have been tentatively estimated from a vast number of sources. Further data for revised estimates are being made.

As time permits, a supplemental study of chemical fertilizer requirements by provinces, along with geographical distribution of supplies, including imports, will be made.

Following is an analysis of chemical fertilizer requirements. The population assumed on January 1, 1976, is taken as 869 million:

1. Assuming an increase of 1.75 per cent (Aird's* Model IV C) food grain requirement at 290 kg/pc = 252 MMT net from yield.

2. Assuming 5M from imports and 7M from increased crop area equals 240 MMT.

The per capita requirement is estimated at 290 kg. revised from previously estimated 300 kg. due to more efficient use under the Communist regime.

----

*John S. Aird is Chief of Foreign Manpower Section, U.S. Census Bureau.

TABLE 9

Trial Method of Estimating Chemical
Fertilizer Requirements for the
Production of Food Grain and
Other Crops to 1975/76

Crop nutrients required by 240 MMT at revised figures per MT food grain, viz., N, 27; P_2O_5, 12; K_2O,
20, equal in 1,000 MT:

N   = 6,480 ÷ .85 for all crops 7,620
P_2O_5 = 2,880 ÷ .85 for all crops 3,400
K_2O = 4,800 ÷ .85 for all crops 5,640

Crop nutrients available from organic fertilizer
(see following calculations, Table 10)

                    MMT

N   = 5,228
P_2O_5 = 2,330
K_2O = 4,441

Additional required from chemical fertilizer

			000 MT	% of Total
N	− 2,392	at 20% gross =	11,960 =	59
P_2O_5	= 1,070	at 18% gross =	6,000 =	22
K_2O	= 1,199	at 40% gross =	2,997 =	19

Total 20,957 + less 10%   = 23,053 (000 MT)

TABLE 10

Calculated Crop Nutrients in Organic
Fertilizer 1975/76
(in 1,000 MT)

Source
Animal units estimate   160 Mil. X 7 MT per
                         1,120 MMT at 70%
                              784

$$\underline{1,000\ MT}$$
N   at .4% = 3,136
P_2O_5 at .2% = 1,568
K_2O at .4% = 3,136

Night soil at .25 for pop. 869 M = 217 MMT X 70%
available 151.9 MMT

$$\underline{1,000\ MT}$$
at N.5   =   760
   P_2O_5.2 =   304
   K_2O.3   =   456

Oilseed cakes, about 1,957 + 10% =
              $\underline{1,000\ MT}$
              7.700 X 70% available = 5.390

                    % $\underline{1,000\ MT}$
         N   at 7.5 =   404
         P_2O_5 at 1 =   54
         K_2O at 1.5 =   81

Green manure gross 50 MMT X 80% available = 40 MMT
                    % $\underline{1,000\ MT}$
    at N   at .2   =   80
       P_2O_5 at .05 =   20
       K_2O at .2   =   80

Compost   140 MMT at 80% available = 112 MMT
                    % $\underline{1,000\ MT}$
         N   at .4   =   448
         P_2O_5 at .2 =   224
         K_2O at .4 =   448

River and pond mud 200 X 80% available = 160 MMT
                    % $\underline{1,000\ MT}$
         N   at .25 =   400
         P_2O_5 at .10 =   160
         K_2O at .15 =   240

Others at 10% of 6 = 14 total
              $\underline{000\ MT}$ Totals (1-6)
    N   =   45   5,228
    P_2O_5 =   22   2,330
    K_2O =   45   4,441

118

AN ESTIMATE OF CHEMICAL FERTILIZER
PRODUCTION IN 1966

China's Requirements of
Chemical Fertilizers

China's farm economy has for a few thousand years been meshed in a biophysical-chemical cycle in which farmers have to replenish soil fertility by means of human and animal excreta, plant residues, pond mud, etc. in order to produce the necessary foods and feeds that they need to carry on their livelihood. But these organic fertilizers tend to be reduced in quantity and effectiveness at each round of the cycle, and the soil is constantly losing its productive capacity through long ages of depleted crop nutrient.

Evidently the most effective way--perhaps the only way--to save China's soil from utter exhaustion is to apply increasing amounts of chemical fertilizer along with available amounts of organic fertilizer, as Japan and Taiwan have successfully practiced for a few decades.

The Chinese National Agricultural Research Bureau conducted an experiment of chemical fertilizer application from 1935 to 1940, covering sixty-eight testing grounds of seventeen main crops in fourteen provinces, and found that 84 per cent of these testing grounds were responsive to N application, 47 per cent responsive to P_2O_5 application, and 16 per cent responsive to K_2O application. The testing grounds that revealed highest percentages of responses were as follows:[8]

	Wheat	Rice	Corn	Rapeseed	Cotton
N	71	86	88	84	43
P_2O_5	40	50	38	53	18
K_2O	9	14	29	17	11

China began to adopt chemical fertilizer in 1904, but it was almost confined to ammonia sulfate alone, and used mostly on economic crops in the coastal provinces. Even between 1925 and 1935, the highest amount of application never exceeded 200,000 tons. China's annual consumption of ammonium sulfate between 1925 and 1935 was as follows:[9]

1925	20,000 tons	1931	110,000 tons
1926	40,000	1932	140,000
1927	50,000	1933	82,000
1928	80,000	1934	74,000
1929	100,000	1935	92,000
1930	185,000		

As domestic output in chemical fertilizer was very much limited in pre-Communist days, its annual supply was largely dependent upon external sources; the annual import between 1928 and 1933 ranged from 100,000 tons to 150,000 tons.[10]

China's Chemical Fertilizer Industry

China's chemical fertilizer output has risen dramatically in recent years, following a reordering and expansion of resources provided to the industry.[11] Production has climbed from 1.7 million tons in 1960 to 10.5 million tons in 1966, roughly equally apportioned between nitrogenous and phosphatic fertilizers.

Of the 1966 output, roughly 40 per cent was contributed by large nitrogenous plants, including the six foreign-aided plants, the three Chinese-constructed plants, and the by-product production of other large plants. About 10 per cent was produced by some 150 small nitrogenous plants with an average annual output of nearly 7,000 tons each, consisting chiefly of ammonium bicarbonate. About 10 per cent consisted of the output of large phosphate plants, consisting largely of calcium superphosphate; the remaining 40 per cent was produced by around 150 small phosphate plants averaging nearly 30,000 tons annually each, comprised of

calcium superphosphate and fused calcium magnesium
phosphate.*

The growth of the industry has been shaped by
technological and resource limitations, as well as
the urgent priority for rapid expansion to meet agricultural needs. Cost has been no object; fragmentary data suggest factory production costs, in
United States dollars, of $150-$200 per ton or
higher. This would require huge subsidies to supply the fertilizers for the farm areas at reasonable
prices. Moreover, industry officials recognize that
the plant system is obsolete and inefficient. They
plan to replace it within ten years, when industrial
and technical advances will permit reconstruction
with a new plant system. It will embody modern and
efficient technologies for ammonia production, and
particularly urea production. Domestic output is
being supplemented by large imports that will amount
to 5.8 million tons in 1967, costing $30 F.O.B.
(shipped) or $35 C.I.F. (picked up) per ton.

Brief History of the Chinese
Fertilizer Industry

In 1949, the Chinese chemical fertilizer industry consisted of two major plants, at Dairen and
Nanking, together with some by-product facilities
attached to other industries. For the first five
years the effort was directed at rehabilitating and
raising the output of the existing industry. However, midway through the first Five-Year Plan
(1953-57), systematic expansion began with construction on four large plants at Kirin, Lanchow,
Taiyuan, and Szechwan. In 1956, the initial fertilizer output goals of the second Five-Year Plan
(1958-62) were placed at 3.0 to 3.2 million tons,
which probably represented the nitrogenous fertilizer output of these six large plants, after the
completion of projected expansion projects.

---

*The commonly used term NPK means phosphate,
nitrogen, and potassium.

A year later, at the end of 1957, a more comprehensive output target of 7 million tons was announced for 1962. This figure included 2 million
tons of phosphate fertilizer and probably 1.0 to
1.5 million tons of nitrogenous fertilizer from
local plants, leaving the major plant targets es-
sentially unchanged at 3.0 to 3.5 million tons.
Six months later, with the "Great Leap" under way,
the 1962 targets were raised to 15 to 20 million
tons; local nitrogenous and phosphate plants were
to account for 80 per cent of this target, indicat-
ing the large plant targets, at 3 to 4 million tons,
were still unchanged.[12]

Output in 1957, which had hardly yet been affected by the new construction, reached 800,000
tons, including 120,000 tons of phosphates.[13] Nitrogenous fertilizer production through 1962 was
almost totally limited to the large plants, as the
small plant program, owing to technical difficulties, produced only negligible amounts. However, a
very large expansion in large plant capacity occurred during 1957-60. Synthetic ammonia production rose from 150,000 tons in 1957 to 334,000 tons
in 1959. In 1960 and 1961, the large plant operations were greatly disrupted by the withdrawal of
Soviet technicians, but in 1962, when partial recovery had been achieved, synthetic ammonia output
reached 540,000 tons.

In contrast, the small plants were far more
important in the development of phosphate production. Owing to the lengthy time in construction of
large plants, with supporting sulfuric acid facilities as well as large pyrite and phosphate mines
to assure a stable source of supply, the large
plants developed their output slowly. The small
plants, relying on local ores and simple equipment
and techniques, were able to enter production quickly. However, the absence of technical controls resulted in a poor quality product, and indeed much
of the product seemed to be merely ground phosphate
rock. More important, the Chinese farmers were un-
familiar with mineral phosphate fertilizers, and

agricultural studies on the areas and techniques of application had not been done. By the end of 1960 there were large stocks of phosphate fertilizer, produced at high cost and with enormous subsidies, and a disillusionment with the effectiveness of phosphate fertilizer on the part of farmers and local officials. In consequence, phosphate production declined sharply in both 1961 and 1962.

During 1962 and 1963, a major effort was mounted to overcome the technical difficulties confronting the industry. In the nitrogenous sector, new attention was given to the small plants, particularly in training large numbers of technicians and skilled workers to take over their operation. For the large plants, research and development efforts centered on improving compressors and high-compression vessels to permit domestic construction of plants; while in the plants experiments were conducted on catalysts, gas purification, temperature control, and pressures. The Chinese asserted that the Soviets had given them plants constructed to the technology of the 1940s, which they could rebuild to substantially higher efficiencies with the technology of the 1950s and the feasible technologies of the 1960s. Over the next ten years, as Chinese technical capabilities improve, they intend to reconstruct the large plants into a urea-based industry employing modern techniques with a capacity of some 20 million tons of fertilizer. During the 1960s China installed new ammonia capacity nominally rated at 175,000 tons annually at Shanghai, Canton, Shihchiachuang, Hainan, and Nanking, while importing a plant with a rated capacity of 100,000 tons annually. Nearly all of these plants, together with the formerly existing plant, have been reported to be operating above rated capacity. By 1966, the ammonia output of large plants was probably over one million tons, augmented by an output of 200,000 to 250,000 tons from the small plants.

In the phosphate industry, the agricultural departments of southern provinces carried out large-scale programs of soil testing, crop experiments,

and extension activities to promote the use of
phosphate, while within the industry efforts were
directed toward improving and controlling quality
and toward reducing costs.

These development activities in 1962 and 1963
led to a major expansion construction program, beginning in 1964, as well as to claims of marked improvements in plant efficiencies. A new domestic-
built plant with a nominal capacity rating of
175,000 tons of synthetic ammonia was installed at
Shanghai, Canton, Shihchiachuang, Hainan, and Nanking, while an additional 100,000 annual tons of
capacity was secured in an imported ammonia-urea
plant. Most of these plants, together with previously existing large plants, are reported to be
operating substantially over design capacity at
present, suggesting that ammonia production from
large plants in 1966 was well over one million tons.
Small nitrogenous plant construction had by the end
of 1966 brought into production well over 150
plants with respective annual ammonia output capacities of 800, 2,000, and 5,000 tons, suggesting a
1966 ammonia output of about 250,000 tons.

With the earlier overexpansion of phosphate
capacity, phosphate output has increased more rapidly than nitrogenous fertilizer output; phosphate
output is now approaching equality in volume with
nitrogenous output. The growth of output appears
to have been limited by farm receptance and a con-
cern for costs and quality. There has been substantial development of phosphate mines and supporting transport facilities. Calcium superphosphate has comprised the larger portion of phosphate
production, although fused calcium-magnesium-
phosphate output has increased rapidly in recent
years. With regard to phosphate ore supplies,
China has imported large amounts in recent years,
including nearly 800,000 tons in 1965 and nearly
700,000 tons in 1966. The development of domestic
phosphate deposits was moving apace in China; and
although figures are lacking, the major mines alone
would account for several million tons of phosphate
rock.

Production Requirements

A chemical fertilizer industry usually demands the most elaborate mechanical equipment in the process of production. The whole outfit of machinery and auxiliary assortments must be highly anticorrosive, with strong resistance to high pressures and high temperatures.

A plant with an annual capacity of 75,000 tons of synthetic ammonia generally takes more than 10,000 tons of mechanical equipment, including 3,000 tons as "fixture" and 7,400 tons as "nonfixture" installations. Even a nitrogen plant of 8,000 tons of the "county-sponsored" scale, for minimum equipment, would require 600 tons of machinery, with the usual assortment of high-pressure containers, high-pressure compressors, gas-blasters, air-blasters, and high-pressure rotating compressors. If no external electricity is available, the plant has to provide its own powerhouse with a minimum capacity of 750 kilowatts. A plant of such small scale will require constant employment of 193 persons, including a technical staff of 20 members, the year round.[14]

Beginning with the early 1960s, the Communists attempted to establish a large series of medium and small plants, to be scattered over the rural areas. These plants were to be designed by Chinese "experts" and equipped with "homemade" machinery. But according to Shigaru Ishikawa, ". . . they encountered great difficulties in manufacturing equipment suitable for these small and medium plants, and difficulties of learning techniques of production and complicated administration."[15]

Hence the question is: Could China's machine builders and chemical producers in the 1960s really provide the nation's fertilizer industry with such a huge quantity of mechanical devices and chemical ingredients in standard quantity, with ample stock for frequent demands of repairs, refilling, and replacement? Again, could China's "instant" training

schools actually provide its fertilizer industry
with many thousands of experts to install and operate many hundreds of large and small plants all
over the country?

It is the opinion of Dawson and Tung that,
under the general depressed conditions in those
post-"Leap" years, possibly some of the very new
projects might never have gone beyond the stage of
blueprints, and that many might have started construction and stopped half way. Still many more
might have begun production, and then suspended
operations for lack of equipment, material, or
technical manpower.

Consumption Limitation

Proper application of chemical fertilizers requires a thorough knowledge of crop behavior, soil
quality, and the corresponding functions of particular types of fertilizers. To a certain extent any
underdosage, or untimely application would do more
harm than benefit to the crops concerned. Chinese
farmers took many generations to learn the proper
response of local soils to various types of organic
fertilizers. It would certainly take time to learn
the combined or separate use of chemical and organic
fertilizers at this pressing stage of development.

Another obstacle to the peasants' demand for
chemical fertilizer is its high cost. The price in
yuan of one ton of ammonium sulfate was reported
as "Y 335 in 1959; as compared with Y 486 in 1950,
and Y 379 in 1953."[16] China's 1957 retail prices
of food revealed that a picul (100 catties) of rice
was marked for Y 12.1 in Shanghai.[17] After the
profit margin for local millers, the wholesale
price (by state agent) would be cut down to about
Y 228 per ton at Shanghai.

According to the 1967 Yearbook on Chinese Communism (Taiwan), the average price differential between purchases and sales of all commodities under
control of state agencies ranges from 45 per cent

to 300 per cent. As the Communists always boasted
of their "reasonable pricing system" in favor of
grain transactions, we may conservatively take 45
per cent as the price differential between grain
sales in the city and grain purchases in the country. If 45 per cent of price differential is deducted from the state sale price of grain at Y 228
per ton, the purchasing price in the rural areas
would be reduced to about Y 125 per ton (55 per
cent of Y 228).

Communist agronomists generally assumed that
the application of every catty of nitrogenous fertilizers (ammonium sulfate) would raise the grain
yield (rice) by three catties.* This means that
one ton of chemical fertilizer would give the user
three tons of additional grain yield from the same
piece of land. We assume a much lower figure for
the chief NPK chemical fertilizers.

Suppose production team A chose to use one ton
of ammonium sulfate to raise its grain yield.**
The additional three tons obtained therefrom would
sell to the state at a net gain of Y 40 (3 X 125 -
335), after deduction of Y 335 as cost of fertilizer.

On the other hand, suppose production team B
should choose hog manure, instead of ammonium sulfate, to raise its grain yield. A rather ideal
situation might occur, but of limited application,
where pig manure can be purchased. According to
Communist estimate, "the stable manure accumulated
by a hog through the year will serve to increase
grain output by 200 to 300 catties." This means
that the manure collection of 20 to 30 hogs in a
year (20-30 hogs X 300-200 catties) could produce
the same result (raising grain output by three tons)

---

*This at a low rate of application.

**Very limited in application owing to supply
of hog manure.

as one ton of chemical fertilizers.* As scavengers
depending to a large extent upon kitchen wastes and
wild grass for fodder, the sale price of meat,
bones, and bristles, etc., from a slaughtered hog
would usually more than cover the costs of its feed
and labor attendance, and thus leave its annual
yield of around 3,000 kilograms of manure almost as
a free gift for the owner. Since a production team
as a rule comprises about twenty or forty households in the commune, it is not unusual for such a
unit to own twenty to thirty head of hogs all the
year around. When their "costless" manures are applied to raise three tons of grain, this additional
output could sell to the state for Y 375 (3 X 125)[18]
without any deduction of "fertilizer cost" as in
the case of using ammonium sulfate. So long as the
grain price is low and the (chemical) fertilizer
price is high, demand for the latter will be highly
limited among the food-producing areas. This is
perhaps why China's chemical fertilizer could find
only a narrow market among the economic crops,
where the state purchasing price was usually set at
a level three, five, or eight times that of the food
grains.

One of the regime's plans to expedite the expansion of production is to finance further building, with profit realized from current sales.

Methodology for Current Estimates

Estimation of China's fertilizer production is
confronted with fragmentary and rather confusing
figures regarding the capacity and output of individual plants on the Mainland. Only a series of
percentage figures have been published about the
nation's annual fertilizer production in the 1960s,
by means of which we may derive a corresponding
series of hard data on the basis of some absolute
numbers of an earlier date. We have learned from

_____

*But supply is limited.

Communist publications that, taking the nation as a whole, China's annual increase of chemical fertilizer output was arrayed as follows:

1962 over 1961   50% (People's Daily, Jan. 3, 1963)
1963 over 1962   40% (Economic Reporter, Hong Kong,
                        Mar. 15, 1965)
1964 over 1963   50% (China Reconstructs, Jan., 1965)
1965 over 1964   70% (Wen Hua Pao, Hong Kong, Feb.
                        12, 1966?)
1966 over 1965   26% (NONA, Peking, Dec. 28, 1966)

The Central Approach

This is the process of calculating China's fertilizer production by means of the published percentages of increase for recent years. Presumably these percentage rates refer only to the fertilizer "end-products" that are annually purchased by, or registered with, the state, to be distributed in the rural areas. The following list is a comparative presentation of three sets of estimates on China's fertilizer output since 1957:

	1967 Yearbook on Chinese Communism[a]	Edwin F. Jones[b]	Shigaru Ishikawa[c]
	(MT)	(MT)	(MT)
1957	800,000	803,000	631,000
1958	1,200,000	1,345,000	811,000
1959	1,800,000	1,837,000	1,333,000
1960	2,800,000 (planned)	1,673,000	2,000,000
1960	(2,200,000		
1961	(2,000,000	1,431,000	2,400,000
1962	(2,500,000	2,146,000	3,600,000
1963	(3,500,000	3,004,000	4,680,000
1964	(4,200,000	4,506,000	7,000,000
1965	(7,700,000	7,660,000	9,000,000
1966	(10,000,000	10,500,000	10,000,000

(1960–1966 entries from the Yearbook marked "(estimated)")

[a]1967 Yearbook on Chinese Communism, Taipei, 1967.

[b]Unpublished manuscript, 1967.

[c]Long Term Outlook of Economy in Mainland China, Tokyo, 1960.

According to Hsiao Chi-jing, Peking's "Great Leap Forward" had pushed China's fertilizer output to 1,673,000 tons in 1960. This agreed with Edwin Jones's estimate. As a result of the breach with the Soviet, however, construction of most medium and large enterprises was soon stopped; the 1961 fertilizer output dropped to 1,431,000 MT. Ishikawa's report on China also indicated that in the years between 1957 and 1960, only five new major fertilizer plants had begun operation, with low rates of plant utilization. Meanwhile, medium and small projects, promoted in the years of 1958-59, encountered many difficulties in connection with mechanical equipment and technical manpower. In the light of these circumstances, the national total of 1,673,000 metric tons is perhaps the most plausible figure for 1960 fertilizer output; and subsequently the figure of 1,431,000 metric tons the most plausible for 1961, as agreed by Jones and Hsiao. Calculated from percentage data in Takung Pao, October 1, 1962, this latter figure may be regarded as the maximum output that could have been achieved under the "depressing pressures" of the disastrous period of 1959 to 1961.

Starting with 1,431,000 metric tons as a basis of calculation, one may then derive China's recent output figures by means of the aforesaid series of published percentages:

Percentage over preceding year	Production (MT)
1962 (50% over 1961)	2,146,000
1963 (40% over 1962)	3,004,000
1964 (50% over 1963)	4,506,000
1965 (70% over 1964)	7,660,000
1966 (estimated 35% over 1965)	10,341,000

The Local Approach

This is the process of using aggregate reported output, results of fertilizer "end-products," from all individual plants. In view of the diversified and controversial nature of data from various sources, we do not rely on this process as our main method of estimation, but use it as a general check over the results obtained from the central approach. Since the central approach gives no separate figures for each type of fertilizer, the local approach helps to find the most probable ratio of production between nitrogenous, phosphatic, potassium, and other products. If separate records are available, the separate figures are used. If only mixed records are found, estimates have to be made for each type on the basis of certain "sample" plants. Output reports from individual plants are as a whole incomplete, contradictory, and often camouflaged under ambiguous terms, so one has had to take steps of "elimination," "classification," and "assignment" by percentage ranges in relation to discrepancies between capacity and output of all plants under investigation.

SUMMARY

Communist China's supplies of chemical fertilizer have greatly increased since 1960, as shown by Table 11.

For 1967, a detailed study of factory capacity and output indicates a production of 10,339,000 metric tons. Details by location and provinces require further research. Production for the chemical fertilizer year September, 1967, to August, 1968, is expected to show some decline, owing to disruptive effects of the Cultural Revolution in important centers. Imports are also smaller than the preceding year by a probable million tons. So the total fertilizer deficit may reach four to five million tons. (See Table 8.) Combined with less favorable crop weather likely in 1968, supplies of grain per capita may show significant declines. However, no doubt the carry-over of both fertilizer and grain would to some extent alleviate the shortage. General progress in improved techniques will also help, but not offset, the prospective shortage.

TABLE 11

Chemical Fertilizer Supply

(in million tons of ammonium sulphate [21% N]
or superphosphate [17% P_2O_5] equivalent)

Period	Output	Imports	Supply			
			Calendar Year		Fertilizer Year	
Jan.-Aug., 1965	5.0	1.7	1965	10.2		
Sep.-Dec., 1965	2.7	.8			1965/66	12
Jan.-Aug., 1966	6.5	2.0	1966	14		
Sep.-Dec., 1966	4.0	1.5			1966/67	16
Jan.-Aug., 1967	7.0	3.5	1967	13		
Sep.-Dec., 1967	1.0	1.5			1967/68	9.5
Jan.-Aug., 1968	4.5	2.5	1968	14		
Sep.-Dec., 1968	4.0	3.0			1968/69	19
Jan.-Aug., 1969	8.0	4.0				

NOTES

1. Aird's Model C Limited Developments. No serious deterioration of civil order.

2. John Lossing Buck, Owen L. Dawson, and Yuan-li Wu, Food and Agriculture in Communist China Published for the Hoover Institution on War, Revolution and Peace, Stanford University (New York and London: Frederick A. Praeger, 1966), pp. 101-2.

3. Aird's, op. cit.

4. Ibid.

5. Aird's Model IV C.

6. Aird's Model C Limited Developments, supra.

7. Ibid.

8. Chu Hai-fan and Chang Son-Ching, China's Current Situation of Fertilizer Application (n.p., n.d.), 1 vol.

9. Ibid.

10. T. H. Shen, Agricultural Resources of China (Ithaca, N.Y.: Cornell University Press, 1951), 407 pp.

11. Estimated by Edwin Jones.

12. Ibid.

13. Ibid.

14. Chang Pin-Chun, "How to Construct a Nitrogen Plant of 8,000 Ton Capacity," Planned Economy (May 9, 1958 [unp.]). See also Wang Hsing-fu and Han Chien-cha, "Great Efforts for the Development of Chemical Fertilizer Industry," Planned Economy (Oct., 1957, [unp.]).

15.   Shigaru Ishikawa, Long-Term Outlook of
Economy in Mainland China (Tokyo: [n.p.], 1950),
1 vol.

16.   James R. Justin, Economic Research (Hong
Kong: United States Consulate, May 17, 1959),
1 vol.

17.   Dwight H. Perkins, Market Control and
Planning in Communist China ([n.p.], 1966), 1 vol.

18.   Chan Sun-Ching and Ma Fu-Tsiang, "Increase
of Fertilization Production and Its National Application," Agricultural Science Bulletin (Nov. 15,
1951), 1 vol.

CHAPTER **8** POWER RESOURCES

FOR AGRICULTURE

INTRODUCTION

The impact of industrial power on China's agricultural situation requires evaluation of the
four types of power: mechanical, electrical, human,
and animal. Tentative conclusions follow.

Mechanization in the sense of large-scale machine operation at present has proved to be feasible only in the northern borders. Here labor is
scarce, fuel is plentiful, farms are larger, and
the land is more suitable for mechanized performances. Small amounts of mechanical cultivation
occur at scattered spots in the interior of China
proper, usually under the ministry-controlled state
farms for purposes of reclamation, demonstration,
or experimental feasibility in chosen areas.

Electric power is used in irrigation, where it
competes with steam produced by coal, gas, oil, and
other fuels. Electric power is swiftly spreading
over the country as a necessary advance in agricultural production. In view of the large plants charac-
teristic of state management, this cheap power is
steadily gaining over the nonelectric facilities.

Human and animal power operate in 93 per cent
of China's cultivated area, and are marked for a
planned scale of gradual transformation. This is
likely to follow the pattern of partially intensive
cultivation practiced in modern Japan, western
France, and the American Middle West; but it could

135

not achieve the more extensive cultivation of Canada, Australia, and the Soviet Union.

MECHANICAL POWER

Communist Policy on Mechanization

The Period of Sporadic
Trial (1950-59)

"Mechanization" was held up by Chinese Communists as a "magic path" to agricultural advancement
in the early years of the new regime. Dazzled by
the quick success of Soviet collectives, the Peking
regime announced (July 31, 1955) its intention to
"mechanize Chinese farms" within a span of twenty
to twenty-five years, whereas the Russians had accomplished it in fifteen years. No mechanization
is really feasible until China's millions of tiny
farms are consolidated into large contiguous areas
of at least 100 hectares or above for each farm.
Mechanical devices, including tractors and combines, were sporadically applied in the newly established state farms and a few collectives in
Sinkiang, Manchuria, and Inner Mongolia.

The Period of "Leap"
Advancement (1960-62)

Mao Tse-tung in a speech in May, 1959, explic-
itly named "mechanization as the basic outlet for
Chinese agriculture" as proposed in his "Great Solution within Ten Years." The specific program for
this "Great Solution" was:

1. Four years (1959-62) of "Small Solution"--
efforts concentrated on improvement of farm tools
in general and partial mechanization of farms in
the suburban areas around big cities, the important
centers of "commercial grains" (surplus grains for
marketing), the main areas of economic crops (especially cotton and oilseeds), and certain pastoral
areas in the borderlands.

2.   Seven years (1959-65) of "Medium Solution" --within the years 1963-65, half of China's cultivated area was to be fully mechanized. This period of three years added to the preceding four years (1959-62) is called "Seven Years of Medium Solution."

3.   Ten years (1959-68) of "Great Solution"-- within the period 1966-68, cultivated areas of the whole nation must be "basically mechanized," together with the mechanization of conservation installations and the practical electrification of all rural activities. These last three years combined with the preceding seven years (1959-65) are called the "Ten Years of Great Solution" of China's farm mechanization.

The Period of Postponed Realization (1962-present)

Mao's "Great Solution" scheme, together with his "Leap" programs and the commune system, collapsed in the years between 1959 and 1961. The Tenth Plenum of the Eighth Central Communist Party, Central Committee (CCPCC) made a vague declaration (People's Daily, Nov. 9, 1962) that "after 20-25 years from now [1962], China's farms would be surely mechanized as the Party has planned." No national program has been put out since that date. Several provinces have announced some ambiguous schedules for mechanization, but these appear to be more for propaganda than for practice. No reports of achievements have followed these schedules.

Communist Estimates of Mechanization Requirements

Several estimates have been made by Communist experts on the mechanical requirements for China's farm modernization. The figures proposed by Liu Jeh-hsing are too high, but they are cited here:[1]

Mechanical facilities	Total requirements
(1) Tractors (at 1 unit for each 100 hectares, on the basis of 80 million hectares of cultivated area for which tractors are applicable)	800,000 standard units (15 H.P.*)
(2) Combine harvesters (at 1 unit for each 230 hectares, on the basis of 106 million hectares of China's cultivated area)	450,000 units
(3) Farm trucks (at 1 unit for each 267 hectares, on the basis of 106 million hectares)	400,000 units
(4) Mechanical devices for irrigation & drainage (at 1 H.P. for each 2.6 hectares, on the basis of 53 million hectares cultivated area that requires irrigation and drainage)	20 million H.P.
(5) Electricity for farm use (at 150 Kwh. for each hectare on the basis of 106 million hectares)	16 billion Kwh.**
(6) "Motivation" machines (at 800 H.P. for each 667 hectares on the basis of 106 million hectares of China's cultivated area)	130 million H.P.

---

*Horsepower.

**Kilowatt hour.

Communist Records of Agricultural
Machinery Production

1. According to Communist reports,[2] by 1958
China had come to possess the following main items
of agricultural machinery, among a great multitude
of mechanical and semimechanical implements and
accessories:

Tractors	45,330 units	(standard, 15 H.P.)
Combined harvesters	3,452	"
Grain threshers	5,516	"
Farm trucks	12,700	"
Machinery for irrigation & drainage	1,600,000 H.P.	
Machinery for ranch use	5,700 units	
Machinery for plant protection	11,100	"
Machine-pulled implements	80,000	"

2. Taking the increase of tractors alone, the
following figures from Communist sources (as cited
in Agricultural Notes, No. 16, 1965) may be presented for consideration:

Year	No. in Service	No. Increased During Year
1957	24,629	5,262
1958	45,330	20,710
1959	59,000	13,670
1960	79,000	20,000
1961	95,000	16,200
1962	110,000	14,790
1963	115,000	5,017
1964	123,145	8,128
1965	134,794	11,694

In view of the steady increase in the last few
years, we may conservatively estimate the total
figure for 1966 as 145,000 and that for 1967 as
150,000 units, both in the standard unit of 15
horsepower.

3. It will be interesting to note that, since
the mid-1960s, Chinese tractor factories have concentrated on the production of six new types of
tractors, which are officially approved as being
most adaptable to various farm uses at the present
stage of development (People's Handbook, 1965,
p. 554):

(a) "Eastern Red 54."

(b) "Eastern Red 75."

These two types of tractors, possess-
ing 54 H.P. and 75 H.P. respectively, are highly
efficient in tilling, harrowing, sowing, etc. They
run at comparatively high speed, "able to cultivate
5 hectares per hour." Both types are adaptable to
the plain areas of North China and Manchuria.

(c) "Red Banner 100." This type of tractor is designed for reclamation over vast areas and
for heavy duties in conservation projects or other
construction work. With its 100 H.P. of force, it
is quite efficient in earth moving, mud dredging,
ground leveling, weight lifting, or any other work
in connection with large-scale engineering tasks.

(d) "Eastern Red 28." This is a small
model with rubber-tired wheels, specially designed
for use in cotton fields and corn fields where
nimble movement is required. At highest speed, it
can reach 25 kilometers per hour. It is most efficient in tilling, harrowing, and sowing, and can
also do well in weeding and top-dressing of fertilizers.

(e) "Bumper 35." This is a lightweight
(1-1/2 tons) tractor with 35 H.P., specially designed for use in paddy fields of the South. It is
easy to handle and nimble in movement. It could
move freely on small fields 3-5 mow in size. Capable of cultivating 5 mow per hour.

(f) "Worker-Peasant 7." This is a "hand-
control" tractor of 7 H.P., specially designed for

use on vegetable gardens, orchards, or on the terraced fields of hilly slopes where other types of
tractors cannot operate. It has been pushed for
mass-production in all parts of the country.

Discussion on the Feasibility
of Farm Mechanization

Despite Mao Tse-tung's frenzied efforts to
achieve his "Great Solution" within ten years, the
feasibility of farm mechanization became a controversial issue among the Communist agro-technologists
throughout the late 1950s and early 1960s. Although
no one is opposed to "mechanization" as a principle,
the debate has focused upon the question of pace
and procedure to attain such a goal.

1. Advocates for quick mechanization generally stress the urgent need of deep-plowing and
ground-leveling, of effective irrigation and
drainage, and of extension of the "double-cropping"
system in the North and the "double-rice" system in
the South. Human and animal power must be swiftly
replaced with mechanical power in order to get
quick results for agricultural advancement, as illustrated by some basic facts.

(a) One man with a spade can cultivate
only one third mow per day; one ox with a plow can
cultivate only three mow; but a tractor with a
mechanical plow can cultivate at least 130 mow.

(b) Human power with traditional apparatus
can irrigate only two to three mow of land per day;
animal power with traditional installations can irrigate only three to five mows; but mechanical devices of varied horsepower can irrigate from 40 to
400 mows, depending upon requirement of the time
and the locality.

(c) There are twenty days of "rush season"
between reaping of winter wheat and sowing of the
autumn crop in North China; there are only five to
twenty days between the two rice croppings in South

China. Huge amounts of work in harvesting, land
clearing, manuring, watering, and sowing must be
hurriedly done in this short time. Speedy results
could be accomplished only through the extensive
application of mechanical power at rush seasons.[3]

2. Advocates for "gradual mechanization," on
the other hand, emphasized repeatedly the many obstacles of China's physical terrain, inadequacy of
fuel and mechanical supply, and subsequent problem
of rural underemployment.

(a) Among China's cultivated area of
111,300,000 hectares, only about 7,300,000 hectares
may be considered as suitable for mechanical cultivation, with roughly 5,300,000 hectares in the
North and 2 million hectares in the South. Even on
these plain and basin areas, there are numerous
networks of canals, ponds, reservoirs, and wells.
These must be removed or rearranged before large
pieces of contiguous land can be integrated for
mechanical cultivation.

The great number of mulberry groves, fruit
orchards, tea plantations, etc., in both South and
North, where trees and crops are interplanted for
space economy, would also have to be discarded or
demolished in favor of farm mechanization. The
concrete losses from these "transforming" measures
would definitely outbalance the gains for hasty
adoption of mechanical cultivation in places that
are not yet ready for such innovations.

(b) According to experiences of Soviet
Russia, tractor cultivation obtains an efficiency
rate of only 64 per cent on a piece of land 200 m
X 100 m (about 33 mow); the efficiency rate rises
to 85 per cent on a piece of land 2,000 m X 500 m
(about 1,500 mow). The minimum requirement for efficient mechanical cultivation is 1,500 to 3,000
mow. "As a rule 3,000 mow per standard unit of
tractor (15 H.P.) when only ploughing was done, or
1,500 mow with multiple operations."

But in the case of China, 70 per cent of
the paddy fields in South and Central provinces are
located on terraced slopes in tiny patches, where
the existing types of heavy tractors could never be
applied. With the exception of a few stretches of
level ground in North China plain, there is scarce-
ly any place in China that one could find a whole
contiguous piece of flat land over 100 mow in size.
Such a rugged terrain is hardly suitable for extensive mechanization in a short period.

(c) A "Delta Model 54" tractor for example,
usually consumes five to ten tons of fuel oil per
year, depending upon the amount of work to be done.
If the estimated 400,000 units are put on the full
run, the annual oil consumption would amount to
2,800,000 tons--even at the rate of seven tons per
unit. This total amount already exceeds the 1958
planned output of crude oil (2,260,000 tons) not
to count any shares for industry and household uses.
China's petroleum production has improved rapidly,
owing to discovery of new fields; so required supply for tractors may be available, but high distribution costs may be a factor restricting consumption.

(d) The main function of mechanical cultivation is "labor saving." Although the nation as
a whole frequently feels labor shortage in rush
seasons, many farm areas are overcrowded with labor
in other seasons of the year. Investigation in
North China provinces has already revealed com-
plaints against mechanization because "machines are
taking away our work points," as the commune members declare. This is really a serious problem in
those regions where machines begin to displace farm
hands, while industry and construction projects are
not yet ready to absorb this extra amount of labor.
The only feasible way is to coordinate the pace of
farm mechanization with that of industrial expansion and the general advancement of national economy in a broad scale.[4]

The Peking regime has proclaimed no definite
policy on agricultural mechanization since 1962.

The general trends followed by provincial authorities seem to have inclined toward (a) gradual mechanization, (b) partial mechanization, and (c) selective mechanization with the following manifestations:

    1. Mechanization is less applied to land resources but more to water resources, as shown by recent boost of power facilities for irrigation, drainage, and water control in river dams and lake regions.

    2. Mechanization is less used in wet fields for rice but more used in dry fields for wheat, miscellaneous grains, cotton and other fibers, soybean and other oilseeds, beets, sugar cane, and other economic crops.

    3. Mechanization is less promoted in densely populated areas but more promoted in labor-scarce regions such as Northern Manchuria, Inner Mongolia, and most parts of the northwestern provinces.

Special Features in Recent Development of Farm Mechanization

Under the principles of gradual, partial, and selective mechanization, distinctive features in China's recent development toward agricultural modernization are notable. One is the transformation of the agricultural machinery stations, marked by progress in scientific experimentation and initiative.

Agricultural machinery stations, at their beginning stage, were actually "tractor stations" of the Soviet model, designated primarily to sell mechanical services to collective farms in plowing, raking, sowing, and other field operations. The first agricultural machinery station was established in Liaoning in 1950. Numbers were increased to 11 in 1953, to 138 in 1955, and to 383 in 1957. As their services were primarily confined to mechanical cultivation, distribution of these stations was naturally concentrated in Manchuria,

Sinkiang, Inner Mongolia, and a few places on the
North China plain, where tractors could be employed
without undue difficulties.

"In 1962, nearly 500 such stations were situated in Heilungkiang and 400 in Liaoning; two thirds
of the total were probably in the three Northeastern
Provinces."[5] But beginning with 1964, the number
of agricultural machinery stations suddenly jumped
up to 1,500 in 1964; to 2,263 in 1965. It could
quite easily have risen to a peak of 2,500 in
1967, if the communal substations were also
counted. According to the People's Daily (Oct.
20, 1964), "By 1964, more than 70 per cent of the
Hsien [counties] in China were reported to have at
least one agricultural machinery station each."
This not only signifies an abrupt increase in
number, but a much more even distribution among
all localities in rural China. Two substantial
causes may be traced to this significant transformation:

1. The Peking regime had in the early 1960s
started a mass movement for scientific experimentation and rural construction. This created an urgent
need for diffusion of mechanical skills, training of
technical personnel, practical assistance in installation, replacement, and repair work among local
industries, collaboration in various local projects
in water conservation, power generation, or the
processing of farm products, etc.

Thus these agricultural machinery stations, old
or new, have found themselves burdened with many
technical functions that are perhaps more important
and more urgent than the original service of tractor
operation.

2. Power decentralization since the late 1950s
and the early 1960s has stirred "local initiative"
for construction work among the provinces and the
counties. Revival of "small freedoms" under the
new agricultural policy has released the private incentive of rural masses and also improved their

material livelihood in the forms of cash income and
grain reserves. By the mid-1960s, these local authorities, in collaboration with communal units,
were not only obliged but also willing and able to
take up various medium and small projects for the
full utilization of their land, water, and power
resources. Expansion of the former agricultural
machinery stations, both in units and in function,
is the logical answer to the increasing demands
from these local projects. This may help very little in extending the areas under mechanical cultivation, but it has certainly made some substantial
contributions in bringing up the technical standard
of China's farm economy as a whole.[6]

Net Results of Farm Mechanization

Area Under Mechanical
Cultivation

     In assessing the nation's area under mechani-
cal tillage, one should give due attention to the
important role played by state farms. This, in
fact, contributed the biggest share of mechanized
farming throughout the seventeen years of Communist
administration. According to the Ten Great Years
(Peking, 1959), there were 710 state farms in 1957
under the jurisdiction of the Ministry of Reclamation at Peking--not counting the small units under
control of the provincial or local authorities.
Together with the small units, there were 2,490
state farms in 1961 for the nation as a whole as
reported by Wang Cheng, the Minister of Reclamation. (Agricultural Notes, No. 39, 1965).

     The task of mechanized farming, however, was
primarily charged to the ministry-controlled group
of big farms, most of which were situated in Manchuria, Sinkiang, and other borderlands, and carry-
ing on work of reclamation or other construction
projects. "In 1964 these state farms were reported
to possess 32 per cent of the nation's tractor power, 50 per cent of the farm mechanical tools, 82.5
per cent of the combine harvesters, and 68 per cent

of the heavy-duty motor vehicles used in agriculture."[7]

The largest area ever claimed as being under the cultivation of all state farms was 5,200,000 hectares in 1961.[8] If 70 per cent of this area is considered as "mechanized," it amounts to 3.37 per cent on the basis of China's cultivated area in 1958. Even if the whole area is considered "mechanized," the result is only 4.82 per cent on the same basis. It is generally recognized that because of practical difficulties, as previously stated, very few of the "people's farms," either before or after collectivization, had really resorted to mechanization for their regular operations--perhaps with the exception of some labor-scarce areas such as northern Manchuria, southern Sinkiang, and a few spots in other borderlands. Collective units in China's northern provinces might be obliged to employ a certain amount of machine services (as afforded by the agricultural machinery stations) in the rush seasons, for special tasks, or at times of emergency as a result of natural calamities. But this is quite different from the regular full-scale mechanical cultivation as performed by the big-sized state farms. It is hence quite evident that despite the clamor about "agricultural mechanization" for these years, the achievements of Communist state farms up to 1960 were pitifully small, and those of the collective units were negligible in all accounts.

Thus the Communist writer Li Ching-yu openly stated that, ". . . at the end of 1958, only about two per cent of the country's arable land was mechanically cultivated."[9] Again, Vice Premier Li Hsien-nien reported in 1959 that China ". . . expects to achieve a mechanized area of 6,600 hectares [about six per cent of 1958 cultivated area] in 1960" (1967 Yearbook on Chinese Communism). It is thought that perhaps Minister Chen Cheng-jen, Ministry of Agricultural Machinery, had made an honest admission when he said, "By the end of 1959, about five per cent of China's cultivated area had

already realized mechanization."[10]   This five per
cent now amounted only to 5,400,000 hectares on the
basis of the nation's cultivated area (107,800,000
hectares) in 1958.

Undoubtedly mechanization together with other
farm activities suffered a great setback during the
disastrous years of the post-"Leap" period. But
along with gradual agricultural recovery in the
early 1960s, several moderate movements slowly but
steadily advanced toward degrees of mechanization
in all parts of the country:

1.   State farms as well as collective units
kept on reclaiming new lands in the border regions
or among hilly regions in the South and Southwest.
Most of the new fields were usually opened up with
machines and made to suit mechanical cultivation.

2.   Increasing amounts of flat, contiguous
fields in the interior provinces were established
through the recent nationwide drives for ground
leveling in which depressions were filled, knolls
cut down, and rocky barriers removed for the farm
machinery operation.

3.   Owing to promotion of multiple-cropping
systems in both northern and southern provinces,
more rush seasons between two croppings have been
created. During this, mechanical services are
needed to do quick work in crop reaping, land
clearing, manuring, watering, and sowing, etc., all
in a span of one to three weeks.

4.   With the increased accumulation of cash
income and grain reserve in recent years, many
large and wealthy communes have found it advantageous to hire more machine services or even to own
some machines themselves, so that regular work on
the common fields can be quickly done and their
members can spend more time and energy on sideline
occupations. They augment their earnings with auxiliary products.

5. Specific types of tractors have been developed to suit the diversified terrain features in
all parts of China, especially the lightweight,
low-capacity models. These can be easily applied
to paddy fields, vegetable gardens, or small
patches of terraced lands on hilly slopes. This
has greatly helped in the extensive adoption of
mechanical cultivation in China's central and
southern provinces.

It is on the basis of these considerations
that we have liberally set China's current mechanized area at seven per cent, or about 115,534,000
mow (based on 1,650,430,000 mow of cultivated area),
including crop fields in both state farms and collective units. These are regularly under mechanical cultivation, either through hired services or by
means of owned facilities. Compared with the status of 1959, the total increase is only 2,300,000
hectares; the average annual increase is about
300,000 hectares for the last eight years. This
annual rate of increase, however, will be constantly modified by the interplay of relevant factors,
such as adequacy of fuel oil, availability of technical staff, depreciation rate of machinery in use,
output capacity of machine industries, and the
costs involved in mechanical operation, as compared
with that of human and animal labor.

Area Under Mechanized
Irrigation and Drainage

While different types of machinery may be varied in their capacity for power generation, the
amount of work produced by each unit of power is
the same for all mechanical devices. Communist experts have set 2.6 hectare per horsepower as the
work norm for mechanical facilities in irrigation
and drainage operations, either as mobile or as
stationary units, and motivated either by electricity or by other forms of power (derived from mineral energy).

1. The total capacity of power facilities for

irrigation and drainage was reported as 6 million horsepower in 1964 (NCNA, Sept. 20, 1964, cited by Agricultural Notes, No. 1, 1965), with 2,040,000 horsepower attributed to electrical pumps and 4 million horsepower attributed to nonelectrical power pumps operated by "camel boilers" (steam engines), coal-gas engines, diesel engines, etc. Estimating at the increasing rate of 1 million horsepower per year, the total capacity for 1967 was put at 9 million horsepower--with electrical pumping facilities sharing 60 per cent and the other facilities 40 per cent.

2.   On the basis of 40 mow per horsepower, the cultivated area served by all mechanical facilities would amount to approximately 24 million hectares, or 60 per cent of our estimated effectively irrigated area (40 million hectares) for 1967. The area served by electrical pumps would amount to 14,400,000 hectares, or 36 per cent of the total irrigated area, and that served by nonelectrical power pumps would be 9,600,000 hectares or 24 per cent of the total irrigated area, with the former outrunning the latter in the last three years.

Expansion of the "Power-
Pump" Facilities

Power pumps for irrigation and drainage were introduced in China long before the Communist advent in 1949. While sporadic adoption of nonelectrical pumps was promoted under the general mechanization scheme of the 1950s, a systematic campaign for the extension of electrical pumping stations was carried out in the early 1960s. Then extra power capacities were found "idle" in many industrial and mining areas that could be utilized through the installation of long-distance transmission lines. Although electrical pumps have come to enjoy the first priority of promotion efforts in recent years, the nonelectrical power pumps had an earlier start in development, and were endowed with other advantages at places where the supply of electricity is inadequate or too expensive for farm

users. According to NCNA (Sept. 20, 1964), there
were in 1964 approximately 2,040,000 horsepower in
electrical pumping facilities and 4 million horsepower in mechanical pumping facilities (that is,
driven by power other than electricity). The ratio
between nonelectrical and electrical pumping capacities is two to one. In view of its swift ascendancy in the last few years, however, the electrical pump will catch up and then outdistance the
mechanical pump within the next decade. Let us
briefly sketch these two types of power facilities
as follows:

    1. The mechanical pumps. This category con-
sists mainly of three types of power engines:

        (a) The "camel boiler," a steam engine
with a waterwheel attached.

        (b) The coal-gas engine, run by coal gas,
with a waterwheel attached.

        (c) The diesel engine, motivated by inter-
nal combusion of fuel oil, usually with a water
turbine attached.

    Communist experts had made a sort of efficien-
cy study of the engines in comparison with human
and animal power for the performance of irrigation
or drainage, with the following results:[11]

Types of power facilities	Area served per day (mow)
Human power with waterwheel	2-3
Animal power with waterwheel	3-5
"Camel boiler" with waterwheel	) 40 mow per H.P.
Coal-gas engine with waterwheel	) average
Diesel engine with water turbine	)

    2. The electrical pumps. The pumps in this
category draw their power primarily from two
sources:

        (a) The numerous small-scale hydroelectric

projects established in recent years, with large numbers concentrated along river tributaries in mountainous regions of southern and southwestern provinces.

(b) The main source is in various power centers of big cities and the important mining and industrial areas on the Mainland, from which extensive networks of transmission lines are set up for power transference.

Coincidentally, China's most important grain-producing areas are generally situated around great metropolises in which population and industries are concentrated with the endowment of power centers. Thus pumping stations on the Pearl River delta can always draw power from Canton; the Han Chiang delta from Swatow; and the Yangtze delta and Hangchow Bay areas from Shanghai powerhouses and the Hsin-Aun Chiang power station. The same situation exists between the Tung-ting Lake region and Wuhan; between the Po-Yang Lake region and Nanchang; between North China plain and its power centers at Tsingtao, Tsinan, Kaifeng, and the Sanmen Gorge Dam, when the power installation is completed.

Our estimate of the 1967 power facilities for farm use (mainly pumps) is 9 million horsepower, covering the whole range of mechanical pumps, electrical pumps, and equipment for the machine wells. Assuming a bigger share of 60 per cent (33 per cent in 1964), the electrical pump facilities would amount to 5,400,000 horsepower for that year. On the basis of 40 mow per horsepower, this amount of power capacity would serve 216 million mow of cultivated area in irrigation. Based on our estimated area under irrigation of 37 million hectares for 1967, 36.84 per cent of that area would be provided with electrical pumping facilities.

ELECTRICAL POWER

Rural electrification in China signifies a drastic change in the evolution of its economic

policy, after ten years of Communist rule. It was
"all power for industry" before 1960; but it has
changed to "all power for agriculture" since that
date. It should be noted that the "Great Leap"
movement was really meant to decentralize industry
from urban areas to the countryside. And the commune system was designed to build up numerous agro-
industrial-political cell bodies at the local level,
to serve as a solid base for the Communist structure. Thus China's rural areas have been charged
with a double duty since the early 1960s:

1. The growing demand of farm production together with various local projects on water conservation, soil improvement, erosion control, plant
protection, etc.

2. The additional burden of rural industries
along the lines of food processing, fodder preparation, oilseed pressing, cotton ginning, tool repairing, and so forth.

In spite of China's great mass of farm laborers
with their inborn aptitude of perseverance, no human power with the aid of animal power could cope
with such an immense multitude of tasks, all crowded in time and space, and with the limited amount
of energy supply. This situation naturally called
for a comprehensive program of power generation and
distribution on a nationwide scale, to which the
Peking regime responded with two extensive schemes
during and after the "Great Leap" period.

1. The minor power projects. Local authorities and collective units were encouraged to carry
out numerous medium and small projects to utilize
energy resources such as coal and gas mines, water
and wind power, thermo or hydroelectrical facilities.

2. Regional power grid. Local power-pumping
stations of various capacities were promoted to be
connected with big power centers (thermo or hydroelectric) through networks of high-tension lines

for transmission of electricity at low cost to the
farm units.

After haphazard attempts for several years,
the "minor projects" scheme, with a few exceptional
cases, was found to be rather disappointing and
fruitless for the following reasons.

1.   Local skill and native materials were usually inadequate to install such projects in full
scale and to maintain them in proper condition for
any length of time.

2.   Power demand and supply do not always
agree in any one locality; lack of coordination between localities constantly created enormous wastes
in labor, power, and fixed assets.

3.   Construction and maintenance of these local stations, together with other industrial projects in rural areas, took too much time and labor
away from the regular farm performances and thus
seriously cut down agricultural production in the
post-"Leap" period.

The regional power grids, on the other hand,
have proved to be conspicuously successful since
the early 1960s

> . . . as a by-product of the indus-
> trial recession. . . . The steep fall
> in industrial and mining activity from
> 1961 led to under-utilization of the
> expanded generating capacity in the
> cities. As part of the new policy of
> priority for agriculture, a program
> was set forth for the installation of
> high-tension transmission lines from
> industrial and mining centers with
> surplus generating capacity to the
> surrounding rural areas.[12]

In 1957, there were only 18,500 kilometers of
high-tension transmission lines existing in China.

Over 70,000 kilometers of such lines were installed
in the rural areas from the summer of 1958 to the
summer of 1963.[13] By the end of 1965, 126,000
kilometers of transmission lines had been added to
the number for 1957. This would make a total of
144,500 kilometers for that year.[14] In view of its
swift extension in the last few years, the mileage
of this rural wire network would probably have
reached 180,000 kilometers at the rate of 15,000
kilometers increase each year. (The annual rate of
increase was about 14,000 kilometers between 1958
and 1963.) While many factors have contributed to
the steady growth of this grid system, the concerted efforts of state (as represented by provincial
and county authorities) and communes (brigades,
teams, and households) played an essential role, as
manifested in the following arrangements.

     1. As 70 to 90 per cent of investment on
electrical pumping stations consists of machinery
and equipment, the construction work is financed
mostly by state grants or loans (actually local
shares in the national budget), with contributions
from communal units in the form of labor, food, and
local materials. The state (provinces and counties) is also responsible for all trunk lines and
most branch lines of the transmission network, with
subbranch lines to be provided by the communal
units closest to their location.

     2. The capacity of these power stations is
only partially used for purposes of irrigation and
drainage. About 1,000 hours in the South and 500
to 700 hours in the North each year are actually
spent for water operations. The rest of the time
is generally utilized for such rural industrial
work as food processing, fodder preparation, tool
repairing, oil pressing, sugar refining, and various types of handicrafts. As more than two thirds
of these stations are owned and operated by communes alone or jointly with state agencies (under
control of provincial or county authorities), fees
are charged for any public services rendered to
purely state organizations at all levels.

3. These regional networks (while currently
taking water utility as their primary function)
could be extended, rearranged, or redirected at a
future date to suit any shift of population centers
or industrial sites, to expand their station apparatus on all types of terrain, or to multiply their
function over many posts of nonfarm work. They
are not only an essential force for agricultural
modernization, but also great agents for rural in-
dustrialization.[15]

There is a special feature in the development
of these regional grids of electrical pumping stations. As electricity is drawn mostly from the
extra capacity of big power stations in great metropolises, the rural counties surrounding these
power centers always enjoy the highest benefits
from this transmission system. Thus the Pearl River delta around Canton, the Han Chiang delta around
Swatow, the Yangtze delta around Shanghai, the
Hangchow Bay area near Hsin-Aun Chiang station, the
Kun-nim basin area near the Hai-Ho station, the Po-
yang Lake region close to Nanchang, the Tung-ting
Lake region close to Wuhan, and the vast areas on
North China plain at varied distances from the
giant Sanmen Gorge Dam are either already provided
or will be provided with extensive meshworks of
high-tension transmission lines. While this natural arrangement agrees perfectly with the recent
Communist policy of selective development, there
are still many other productive areas that deserve
some sort of "power lifting" in order to catch up
with the preferred regions. Thus the Communists
adopted a supplemental policy in the early 1960s,
following the failure of numerous small power projects during the "Leap" years. "In areas remote
from cities (and especially in those important as
producers of grain, cotton and other industrial
crops) the policy has been to build power stations
of at least 500 kw [kilowatt] capacity with the intention of linking them to a larger power system
when possible."[16]

According to China News Service (CNS),[17]

> Among China's 2,126 counties in 1965,
> more than 1,300 have been provided
> with electrical power supply--either
> from local plants or through the
> transmission lines. Approximately
> 80 million peasants have received
> great benefits thereby, and 720 mil-
> lion workdays are thus relieved from
> their annual amount of labor.

China's rural consumption of electricity was estimated as 1,924 million kwh (kilowatt hour) in 1963
(about 6.4 per cent of the nation's total power
output of 30 billion kwh). In 1964, rural power
consumption was reported as 2,200 million kwh,
about twenty-two times that of 1957 (Agricultural
Notes, No. 30, 1965). Considering the speedy expansion of electric pumping facilities, supplemented with 500 kw plants at the local level, we have
conservatively estimated the nation's 1967 rural
consumption as 3,500 million kwh. This is above
7.3 per cent of its total output of 48 billion kwh
(estimated).

The percentage of China's rural consumption of
electricity for selected years has been estimated
by Wu Yuan-li in his Economic Development and the
Use of Energy Resources in Communist China (New
York, 1963) and his joint authorship with others of
Economic Potentials of Communist China (Menlo Park,
California, 1963). The estimated figures, by sector, for the percentage distribution of electric
power are:

	1953	1957	1960	1962
Industry	83.0	88.2	92.6	88.8
Agriculture	0.5	1.3	1.7	3.8
Transport	1.4	0.8	0.6	0.7
Household	14.6	10.6	5.4	6.7

The 1967 Yearbook on Chinese Communism has
made a series of estimates on the nation's power
output from 1960 to 1966. Taking its output figures

from 1963 to 1966, we (Dawson and Tung) have made
our own estimates of Mainland China's rural power
consumption for recent years:

		Rural consumption	
National power output		Quantity	Per-
(million kwh)		(million kwh)	centage
1963	30,000	1,900	6.33
1964	35,000	2,200	6.30
1965	39,000	2,500	6.41
1966	43,000	3,000	6.97
1967	48,000 (our estimate)	3,500	7.30

HUMAN AND ANIMAL POWER RESOURCES

This section is intended to assess the requirements and supply of human and animal labor resources in relation to all agricultural activities
that draw power from the farm population and their
draft animals. It covers two broad categories of
farm operations under the Communist system of collective management.

1. Direct farm operations in relation to crop
growing, such as plowing, harrowing, sowing, watering, manuring, transplanting, sprout arranging,
weeding, harvesting, threshing, etc.

2. Indirect farm operations in relation to
crop growing, such as:

(a) Accumulation of fertilizers (collect-
ing animal dregs from grazing grounds, drawing
"mud manure" from rivers, ponds, and lakes, reaping
green manures from fields, etc.

(b) Preparation of fodders (concentrates,
roughages, wild grass, etc.

(c) Repair, maintenance, or expansion of
local conservation projects, or the same work in
connection with other local constructions.

(d) Ground leveling and field consolidation (such as filling depressions, cutting down molds, removing stony barriers, etc.).

(e) Soil improvement (such as moving sandy soil to clayey areas, moving clayey soil to sandy areas, transferring soils and turfs from thick beds to thin beds, desalinization, washing, draining, or other reconditioning processes).

(f) Transportation of agricultural produce and farm supplies between farmstead and the market town.

(g) Others.

The labor situation for both direct and indirect farm operations may be hinged upon or expressed in any of the following factors: (a) farm population; (b) agricultural production; (c) cultivated area; and (d) crop acreage. We have chosen crop acreage as the denominator, because it is the most concrete and illustrative indicator of agricultural development in a country. But the workday requirement or supply per crop-mow should not be interpreted as related to direct farm operations alone. In fact, the indirect operations have tended to grow in volume, and constantly demand an increasing amount of labor supply under the Communist system of collective management.

Vice Premier Tan Cheng-lin (in charge of agriculture) in his assessment of labor requirement in the agricultural sector, apart from the special seasonal work (winter-spring rural construction) carried on every year, also included the following items in his calculation:

1. Commune-controlled forestry, animal husbandry, fishery, and other auxiliary enterprises (not state enterprises).

2. Commune-managed small industries and handicrafts on a local scale.

(3) Collective cultural and welfare works in the community.

According to Tan's estimate, ordinary construction work on the farm (such as ground leveling, field consolidation, soil improvement, erosion control, etc. alone) usually occupied about 20 per cent of the total farm labor units. The percentage would be much higher, if the extra seasonal work (winter-spring) were included.

"Hence the current situation (1960) is that only a little more than 50 per cent of the farm labor units could be devoted to the task of crop production."[18]

In assessing labor requirements in China's farm economy we have to take into consideration the drastic changes that have been brought about through the Communist rule of the past ten years.

1. Institutional changes. Under the Communist system the income and hence the well-being of the communal members depends largely upon the work points they earn from collective work on the collectivized fields. Not only adult men and women strive to get full-time work on lands or for the group, but even aged people, and children above six or seven, want to perform a certain amount of services to augment their work points.

2. Technical changes. Farm technique programs promoted under the "Eight-letter Charter of Agriculture" have demanded a great number of innovations and improvements, such as deep plowing, close planting, increased fertilization, frequent weeding, rational control of irrigation and drainage, seed breeding and selection, pest and disease control, and many other measures. These China's traditional farm economy had failed to initiate or failed to carry through.

While some of these technical measures (such as close planting, seed vernalization, and the

making of "native chemical fertilizers") were
quickly dropped after a brief trial, most of the
innovated or improved techniques have been continued in modified forms to suit local conditions.
Thus many paddy fields in the South have increasingly adopted the practice of fertilizer apportion-
ment and water regulation in accordance to the optimum requirement of the growing plant at different
stages. Wheat fields (and other dry-land crops)
have also achieved an increase in their frequency
of watering and applying the proper allocation of
mixed fertilizers at different stages of crop
growth. For many parts of the nation, land plowing
has been carried from the traditional three to five
inches down to the new depths of (reportedly in
some places) one to one and one half feet. Seed
improvement and plant protection have been gradually extended all over the country through collective
efforts with adequate amount of state assistance.[19]

All these technical measures directly connected with operations of crop growing naturally would
require considerably more additional workdays from
both the peasantry and their draft animals, in comparison with the simple passive requirements as revealed by farm surveys of the pre-Communist days.
Although no national or regional data are available
concerning the labor situation in relation to different crops under the Communist farm system, a few
instances may be cited as an illustration, as follows:

1. In connection with its investigation on
"Labor Input and Production Cost of High-yielding
Rice Fields" in six provinces (Hopeh, Liaoning,
Kansu, Szechwan, Hunan, and Hupeh), Statistical
Work magazine (No. 22, Nov. 29, 1958) has published
the following findings as an average phenomenon of
seven sample areas in rice production:

	Average workday input per mow	Average production cost per mow (in yuan)
Most high-yielding fields	265	206
Medium high-yielding fields	56	56
Common fields	35	24

2. Reporter Wang Yun of the People's Daily has published an article in that paper (Nov. 11, 1958) in which he cites the labor investment on four staple crops by the "Red Banner Commune" of Wei-Nan County, Shensi, with the purpose of contrasting the production records from its "Sputnik plots" (intensive investment of productive factors including labor) and that of the common fields:

	Average input of workdays per mow	Average value of production per mow (in yuan)
Wheat		
Sputnik plots	30.3	230.12
Common fields	13.4	51.0
Corn		
Sputnik plots	42.4	1,036.37
Common fields	16.9	117.65
Cotton		
Sputnik plots	111.6	1,536.37
Common fields	18.1	142.00

Common fields, as cited in the above tables, denote the ordinary croplands in that region, managed with the ordinary input of labor and other factors without any special efforts at intensification. These fields in fact represent the general standard of labor requirement among these four staple crops in the late 1950s in Mainland China.

If these labor requirements are compared with Professor Buck's findings for the same crops in the early 1930s, one would be surprised to notice such a great discrepancy between these two sets of figures:

	Pre-Communist workday requirements per crop-mow 1929-33	Workday requirement* per crop-mow under Communist rule, 1958	Percentage of increase
Rice	13.66	35.00	156.22
Wheat	4.33	13.40	209.46
Corn	3.88	16.90	335.56
Cotton	8.80	18.10	105.68

While these few instances could not be taken as representative of the nation as a whole, it seems quite apparent that per crop-mow labor requirement under the Communist system (even taking the direct farm operations alone) would be considerably higher than that of the pre-Communist days, so far as these four staple crops are concerned. If the indirect farm operations are added to these figures, the total number of workdays required would again be doubled for each crop-mow, according to Vice Premier Tan's assessment for the broad category of agricultural work at large.

However, in view of the gradual introduction of improved farm tools and the rapid advancement of mechanized power facilities in recent years, we shall conservatively set the human labor requirement at 240 workdays per year, and animal labor requirement at 120 workdays per year.

Actual procedures of computation may be briefly sketched as follows.

1. For human labor workdays:

    (a) The 1967 population is estimated as

_____

*Reports may be exaggerated for accumulation of work points.

753,500,000. On the basis of 85 per cent, the farm population is calculated as 640,415,000.

(b) In view of changed demographic structure in China in recent years, we set the fifteen to sixty-four age group as 55 per cent.

(c) Assign working capacity unit 1 for each male of the fifteen to sixty-four group and unit 0.5 for each female of this group, using equal sex ratio for the sake of simplicity.

(d) Deduct 15 per cent from the remaining 45 per cent of farm population as children under six and aged people over sixty-five who are too feeble to work. Then assign working capacity unit 0.2 for the 30 per cent that can perform farm work partially or intermittently as occasion demands.

(e) The working units derived from these capacity ratios are:

Male	175,312,500 units	
Female	87,656,250	
Others	38,250,000	
Total	301,218,750 (or 301,219,000 units)	

(f) Assuming 240 days as the working range for each labor unit, the total number of workdays for 1967 is calculated as 72,292,760,000.

(g) Dividing the 1967 total workdays by the crop acreage (2,439,000,000 mow) of that year, we obtain a result of 29.64 days per crop-mow.

2. For animal labor workdays:

(a) The 1967 draft animal (large animal) is estimated at 97 million head. At 70 per cent availability, the actively working number is 67,900,000 head.

(b) Assign working capacity unit 1 for each head of available numbers; the working units will amount to 67,900,000.

(c) Assuming 120 days per year as the working range of each animal unit, the total animal workdays is 8,148 million days.

(d) Dividing the total workdays for 1967, we obtain a result of fifty days per crop hectare for that year.

FINAL RESULTS OF ESTIMATION

1. Mechanical power (land and water utilization):

A. Status of mechanical cultivation:

(a) Tractors in farm service (standard units of 15 H.P.)

1957	1967	Per cent of increase
24,629	150,000	509.04

(b) Areas under mechanical cultivation

	Area of mechanized cultivation	As percentage of cultivated area
1957:	50,000,000 mow (est.)	less than 1
1967:	115,534,000 mow (est.)	7

B. Status of agricultural machinery stations:

1957	1967	Percentage of increase
383	2,500	552.74

C. Status of mechanized irrigation and drainage:

(a) Total mechanized pumping facilities

		Area served
Capacity (H.P.)	(1,000 mow)	As percentage of irrigated area
1957: 560,000	22,400	4.30
1967: 9,000,000	360,000	61.40

(b) Mechanized pumping motivated by nonelectric
    powers

		Area served
		As percentage of
Capacity (H.P.)	(1,000 mow)	irrigated area
1957: 500,000	20,000	3.84
1967: 3,500,000	144,000	24.56

(c) Mechanized pumping motivated by electric power

		Area served
		As percentage of
Capacity (H.P.)	(1,000 mow)	irrigated area
1957: 60,000	2,400	0.46
1967: 5,400,000	216,000	36.84

    2. Electrical power (power diffusion and rural consumption:

        A. Extension of transmission lines:

1957	1967	Percentage of increase
18,500 km	180,000 km (est.)	873

        B. Rural consumption of power:

1957	1967	Percentage of increase
251,420,000 kwh	3,500,000,000 kwh	1,292
(1.3% of total	(7.3% of total	
power output)	power output)	

    3. Human power (labor units for farm work):

        A. Human labor units:

1967
301,219,000 units

        B. Human labor workdays:

1967
72,292,760,000 days

C. Average workdays per crop hectare:

1967
445 days

4. Animal power (animal units for farm work):

A. Animal labor units:

1967
67,900,000 units

B. Animal units workdays:

1967
8,148,000,000 days

C. Average workdays per crop hectare:

1967
49.7 days

NOTES

1. Liu's estimates of (1) to (6), except (2),
are taken from his article in People's Daily (Peking, June 20, 1963); item (2) is from the Handbook
of Current Events, No. 23 (1962).

2. 1967 Yearbook on Chinese Communism (Taiwan,
1967), p. 962.

3. Hu Yao-Pan, "Create a New Generation of
Warriors for the Great Struggle on Our Agricultural
Front," People's Daily (Peking, Nov. 22, 1960).
    Huang Ching, "Problems of Farm Mechaniza-
tion in China," op. cit. (Oct. 24-25, 1957).
    Tien Ling, "Report of a National Confer-
ence on Mechanization of Irrigation and Drainage,"
op. cit. (Dec. 19, 1957).

4.   Chao Hsieh, "Discussion on China's Problems of Farm Mechanization," Planned Economy (April, 1957 [unp.]).

Huang Ching, "Problems of Farm Mechanization in China," People's Daily (Oct. 24-25, 1957).

Yang Pei-Tsin, "The Problem of Financing the Process of Agriculture Mechanization in Our Country," Economic Research, No. 6 (June, 1963 [unp.]).

5.   NCNA (Chang-chun, Feb. 18, 1965).
NCNA (Shenyang, Aug. 26, 1942).
NCNA (Harbin, Sept. 17, 1921).

6.   Chinese Agricultural Journal, No. 8 (1956).
China Weekly (March 9, 1964).
People's Daily (Jan. 18, 1958; Oct. 20, 1964; April 13, 1966).

7.   Sheng Chih-lung and Ma Ching-po, "Fifteen Years of Agricultural Mechanization on State Farms," Technology of Agricultural Machinery, No. 11 (Nov. 13, 1964 [unp.]).

8.   Wang Cheng, Report (n.p., n.d.), 1 vol.

9.   Li Ching-yu, "Gradual Realization of Agricultural Mechanization through Tool Innovations," Agricultural Machinery, No. 18 (1959 [unp.]).

10.   Chen Cheng-jen, "Speed up Innovation of China's Farm Techniques," People's Daily (April 11, 1960).

11.   Tien Ling, "Report of National Conference on Mechanization of Irrigation and Drainage," People's Daily (Dec. 19, 1957).

12.   Tso Hu, "Several Problems of Agricultural Electrification," Economic Research, No. 3 (March, 1963 [unp.]).

13.   Wang Wen, "A Continuous Supply of Electricity to Villages," Daily Worker (Peking, Sept. 24, 1963).   Totals subject to question.

14.   China News Service (Peking, Sept. 25, 1965).

15.   Tseng Chih, "Exercise Strict Control, Practical and Proper Control over Appropriations for Capital Construction," Finance (Feb. 7, 1963 [unp.]).

16.   Huang Ching-yu, "Certain Problems in the Development of Agricultural Electrification," People's Daily (Sept. 12, 1963).

17.   China News Service (Sept. 25, 1965).

18.   Tan Cheng-lin, "Some Problems Concerning the Realization of Agricultural Mechanization in China," also published in Chinese Journal, No. 6 (March 23, 1960).

19.   Research Institute of Irrigation, Academy of Hydrological Science, "Discussions on Irrigation," People's Daily (March 25, 1959).
         Ministry of Agriculture, Office of Farm Tool Improvements, "On Farm Tool Improvement," People's Daily (May 9, 1959).
         Central Communist Party, Central Committee: (1) "Directive on Fertilizer Application," Aug. 29, 1958. (2) "Directive on Deep Plowing and Soil Improvement," Aug. 29, 1958 (Peiping, Aug., 1958 [2 vols.]).

CHAPTER **9** ESTIMATED LIVESTOCK

SITUATION, 1967

INTRODUCTION

Population, livestock, and food grains constitute the interlocking rings of China's farm economy.
Being interlocking, they are interdependent in supply and demand, and interacting in their "push-and-
pull" movements for progress or stagnation. No one
segment can advance far ahead without being dragged
by the other two from behind. Nor could one segment linger far behind without being drawn up by
the two in front.

We have already set forth estimates of two seg-
ments in China's farm structure:

1. Total population in
   1967-68   753,500,000
   Rural population in
   1967-68   640,415,000

2. Grain production in
   1967   213,883,000 M.B.*

In spite of this seemingly big aggregate of
grain output, however, the 1967 per capita is only
570 catties in unhusked grain, which is actually
two catties lower than the 1957 average. This
means that the output of 213,883,000 metric tons

---

*Metric tons. Figure is higher than most
estimates.

170

constitutes a minimum requirement to keep China's
753,500,000 people near the food requirements level,
and all productive factors must work together to
maintain and to augment the current level of production.

As explained elsewhere in this book, over
93 per cent of China's cultivated area has to be
worked by human and animal labor, and over 60 per
cent of its grain fields depend on organic fertilizer, principally animal and human excreta   Logically
and practically, multiplication of livestock at this
transient stage is possibly more important than the
promotion of mechanized farming and chemical fertilizer. Ever since the mid-1950s, hog-raising under
state aid has been upheld as a main source for
manure accumulation. Beginning with the early 1960s,
breeding of large animals has strongly developed
along three lines through concerted efforts of central and local authorities:

1. Extension and improvement of pasture lands
in the border regions by means of irrigation facilities, seed grass selection, and regionalized grazing
management.

2. Increase of state ranches in Sinkiang,
Chinghai, Inner Mongolia, and several areas in
southern and southwestern China, especially for the
purpose of raising draft animals on a large scale.

3. Establishment of breeding centers and veterinary stations in selected areas of the country
with special emphasis on the improvement and multiplication of draft animals.

While sheep and goats seem to engage little
attention on a national scale, they have enjoyed
special attention under local authorities in pastoral regions where their bodily elements provide
food, clothing, and shelter for the indigenous population.[1]

Considering the quick recovery and steady
advancement of agricultural production in recent

years, it is inconceivable that China could have attained its current status of development without a comparable growth in the segment of livestock, partly as an important source of fertilizing agents as important diet items, and as a main source of motive power for agriculture. Daniel Tretiak at the University Service Center, Kowloon, Hong Kong, investigated China's hogs and sheep (and goats) and large animals. The increase in recent years, largely based upon scattered Communist information, may be cited to illustrate our point.

Hog Situation

Kiangsu: Had hog population of about 10 million in 1957. By the end of 1966, the 1957 figure had been attained again. In view of good conditions in 1967 it seems likely production is now appreciably above 1957.

Kiangsi: 1957 number of 5.27 million was reached by the end of 1965 with further increases likely since.

Kwantung: Hog population suffered drastically during the "Great Leap Forward." The figure for 1957 was put at nine million, which dropped to 4.4 thousand in 1961. By the end of 1964, the 1957 high had been exceeded; by 1965, even the 1958 figure of 10.8 million had been left far behind. The 1968 figure must be still higher.

Heilungkiang: According to the Hong Kong agricultural officer, a 1957 figure of 3.06 thousand had been reached in late 1964 or early 1965.

Szechwan: In 1957, 25 thousand head; in 1958, 30 thousand; but in 1962, only 11.2 thousand. Afterward recovery was rapid, and in 1966, 27 thousand were estimated. It's still larger at present.

Shensi: Pig production does not seem to have declined appreciably during "Great Leap Forward": 2.7 thousand in 1957. This seemed to have actually increased in 1961, but a drop later to 1957 level

was reported.   This hardly seems consistent with developments in other provinces.

Shansi: In 1957, 1.9 thousand are estimated.
For 1962, reported drop to 1.4, but by 1964 had
reached 2.3 thousand, thus substantially exceeding
the 1957 level.

On the basis of the above numerical data for
certain important areas, hog population had exceeded the 1957 level.   Dawson and Tung estimate at
least 10 per cent increase owing to the general
feed situation and continued improvement in sanitary conditions and government encouragement

Large Animals

In 1957, there were an estimated 83.5 million
large animals.   The Consul General, Hong Kong, estimates a drop in 1961 to 50.9; and in 1963, recovery to only 54.3 million, or 65 per cent of 1957.
Explanation of these drastic drops for the country
as a whole are not clearly set forth.   Dawson and
Tung believe that while feed conditions were very
poor in some sections, the animals would not be
allowed to starve, but might be sold to other provinces, where feed was available and draft animals
usually short in supply.

Tretiak takes a higher basis for 1961 (70 per
cent of 1957); and by applying a percentage increase
of 5 to 7 per cent arrives at 77 million for the
figure for 1967.   Dawson and Tung believe a drop of
30 per cent is still too much, and that the figure
for 1967-68 represents not only a recovery but
definitely a higher level than 1957, based on livestock ratios to other agricultural indexes. With
the general upward trend in feed production and the
need for draft animals, the demand has increased.
It is also notable that extensive effort has been
made to improve animal strains and cut down losses
by better sanitary measures.   Specialized centers
are a case in point.   Provincial data are used in
the final estimate.

Sheep

This class of animals did not suffer excessive-
ly during the "Great Leap Forward," and has continued to show significant increases in the main provinces in which they are raised; i.e., Inner Mongolia
Autonomous Region (IMAR), Sinkiang, Tibet, Chinghai,
and Shansi. Tretiak states: "Before the 'Great
Leap Forward,' these provinces produced approximately 75 million sheep. By 1965 they probably
produced over 110 million. . . . In 1957 other
provinces accounted for 25 million more sheep and
goats. If these experienced a similar increase to
the leading four--i.e., 45 per cent from 1957 to
1965--then there were about 145 million sheep and
goats in China by the latter date." We have conservatively estimated over 127 million.

The phenomenal increase indicated shows the
potential importance of this class of livestock.
It has importance for further expansion, but at the
more conservative rate, quality rather than quantity may be emphasized.

Poultry

Poultry is not mentioned in this report, but
no doubt showed large increases in line with increased feed crops.

In the Progress Report of October, 1967, Dawson and Tung tentatively made an estimate on the
provincial distribution of China's livestock, on
the basis of the 1957 figures from State Department
Livestock Notes, supplemented by some fragmentary
data from the Agricultural Notes prepared in Hong
Kong. Following the general trends of "gradual increase" as assessed in that October, 1967, report,
Dawson and Tung's estimate of the 1967 situation
sets forth three categories as follows, in million
heads, or animal units:*

---

*One animal unit equals one large animal, five
pigs, seven sheep, or 100 chickens.

		Million head 1967	Animal unit 1967
1.	Large animals	97	97
2.	Sheep and goats	127	18
3.	Hogs	166	33
	Total	390	148

Total animal units show an increase of 10 per cent over the national total animal units of 1957. There seems to be little question about the recent major increase of sheep, goats, and hogs over their 1957 level. This is confirmed in most cases even by the Communist reports.

LABOR REQUIREMENT OF LARGE ANIMALS

As no complete and consistent information is available for China's large animals, we attempt to measure the current situation in general through the labor requirement in animal hours. According to certain prewar data, as recorded in a Livestock Compendium, the working capacity of China's draft animals per head per day[2] may be estimated as follows:

	Loads Carried		Loads Pulled		Fields Operated
	Weight (kilo- grams)	Distance (kilo- meters)	Weight (kilo- grams)	Distance (kilo- meters)	Sq. Meters
Horses	80-100	40-60	800- 1,000	40-60	2,000- 3,000
Oxen	60-80	30-50	200	15-20	2,000- 3,000
Buffalo	--	--	--	--	1,500 (wet fields)

The Communist Practical Handbook for Agriculture (Shanghai, 1953) again reported the following records of labor requirement in North China, in number of workdays required by major crops:

Crops	Man-Days	Animal-Days	Total
Soybeans	50.3	32.5	82.8
Kaoliang	53.9	25.0	78.0
Millet	52.9	21.2	74.1
Rice (dry-field)	56.5	16.6	73.1
Wheat	50.0	18.0	68.0
Hemp	124.0	20.7	144.7

On the basis of these incomplete data, we have roughly assessed China's annual labor requirement for all draft animals as fifty workdays per crop hectare for direct farm operations such as land preparation, sewing, raking, harrowing, manuring, soil pressing, sprout arranging, weeding (three to four times), harvesting, threshing and storage, etc. Then farm animals must also annually spend some thirty-five days per crop hectare for such indirect performances as fodder preparation, fertilizer accumulation, irrigation and drainage, earth and stone work for local projects, and transportation of agricultural produce and household provisions between the farmstead and the market town (or the points of delivery for state grains). Taking the nation as a whole, eighty-five days per crop hectare seems to be a reasonable requirement for both types of work throughout the year.

The 1967 cultivated area is estimated as 110,032,000 hectare on April 1, 1968. Seven per cent is under mechanized cultivation (7,436,000 hectares) as recently assessed. The remaining 102,596,000 hectares depend upon human and animal power for direct and indirect operation requirements throughout the year.

Multiplied with a multiple cropping index of 148 per cent (actually 147.77 per cent), the result is a total crop acreage of 151,450,000 hectares in round numbers, which requires about 7,572,500,000 animal workdays each year, according to our estimate of fifty days per crop hectare.

The 1967 large animal figure is set at 97 million head--including the usual types of horses, mules, donkeys, cattle, and buffalo--with an average working capacity as one for each unit. Counting on an availability of 70 per cent of the total number for China, the actual working force would be 67,900,000 units for the year. Assuming 120 days as a working gauge each year for agricultural work, the total number of animal workdays in 1967 would amount to only 8,148,000,000 days, which is near the hypothetical requirement of 7,572,500,000 for that year. This means that in order to have attained the 1967 output target of food grain and other crops, approximately 8 billion animal workdays must have been put into the fields.

Judging from the steady improvements of pasture lands in border areas, and special efforts put into breeding and veterinary programs, evidence indicated that China's large animals (despite suffering considerable losses in certain provinces during the "Great Leap" period) have more than regained their 1957 status in recent years. The important reasons are that:

1. The urgent requirement of animal labor would not allow the draft animals to drag behind 1957 numbers.

2. The national efforts for draft animal promotion are quite evident in financial as well as technical programs.

3. The recovery and advancement of grain production have adequately solved the problem of feeds for all animals.

FODDER SITUATION IN RELATION TO
LIVESTOCK DEVELOPMENT

China's livestock development may also be assessed from the adequacy or deficiency of its feedstuff supplies. The Chinese feedstuffs are custom-
arily divided into two broad categories:

1. The concentrates--consisting of grain
seeds, together with bran, chaff, husks, and other
milling wastes; oil-seed cakes and meals; sugar
extraction residues; all sorts of dregs from butcheries, breweries, canning factories, etc.

2. The roughages--consisting of all digestible by-products from grain or nongrain crops such
as stems, stalks, straws, roots, foliage, cobs,
skins, shells, etc.; usually collected for stable
provisions when outdoor grazing is impossible or
unsuitable.

Requirements and Supplies of Concentrates

1. Concentrate Requirements:

The Peking regime, in its 1955 decree on the
unified purchase and unified supply of grains, set
the following standards of concentrate feed rationing (including grains and milling dregs) for several types of animals:

a.	Horses and mules.	4-7 catties of unhusked grains per head per day.
b.	Donkeys and camels.	2-4 "
c.	Mother cows.	4-6 "

d. Quantity of grain for hogs to be determined by local authorities "within the limits of
feed standards in surrounding villages."

e. Presumably the standard for working cattle is the same as for horses and mules.

f. No standard is set for sheep and goats.

According to Hsiao Chi-yung, Issues and Studies (Taipei, Jan., 1968), these standards have never been fully carried out and the annual ration for hogs was "50 to 100 kilograms of fodder per head in 1956 and 50 kilograms in recent years."

Adjusting and supplementing the aforesaid official standards, we assume the annual requirement of concentrates for China's three categories of animals:

a. For large animals--600 kilograms per head (approximately 1.66 kilograms per day on the average).

b. For sheep and goats--30 kilograms per head (sheep and goats depend more on roughage).

c. For hogs--60 kilograms per head (hogs depend more on concentrates).

Calculating on this basis, the annual concentrate requirements of each category result in the following:

a. Large animals (97 million)--41,500,000 M.T.*

b. Sheep and goats (127 million)--3,810,000 M.T.

c. Hogs (166 million)--9,960,000 M.T.

Total requirement for 1967--55 million M.T.

---

*Metric tons reduced to 41,000,000 for agricultural areas.

The Communist official standards are for practical rationing, but are considerably below the theoretical requirement of Western standards.

2. Concentrate Supplies:

In connection with its three "fixed quota rationing system," the Peking regime also ruled that 30 kilograms of fodder were to be included in the ration for each peasant.[3] This means that each peasant was obliged to put aside that amount of grain as feedstuff for his animals each year, the animal's share from the annual ration for each peasant. The farm population for 1967 (as 85 per cent of 753,500,000) is 637,500,000 at the year's end. The animal's share of grain concentrates so calculated would amount to 19 million metric tons.

The same Peking decree also annually set aside 15 kilograms of seed grain from each peasant, which would aggregate to 15,937,000 metric tons per year. With the feed grain and seed grain deducted from the 1967 total output of 213,883,000 metric tons, there remains 166,071,000 metric tons for human consumption, from which secondary concentrates (brans, chaffs, etc.) could be derived for the animals. Calculating on an average conversion rate of 78 per cent (that for rice is 74 per cent, for other grains around 80 per cent), the result is 36,535,600 metric tons of grain residues, which are classified as concentrates in China's feeding statistics.

Again there is a huge amount of processing dregs from nongrain crops such as oil-seed cakes, sugar refining residues, waste materials and butcheries, breweries, canning plants, etc. Oil-seed cakes alone amounted annually from 5 million tons to 6 million tons in prewar years. T. H. Shen gives an estimate of 5,800,000 tons each year.[4] For this composite category of dregs from various sources, our estimate of an annual amount of 7,500,000 metric tons seems to be rather conservative. Thus, we have here three main items of primary and secondary concentrate supplies as follows:

		Metric tons per year
a.	Grain seeds	19,000,000
b.	Milling dregs from grain	36,536,000
c.	Processing dregs from non-grain and other sources	7,500,000
	Total supply of concentrates	63,036,000

It is evident from these calculations that China's concentrate supply is quite adequate to meet the annual requirement of 148 million animal units.

Requirements and Supplies of Roughage

1. The Roughage Requirement

Roughage requirement of animals as a rule varies according to their live weights at different stages of growth, with each type of animal differing from others even at the same stage of life. On livestock export, Chang Chun-kuo has given a list of estimated animal weights in his "China's Livestock Resources,"[5] from which we have deduced the following representative weights for each category of animals:

a. Large animals   475 kilograms on the average

b. Sheep and goats   50 kilograms on the average

c. Hogs   90 kilograms on the average

Estimating on the basis of Wang Teh-chang's "Feeding Schedule for Growing Animals," in his Compendium for Livestock Feeding, the calculated roughage requirements for each category of animal is as follows:

a.   Large animals (475 kilograms)

    Daily requirement   7 kilograms
    Annual requirement   2,555 kilograms

b.   Sheep and goats (50 kilograms)

    Daily requirement   1.5 kilograms
    Annual requirement   547.0 kilograms

c.   Hogs (90 kilograms)

    Daily requirement   1 kilogram
    Annual requirement   365 kilograms

Based on the aforesaid annual rates, the roughage requirements are calculated as:

		Metric tons
a.	For large animals (97 million)	247,835,000
b.	For sheep and goats (127 million)	69,532,500
c.	For hogs (166 million)	60,590,000
	Total requirement	377,957,500

2.   The Roughage Supplies

China's roughage supplies for animals are primarily drawn from the by-products of all grain crops and certain items of economic crops. The term "by-products" covers almost all parts of the crop plant except the grain with its husk. The rates of by-product yield, as listed below, are derived from various documentary sources available at hand:[6]

By-product yields (M.T.) for each ton of grain:

Rice*	1.65	(1)
Wheat	2.57	(1)
Potatoes	0.30	(2)
Miscellaneous grains:		
Corn	4.00	(3)
Kaoliang	2.80	(4)
Millet	2.80	(4)
Other miscellaneous grains	2.30	(2)
Soybeans	1.90	(3)
Peanuts	3.00	(3)
Cotton	2.98	(3)
Other nongrain crops	(varied rates)	

Based on these yield rates of by-products, the amounts of roughage supply for 1967 and for other crops are as follows:

Output of grain (metric tons)	By-products (metric tons)
a. Rice (98,584,300)	162,664,100
b. Wheat (25,892,400)	66,543,500
c. Potatoes (29,828,950) (4 times result from rate 0.3 per ton)	35,794,800
d. Corn (estimated 25 million)	100,000,000
e. Kaoliang (estimated 10 million)	28,000,000
f. Millet (estimated 10 million)	28,000,000
g. Other miscellaneous (14,577,350) (59,577,350 metric tons deducting d, e, and f)	33,527,900
h. Soybean (estimated 9 million)	17,640,000

---

*Rice gives plenty of weight to husks that go with concentrates.

i. Peanuts (estimated 3 mil-
    lion)   9,000,000

j. Cotton (estimated
    1,250,000)   3,725,000

k. Other nongrain crops   70,000,000
                                        ──────────
        Total supply   554,895,300

Since the roughage requirement is only
377,957,500 metric tons for the 1967 animals, there
remains 176 million metric tons of by-products to
be used as fertilizers, fuel, and building materials,
as the Chinese peasantry used to apportion their annual collections for various purposes according to
needs of the time.

Hence from the viewpoint of fodder supply in
both concentrates and roughages, China's current
animal population of 148 million animal units (as
we have estimated) is by no means an overburden on
the nation's farm economy.

                            NOTES

    1. See Agricultural Notes (1964-68); Yearbook
on Chinese Communism 1967; and China Monthly (1965-
67).

    2. Tang Yuan-chih, Roads to Production En-
hancement in Chinese Agriculture (Taipeh [n.p.],
1953), 1 vol. Cited this compilation by Ko Fu Chang
and others.

    3. China (People's Republic, 1949-) laws,
statutes, etc. Decree of Unified Purchase and Unified Supply of Grains (Peiping, 1955).

    4. T. H. Shen, Agricultural Resources of
China (Ithaca, New York: Cornell University Press,
1951), 407 pp.
    For documents on rationing, see Chao Kuo-
chun's Agrarian Policies of Mainland China; a

Documentary Study, 1949-56 (China's Economic and
Political Studies, Special Series; Cambridge, Massa-
chusetts: Harvard University Press, 1957).

    5. Chang Chun-Kuo, China's Livestock Resources
(Shanghai [n.p.], 1947), 1 vol.

    6. See A. P. Brodell and others, "Estimated
Production of Straw per 1,000 Bushels of Grain Harvested," Agricultural Yearbook, 1947 (Washington,
D.C.: Government Printing Office for the United
States Department of Agriculture, 1946) Preliminary (?).
        See also Dawson's and Tung's estimates
based on Brodell, and the following: Chu Hai-fan
and Wang Teh-chang.
        Chu Hai-fan, "Application of Fertilizers
in Relation to Increase of Agricultural Production,"
in Teng Yuan-chih's Roads to Production in Chinese
Agriculture (Taipeh [n.p.], 1953), 1 vol.
        Wang Teh-chang, Compendium on Livestock
Feeding (Shanghai [n.p.], 1952), 1 vol.

CHAPTER **10** FOOD GRAIN AND
COTTON PRODUCTION
SERIES, 1952-67

FOOD GRAIN

Since the inception of the Communist regime,
there have emerged various reactions and views
regarding progress in food grain production and
adequacy of supplies to meet consumption requirements.

The author's main work in prewar China was to
report on the supply and demand of important agricultural products for the U.S. Department of Agriculture, and has been following the situation
closely since the Communist take-over based on
Nationalist Government reports and news reports for
different areas, as reported from Hong Kong and
directly by the press.

He has set up a series of food grain estimates,
as shown in Table 12, with calculations on available food supplies per capita and caloric equivalent. In general the calculations show food grain
availability near the minimum requirement. On an
index basis with 1952-53 = 100:

Food Grain Production   1967-68 = 125
Population   130

Food supply will support the population of
1975/76; as shown in Chapter 7 on Fertilizer, with
greater use of fertilizer and improved techniques,
augmented by moderate imports, and underlaid with
moderate economic progress.

TABLE 12

Estimated Food Grain Production, 1952/53-1967/68

	Food Grain Production[a]	Net Trade & Change in Stocks	Gross Food Grain Available	Population[b]	Gross Food Grain Per Capita	Food Use[c]	Food Net[d]	Available Daily	Available All Foods[e]	Daily Minimum Adequate[f]
	1	2	3	4	5	6	7	8	9	10
	MMT	MMT	MMT	Mil	Kg	Kg	Kg	Cal	Cal	Cal
52/53	175	-5.9	169.1	578	292.6	240.0	192.0	1,815	2,187.1	2,100
53/54	166	- .9	165.1	588	280.8	210.3	168.2	1,590	1,916.0	"
54/55	170	-1.1	163.9	599	282.0	221.2	177.0	1,673	2,016.0	"
55/56	185	-6.3	173.7	611	292.5	239.9	184.9	1,748	2,106.3	"
56/57	175	-1.7	173.3	624	275.6	226.0	180.8	1,709	2,059.4	"
57/58	185	- .9	184.1	637	289.0	238.9	191.1	1,806	2,176.2	"
58/59	205	- .11	194	650	300.0	246	196.8	1,863	2,244.9	"
59/60	175	+ .8	183	662	276.4	226.6	181.2	1,713	2,064.2	"
60/61	160	+8.5	163.5	673	250.3	212.9	170.3	1,644	1,981.0	"
61/62	170	+6.0	175.0	682	258.1	211.8	169.4	1,601	1,929.2	"
62/63	180	+3.3	183.5	691	265.6	225.8	178.1	1,683	2,028.0	"
63/64	185	+3.0	183.0	702	267.8	219.6	175.7	1,660	2,000.3	"
64/65	195	--	195.0	715	272.7	226.6	181.3	1,713	2,064.2	"
65/66	207	+4.0	211.0	728	289.8	237.6	190.1	1,797	2,165.4	"
66/67	205	+6.0	211.0	741	284.8	233.5	186.9	1,766	2,128.0	"
67/68	214	+5.0	213.0	754	290.5	238.2	190.6	1,802	2,171.0	"

[a]Estimated by the author.

[b]From John S. Aird, Estimates and Projections of the Population of Mainland China: 1953-1968, U. S. Bureau of the Census, International Population Reports, Series P-91, No. 17 (Washington, D.C.: 1968), p. 43 Model IV, p. 47 Model C.

[c]Based on "other uses for feed, etc." from T. H. Shen, Agricultural Resources of China (Ithaca, N.Y.: Cornell University Press, 1951), Appendix IV.

[d]Food net equals column 6 x .80.

[e]Shen, ibid., shows food grain as proportion of total food .79.

[f]J. L. Buck, Land Utilization in China (Shanghai, China: Commercial Press, 1937), p. 411, shows grain and potatoes .87 (.83 used here is midway between Shen's and Buck's figures.)

187

In our 1967 estimate for food grain, shown in this chapter, we have made an intensive study of available provincial data to build up a national figure. Some of these estimates are fragmentary and inconsistent for certain provinces; but, as a whole, they have been helpful in presenting a fuller view of the national situation than we had before. The picture seems plausible and realistic, in view of technical improvements shortly due. Further study can bring out the estimates more definitely. A study is now under way to describe apparent surpluses and deficit food grain production, by provinces and according to factors governing the trend.

Estimates of food grain crop production in Communist China since 1952 by other China specialists have sometimes been lower than our estimates-- partly due to a belief in lower population figures. But our assumption on population seems conservative and, at present, possibly low. Yet we welcome constructive criticism of Dawson's series of estimates for 1952-67. Three factors must also be given due weight in effective utilization of available surplus:

1. A great saving in prevention of losses. See the chapter on fertilizer and agricultural drugs.

2. Fuller use of protective foods in the diet, such as vegetables, fruits, meat, and fish, to supplement the food grain diet with a lesser requirement of calories.

3. More equitable distribution of available food to the population through rationing.

An authority[1] on nutrition in China expressed the opinion to the author that the diet in Communist China, while less in national average, was better per capita than in prewar China--with exception of the really bad years of 1960 and 1961.

The next most important crop in China is cotton, for which progress has been outstanding.

COTTON

Cotton Production and Utilization

Cotton is a pivotal factor in China's economy. It provides 90 per cent of the material for clothing and is the main source of foreign exchange for exports of piece goods. Increases in cotton production in Communist China from 1952 to 1959 exceeded the rate of growth in population, but production declined severely in 1960. It has, however, shown a steady recovery since that time, encouraged by government support.

If cotton production increases to 2.2 million metric tons by 1975-76, which with rational planning is possible, it should be able to supply the population with a minimum adequate cloth ration of twelve to fifteen meters; and, with imports running at present levels of 700,000 to 800,000 bales, maintain or increase exports of 500-600 million yards. It is expected that China's proportion of the world market of piece goods will be maintained, if not increased.

These developments will be an aid to farmers, mill workers, and import and export agencies--as well as stimulating the morale of the people, who have been on meager cloth rations during most of the period since 1949.

Man-made fibers are also increasing in production, and should prove a significant supplement to the position of cotton.

China is the world's third largest producer of cotton, surpassed only by the United States and Soviet Russia. It is, nevertheless, a large importer of raw cotton, as well as a large exporter of cotton piece goods and garments.

After food grains, the most valuable crop is cotton--the major fiber crop and the outstanding economic crop. It is the most important single

element in the light industrial group, and is a
major source of foreign exchange. According to the
U.S. National Cotton Council, over 200 million people (over one fourth of the population) are concerned directly with production or processing of
cotton in China--not counting those engaged in the
trade. Nevertheless, the acreage planted in cotton
has been small compared with food grains. The comparison is striking when it is noted that each per
capita increase in population requires only some
five pounds increase in cotton production, whereas
for food grains some 600 pounds are required.

Cotton and Food Grain Acreage

Food grain and cotton together took up some 90
per cent of the planted area in 1952 to 1958.
Since that time, a moderate increase in total cultivated area seems to have occurred, with food
grains accounting for most of the increases, while
the cotton area remained about the same. In 1961,
the cotton area fell off by some 30 per cent. It
has now recovered to about five million hectares,
while food grain acreage (including tubers) has
reached about 136 million hectares. Cotton planting conditions in the last three years, as well as
improved incentives from the government, seem to
support the above cotton acreage level. Yet any
future expansion in acreage is expected to be moderate. Policy now is to concentrate cotton where
it is best adapted and to increase yields. Government policy was set forth in 1963 as follows:

> To insure cotton acreage, production,
> and state procurement, the main poli-
> cy is to increase cotton acreage in
> areas where cotton growing is already
> concentrated--and not to increase in
> marginal areas. Production teams
> should not only obey the state acreage
> plan, but also plan their cotton grow-
> ing according to local soil conditions
> and practical production possibilities.
> The state will enter into contracts

with production teams, and make advance payments for cotton purchases.
Moreover, it is specifically recognized that for production teams primarily engaged in cotton production,
the standard of food grain made available should not be lower than those
of surplus grain-producing teams.[2]

Cotton Products

Besides the value of lint cotton, the value of
by-products is substantial.

The value of the seed and oil from a 5,000,000-
bale crop carries:

	Kg/ha
Lint	269
Seed	538
Oil	135
Oil meal and cake	215 (40% of seed)

These are substantial items for food, feed,
fertilizer, and export. A good yield of lint,
which could be obtained in the next few years (with
expansion in the use of chemical fertilizer and
improved varieties), might well be:

350 kg/ha lint @ $0.44 =	$154.00
Value of seed oil and cake	38.00
	$192.00

Future Cotton Production and Imports

Cotton production is a pivotal factor in Communist China's economy; where the land is adaptable,
cotton pays excellent returns. Imported lint cotton, which now approaches record levels, also pays
an attractive margin in value of piece goods exports. Cotton may displace a small amount of wheat
in North China, but the difference can easily be
made up by imports.

TABLE 13

Cotton Acreage, Yield, and Production
(thousand metric tons)

	Area (1,000 ha)	Yield (kg/ha)	Production (1,000 MT)	Based on Utilization*
1949	2,770	165	445	587.0
1950	3,786	183	693	839.7
1951	5,486	188	1,031	946.5
1952	5,570	234	1,304	1,105.0
1953	5,180	228	1,179	1,173.4
1954	5,562	192	1,065	1,217.8
1955	5,800	262	1,519	1,258.0
1956	6,255	231	1,445	1,244.7
1957	5,774	284	1,640	1,494.0
1958	5,722	369	2,100	1,696.0
1959	5,791	416	2,410	1,663.0
1960	5,720	269	1,410	
1961	3,700	257	1,090	
1962	3,400	276	1,134	
1963	4,300	272	1,173	
1964	4,400	282	1,240	
1965	4,600	260	1,200	
1966	4,800	260	1,260	
1967	5,000	269	1,300	

*Mill and nonmill consumption.

Sources: The figures for the 1949-59 period are official statistics. The remaining ones are U.S. Department of Agriculture and U.S. Consulate General (Hong Kong) estimates.

Chart 1 presents the estimates of China's cotton production projected to 1972. It shows the official estimates of China's cotton production from 1950 to 1959 and adjusted estimates based on utilization including mill and nonmill consumption, net trade, and change in stocks. For 1960-66, estimates are by the U.S. Department of Agriculture, Foreign Analysis Division, Cotton Section, based largely on reports from the Hong Kong Consulate General. Projections to 1972 were made by a study of trends in area and yield, and crop improvement developments due to improved techniques such as increased use of chemical fertilizer, expansion in irrigation, improved varieties, and shifts of planting to more adaptable areas.

Extension of projections to 1975-76 is in preparation.

Following the 33-1/3 per cent decline in cotton production from 1960 to 1961-62 (with mill production proportionately reduced), exports of piece goods declined substantially. These are now returning to a level of about 500 million yards per year. Raw cotton imports, in 1962-63, totaled 357,000 bales (76,000 metric tons) and 800,000 bales (173,000 metric tons) in 1963-64. Imports come from East Africa, Egypt, and Pakistan; these trade deals have in part been motivated by political goals. However, the Chinese can use whatever cotton is purchased for conversion into manufactured products for export markets. The 1963-64 amount is the largest amount of raw cotton imported since 1932. Imports of some 70,000 metric tons are needed to offset exports of piece goods in terms of equivalent raw cotton. The remainder is available for home consumption and for replenishing stocks.

Summarily, it seems that China is likely to revive or exceed previous high production levels in the next two or three years, but still continues to import moderate amounts of cotton, especially certain qualities. The cloth ration may be increased to a moderate level, and required supplies made

CHART 1

China's Cotton Area and Production

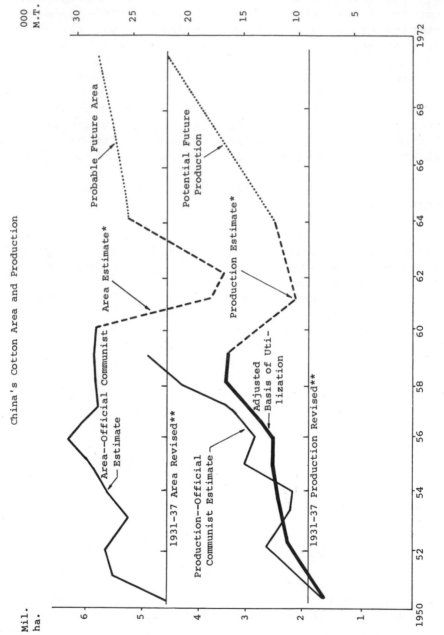

*Estimated by author.
**National Agricultural Research Bureau estimate, revised by author.

194

available for other uses. Strenuous efforts will
be made to expand export markets for piece goods,
especially in underdeveloped countries, as well as
to earn hard currencies (e.g., British sterling).
Success will depend on negotiating favorable trade
arrangements and manipulation of prices. Satisfactory to the Chinese, future developments should
prove of much interest in assessing impacts on
other countries and the effect on China's domestic
economy and morale.

MAN-MADE FIBERS

The entry into man-made fibers was started in
the 1960s, when China was suffering from a shortage
of cotton.

The production of rayon yarn staple fibers in
1962 was estimated to reach 75 million pounds.
Production of noncellulosic fibers, at 1 million
pounds in 1962, by 1965 would reach 3 million.

Two vinyl-producing plants ordered from Japan
in 1963-64 have been delivered.

In the July 16 issue (1965) of the Peking Review it was stated that a group of new man-made
fiber mills had been built, which had a capacity to
produce enough viscose fiber for 300 to 400 million
meters of fabrics a year. The new mills, all
opened in 1965, are spread over several provinces
in central, northern, and Kwantung areas.

This movement toward man-made fibers will have
an impact on the cotton textile trade, which will
be watched with interest.

APPRAISAL OF FOOD GRAIN ESTIMATES, 1967

Our estimates of the 1967 grain output are
based upon the counterbalancing results of various
favorable and adverse factors. To sketch in brief:

Favorable Factors

1. Good weather--"It is believed that the
weather [in 1967] may have been the most favorable
for agriculture production since the Communists
gained control of the Chinese mainland." (Agricultural Officer, American Consulate General, Hong
Kong, Nov. 17, 1967.)

2. Local initiative--The Peking regime has
adopted a policy of "selective development" in
place of the former "equalitarian schemes." Under
this system, only the most promising areas for
grain and cotton yield can receive the concentrated
investments of money, labor, and technical equip-
ment--either from the state (represented by provincial and county authorities) or from the communal units in the localities concerned. Hence,
highly endowed and economically advanced provinces
are able to proceed full speed upon their own resources, without being dragged from behind by the
"backward areas" as before.

3. Private incentive--The peasantry has received a great impetus from the new agricultural
policy with its "small freedoms." Their cash income has been augmented through operations on private plots, household reclamation, sideline occupations, and free trading in the local markets.
Through daily work on the communal fields, they
have also steadily accumulated grain reserves from
annual surpluses in both the collective and individual accounts. It is by means of this surplus
income and reserves that in recent years, many
small-scale projects of rural construction have
been carried out in the spirit of "self reliance."

4. Technical factors--Peking since the early
1960s has promoted four basic principles for agricultural modernization:

(a) Mechanization. Although full-scale
farm mechanization advances rather slowly, semi-
mechanized implements and improved tools have

gained ground in many parts of the country. The
installation of power-pump facilities has especially increased in great speed in Central and South
China, making substantial contributions toward the
nation's grain output boost.

        (b) Chemicalization. Increasing produc-
tion and application of chemical fertilizer and
agricultural chemicals have rendered great help to
China's agricultural production, especially in the
field of economic crops.

        (c) Rural electrification. Large numbers
of small projects are constructed for hydroelectric
power generation in South China and southwestern
provinces. Besides, around the big power centers
of industrial and mining districts (where extra
capacity is available as a result of industrial re-
cession in the post-"Leap" period), extensive networks of high-tension lines have been built to
transmit power to the surrounding rural areas for
various types of farm operation.

        (d) Water utilization. Generally speak-
ing, the large-scale state enterprises have contributed more toward flood control--as in the case
of Yellow River, the Huai River, Han River in the
Yangtze Valley, West River in the Pearl basin, and
the Liao River in Manchuria. Local irrigation and
drainage, with a few exceptions, almost entirely
depend upon the joint enterprise of county authorities and the communal units. Large and medium
projects for irrigation or drainage usually call
for the combined efforts of a group of counties and
communes, with the guidance and support of provincial authorities; as illustrated by the drainage
projects in the provinces of Hopeh, Shantung, Hunan,
and Anhwei.

                    Adverse Factors

     The chief factor that could adversely affect
China's grain production is the Cultural Revolution, which has created great disturbances in

Shanghai, Peking, Canton, Wuhan, Chungking, and
several other provincial capitals. It should be
noted, however, that throughout the whole period of
1966-67--with the exception of a few suburban counties around the big cities--China's vast area of
over 2,000 counties (with its 74,000 communes and
5 million-odd production teams) has remained practically undisturbed.

1.   The Peking regime has purposely kept the
rural areas out of the "rebel movement" in order to
maintain the nation's agricultural production.

2.   The Red Guards can operate effectively
only as groups in the cities. Once dispersed among
the villages, they are weakened in strength and
frequently exposed to local ambushes.

3.   The real power in the farm areas is held
in the hands of production team leaders. Most of
them are non-Communists, and will take no side in
the faction fight of the Communist Party.

4.   The team leaders, being field workers
themselves, usually stand up against unreasonable
Party demands, and have generally enjoyed the full
support of the team members. They are popularly
elected, and could not be whimsically disposed of
by the Party authorities.

Military commanders have taken over the provincial administrations in all provinces; their
sole purpose is to maintain grain production--in
order to feed their soldiers and to consolidate
control over all economic activities in the province. Taking the nation as a whole, the adverse
effect of the Cultural Revolution on China's 1967
grain production is rather slight and superficial--
in the face of substantial and sustaining influences as exerted by the large number of physical
and technical factors.

The final results of our estimation on China's
1967 grain production is summarized below:

1. The cultivated area   110,032,000 ha.

2. The crop acreage (with
   multiple cropping index
   of 147.77)   162,600,000 ha.

3. The grain acreage (79%
   of crop acreage)   128,457,000 ha.

4. The average unit yield   222 (catty/mow)
   of total grain   or 1,665 kg/ha

5. The grain acreage distribution of four categories:

	1957 (mow)	1967 (mow)	Percentage increase (1967 over 1957)
Rice	483,620,000	506,900,000	4.81
Wheat	413,120,000	419,400,000	1.52
Potatoes	157,420,000	200,870,000	27.61
Misc. grains	759,110,000	799,690,000	5.34
Total	1,813,270,000 mow	1,926,860,000 mow	
	(120,885,000 ha.)	(128,457,000 ha.)	

6. The average 1967 unit yield of the four grain
   categories:

                        (catty/mow)
   Rice   388.97   8.35% over 1957 (359)
   Wheat   123.47   8.30% over 1957 (114)
   Potatoes   296.99   6.84% over 1957 (278)
   Misc. grains 149.01   7.20% over 1957 (139)

7. The 1967 production in four grain categories:

	1957 (MT)	1967 (MT)	Percentage increase (1967 over 1957)
Rice	86,800,000	98,584,300	13.57
Wheat	23,600,000	25,892,400	9.71
Potatoes	21,900,000	29,828,950	36.20
Misc.grains	52,650,000	59,577,350	13.16
Total	185,000,000	213,883,000	15.61

Methodology

The process of assessment is briefly as follows:

1. The 1967 acreage for provinces is largely based upon the 1957 acreage as reported in the Economic Geography of China (Peking, 1958-60), with adjustments conditioned by Buck, NARB, and estimated increase from 1937 to 1957.

2. The 1967 unit-yields are derived from the 1957 yield rates for the provinces with comparable adjustments.

3. The production figures are obtained by multiplying the 1967 acreage by the derived 1967 yield rate, with necessary rounding on the lower digits for the yield and acreage figures.

4. The process of assessment for potatoes and miscellaneous grains is practically the same as that for rice and wheat.

Salient Features of the 1967
Grain Situation*

The 1967 grain situation represents the cumulative results of agricultural revival in China for the last five years, starting with 1963 when farm production began to gain momentum due to the combined action of natural and technical factors. As suggested in the Progress Report of October, 1967, grain output had already surpassed the 1957 level by the mid-1960s, with an average of 205,552 billion tons for 1964-66. If not for the slight disruption of its recent Cultural Revolution, China's 1967 grain output could posibly have reached a high mark of 218,000 billion tons, with a per capita share of 290 kilograms (286 kilograms for 1957). As it now

---

*Figures cited are higher than most.

appears under our conservative estimate, after bal-
ancing off favorable and adverse influences, the
net result is a moderate estimate of 213,883 billion tons--based on an estimated acreage of
128,457,000 hectares, with an average yield of
1,665 kilograms. The per capita share thus derived
for 1967 is about 284 kilograms per year, for a
population of 753,800,000, which is even a little
lower than the 1957 figure of 286 kilograms.

This moderate advancement of recent years, as
reflected in the 1967 situation with all its implications, may follow two broad aspects of the Chinese farm structure:

1. Increase of crop acreage resulting from:

A. Extension of cultivated area in the
borderlands through reclamation of "raw-waste"
areas, notably in Manchuria, Sinkiang, and Inner
Mongolia.

B. Extension of cultivated area in China
proper through:

(a) Terracing of hilly slopes either
for paddies or for dry fields, as is being done in
the upper Yangtze and the upper Si-Kiang provinces.

(b) Conversion of marshy basins into
croplands, as is being done in the lake regions of
central and lower Yangtze provinces.

(c) Dealkalinization of salty lands on
coastal plains and interior depressions, as is being carried out in Kiangsu, Shantung, Honan, Hopeh,
and Liaoning.

(d) Restoration of abandoned "ripe-
waste" areas by means of irrigation and drainage,
as is being done on the "flooded areas" of the Yellow River and the Huai River basins.

C. Expansion of double-cropping systems

in the North China plain by reducing "idle lands"
formerly set out for the following winter or summer.

D. Expansion of multiple-cropping systems
in southern China and the south-bank Yangtze provinces by intensified cultivation and/or introduction of quick-ripening crop varieties.

2. Increase of unit yield resulting from:

A. Alloting a greater portion of acreage
to high-yielding crops such as rice, corn, and potatoes, while restricting that of the low-yielding
crops such as kaoliang, millet, barley, beans,
peas, etc.

B. Raising the unit yield of grain crops
through:

(a) Extensive construction of conservation works, with emphasis upon small projects.

(b) Intensive application of fertilizers, with emphasis upon use of available organic
nutrients.

(c) Extension of good-quality seeds,
especially those of rice, wheat, corn, potatoes,
kaoliang, and millet.

(d) Adoption of mechanical or semimechanical devices in connection with irrigation,
drainage, flood prevention, erosion control, or
field operations wherever possible.

(e) Full utilization of power resources
(water, electricity, gas, oil, coal, human, and
animal) in combination with mechanical devices, especially to gain time at rush seasons for sowing or
harvesting, and to stave off disasters when threatened by drought, flood, waterlogging, or other
forms of natural calamity.

General Pattern of 1967
Grain Distribution

China's grain economy has been practically
stereotyped for many years through continuous interaction between natural elements and human endeavors in a confined domain of 9,561,000 square
kilometers (956,100,000 hectares), with an 11 per
cent cultivated area of 110 million hectares
(1,650,480,000 mow). Although the basic pattern
of crop distribution has remained practically unchanged since it was mapped out by Professor Buck
in the early 1930s, the grain distribution area has
undergone a gradual transformation in the last seventeen years as a result of Communist "expansion
policy," which appears to proceed in five directions:

1. "Outward Expansion," manifested by movements for the "Conquest of Swamps and Deserts in
the Borderlands."

2. "Upward Expansion," manifested by schemes
for "Mountain Exploitation," "Terrace Development,"
and "Staircase for the Tablelands."

3. "Double-deck Expansion," as manifested by
the extension of multiple-cropping systems over the
North China plain as well as in the central and
southern provinces.

4. "Substitute Expansion," manifested by the
acreage adjustments to replace low-yield crops with
high-yield crops, resulting in the ascendancy of
rice, corn, and potatoes, with some decline in
kaoliang, millet, barley, and other coarse grains.

5. "Interlocking Expansion," manifested by
the various space-saving systems in field utilization, namely: transplanting from crop nurseries
(except rice), mix-planting (two crops sown by al-
ternate rows in the same field), and overlap planting (with two consecutive crops partially overlapping in their growing seasons); these systems have

been sporadically adopted in many parts of China,
wherever natural conditions and input factors permit.

As a result of these "evolutional processes,"
China's grain structure has been modified considerably both in form and in magnitude. The current
rice belt takes the shape of a huge crescent, with
its swollen midsection covering all provinces of
the Pearl River basin and the Yangtze Valley in a
consolidated patch of paddy fields; its right arm
stretches northward along the coast and then enters
Manchuria with narrow strips of "fingertips"; the
left arm, after embracing the Red basin and the
Wei-ho plain in its fold, stretches northwest until it reaches the Tarim basin of Sinkiang.

At the same time, China's spring wheat belt
on its northern frontier, growing in width and
length through recent reclamations, has stretched
in an east-west direction to grasp both arms of the
rice crescent away down south--with its eastern end
joining one crescent arm in the marshes of Heilungkiang, and its western end joining the other crescent arm at Sinkiang's Tien-Shan foothills.

The central areas between the spring wheat
belt in the north and rice crescent in the south
enfold the whole North China plain, the southern
part of Manchuria, and the eastern part of the
loess plateau. This constitutes the "home grounds"
for China's winter wheat and the miscellaneous
grains, with millet dominating the western section,
kaoliang dominating the eastern section (including
South Manchuria), and corn spreading over the whole
region and penetrating northeastward into Manchuria
and southwestward into the upper reaches of the
Pearl basin and the Yangtze Valley beyond the mountainous gorges.

Among all food grains, potatoes--owing to
their superior qualities of high yield, strong resistance, and great adaptability--are regarded as a
"gap-filler" on all occasions and at all places.

They are the "mountain climbers," the "swamp dwell-
ers," and the "ground hoppers" on all "badlands"
that have frequently shunned over these years the
more delicate crops. Thus their producing areas
may be found anywhere in the country, with Irish
potatoes prevailing in cool, dry, rugged regions,
and sweet potatoes prevailing in warm, moist, level
lowlands.

      It should be noted, however, the Communist
scheme for grain promotion has experienced a notable
change from that of the first Five-Year Plan, pertaining to its shifting of emphasis among the four
categories:

      1. Rice has continued to enjoy the highest
priority of all production efforts, as shown by its
increase of 4.81 per cent in acreage, 8.35 per cent
in yield, and 13.57 per cent in output, 1967 over
1957.

      2. Potatoes have been persistently promoted,
although slight concessions have been made recently
in favor of the miscellaneous grains. Potatoes
still show an increase of 27.61 per cent in acreage, 6.84 per cent in yield, and 36.20 per cent in
output, 1967 over 1957.

      3. Wheat, in spite of its low-yielding sta-
tus, was put in the same rank as rice, corn, and
potatoes in China's promotion schemes during the
plan period (1953-57). This is indicated by its
acreage increase of 11.12 per cent and output increase of 30.66 per cent, 1957 over 1952. But
wheat acreage has been constantly limited since the
post-"Leap" years, although its unit yield has never been neglected, as shown by its 1.52 per cent
increase in acreage, 8.30 per cent in yield, and
9.71 per cent in output, 1967 over 1957.

      4. Miscellaneous grains (with the exception
of corn), owing to their low-yielding status, have
suffered acreage restriction or curtailment, both
through the plan period and the "disaster years"--

until the last two or three years, when Communist
authorities began to call for "Restitution of the
Dry Land Grains" (partly because of the growing demands of feedstuff in the North that had been mostly supplied by coarse grains in the past). There
is quite a noticeable tendency for the recovery of
this group, as shown by an increase of 5.34 per
cent in acreage, 7.20 per cent in yield, and 13.16
per cent in output. As corn of this category is
especially high-yielding, this recent ascendancy of
output is probably due to corn in a large measure.
Reportedly, the late adoption of improved seeds for
kaoliang and millet may help to further raise this
figure.

COMMUNIST CHINA'S AGRICULTURAL POTENTIAL STUDY

Summary and Outlook

The salient features of the study show that
the potential increase in arable area is narrowly
limited by reclaimable land. Water supply as a
whole is bountiful; but uneven seasonal distribution and great periodical variability cause grave
problems. The main causes are frequently floods,
waterlogging, and drought. China has been farmed
for centuries and has maintained yields at surprising levels through returns of organic fertilizer to
the land. Records are not available, but there
must have been a gradual decline in the store of
soil crop nutrients. In the last ten years, the
crucial necessity of adding chemical fertilizer to
increase yields has been realized along with improved varieties to utilize successfully the heavy
supply of crop nutrients.

Prewar China had a select corps of high-grade
specialists in crops and livestock, and intensive
surveys were made to appraise agricultural resources and requirements--especially for food.
These are all described in Chapter 1. Although notable improvements were made, there was little time

to make a major advance on the whole problem before
the Communist intrusion.

The Communists inherited a host of problems
along with many well laid-out specific plans for
coping with them set forth by the China-American
Agricultural Mission.

Many improvements have been made in agricultural techniques by the Communists, such as plant
and animal improvement and use of mechanical power.
Notable advances were made in coping with plant and
animal diseases, and in reducing crop predators
such as rats.

Disruption in progress was caused by emphasis
on ideology in 1955 and later to the detriment of
needed rapid progress in agricultural production to
cope with the requirements of a mounting population.

With a more realistic agricultural policy becoming evident and farmers' incentives to increase
production, it is our belief that the advances
shown on Table 14 are possible, barring any major
political upset.

Comments on the 1967 food crop outlook follow.

Population, livestock, and food grain constitute interlocking rings of China's farm economy.
They are interdependent in supply and demand, and
one section cannot move far away from the others
for very long.

In 1960-61, livestock numbers fell off considerably, particularly for pigs. Draft animal numbers also fell off greatly in some provinces, but
only moderately for the country as a whole. With
increases in the feed situation, steady improvements in health conditions, and promotion of breeding centers, livestock numbers increased rapidly
and surpassed 1957 levels. Many provincial reports
enabled reasonable estimates of pigs, sheep, and
goats. For large animals, information is not so

complete or consistent, so we have in part measured the current situation through labor requirements checked against feed availability.

Future Outlook for Food Grain and Other Crops

Rice, among the four categories, has for the past seventeen years received the best allotment of basic factors (land and water resources) and the highest investment of the productive factors (fertilizers, agricultural chemicals, power facilities, mechanical devices, etc.).

If Peking's rice policy, coordinated with other grain policy, continues with redoubling efforts in the following twenty or thirty years, a population-food balance can be achieved. Rice will continue to dominate China's grain economy with its over 26 per cent of grain acreage and over 46 per cent of grain production.

Wheat has a better prospect for acreage extension through promotion of the "spring type" on the northern borderlands. There are only slight chances for the expansion of winter wheat areas, either in the northern belt of th• Yellow River basin or in the southern belt of the Yangtze Valley. This category as a whole will probably drag along in its present status with 21 per cent in acreage and 12 per cent in output among the nation's grain totals.

Potatoes will continue to increase but probably with fluctuating rates of multiplication, so long as the nation's food supply remains in a precarious position, and so long as there are plenty of marginal lands to be reclaimed and utilized for food production. The present 10 per cent of acreage and 14 per cent output may be gradually increased with the opening up of new areas for cultivation.

Miscellaneous grains as a group will slowly

regain or even improve former status with advancement of water conservation in North China, consolidation of frontier settlements in the borderlands,
and the breeding and promotion of high-yielding
strains of kaoliang, millet, and the superior type
of hybrid corn. The present 41 per cent in acreage and 28 per cent in output could hardly antici-
pate substantial changes without a general expansion of cultivated areas.

Cotton is the most important nonfood grain
crop, providing the population with about 85 per
cent of the clothing requirement; it is also an
important source of exports. It has showed phenomenal development under the Communists, about doubling prewar production. Area is restricted owing
to demands of food grain, but yields have increased
greatly. The future outlook is favorable for improving cloth ration for the people and for maintenance of exports.

Silk production was encouraged by the Communists and increased exports have developed.

Ramie hemp, jute, and kenafe are important
fibers and have shown a material increase since the
prewar era. Man-made fibers are expanding greatly.

Besides food grain and cotton, which constitute some 85 per cent of the planted area, oil seeds
are next in importance. These include soybeans,
peanuts, rapeseed, sesame seed, castor beans, sunflower seed, and tea seed. These are all discussed
in the Appendix, based on the research of Dr. Wu
and his associates of Asia Science Research Associates, Palo Alto, California. They conclude, in
general, that production had not exceeded prewar
levels in 1965-66; current production of these oil
seeds, however, may have attained or surpassed prewar levels. Cotton-seed oil production has greatly
exceeded prewar production, making total vegetable-
oil seed production well above prewar levels.

Flue-cured tobacco registered a tremendous

increase of over 300 per cent over prewar levels,
according to ASRA's analysis. A like increase was
estimated for sugar; but this is still below consumption level, which has increased at a rapid rate
per capita. It was only 2.86 kg in 1965, compared
with 10.05 kg in Taiwan.

Forestry and fisheries are discussed in the
Appendix.

Forestry is an important national resource of
China. The Communists have made strong efforts to
conserve and increase production, but it is still
much below requirements. In a few years, a self-
sufficient program may be under way.

The fishing industry in China has made a rapid
increase in the last few years, especially in
freshwater culture. Shortage of equipment hampers
deep-sea production. Despite the large increase in
production, per capita output of aquatic products
at some 9.4 kg is far below that of Japan at some
29.2 kg, and should be doubled or tripled depending on strong government support. Many fish products are exported, but the total is only a small
part of production.

Basic Agricultural Ratios Calculated
from 1952/53 Estimates and
Projections to 1975/76

Table 14 has been compiled to show the relationship between population, cultivated land, food
grain production, and livestock animal units.
These rations have proven useful guidelines for
forms or studies keeping estimates within consistent bounds and also for comparison with similar
estimates of other countries, particularly those in
the Far East, such as Taiwan.

The projected estimates in the frame of productive factors assume actively consistent progress
in agriculture to effect a moderate improvement
in living standards. A similar or more rapid

TABLE 14

Communist China Basic Ratios (based on animal and human population, agricultural production, and productive factors)

	Col. 1 1952-53	Col. 2 1957-58	Col. 3 1967-68	Col. 4 1975-76	% Col. 4 to Col. 1
1 Cult. Area Mh[a]	108	112[b]	110[c]	113	104.7
2 Crop Area Mh	141	157	162.6	169	120
3 Crop Index Ratio	130	142	148	150	115.4
4 Food Grain Area Mh	119	121.9	128.5	136	111.7
5 4 - 2 Ratio	80	78	79	80	100
6 Animal Units Mil. Head	102	133	148	163	160
7 Draft Animals Mil. Head[d]	67	90	97	107	145
8 6 - 1 AU Cult. Area Ratio	.91	1.19	1.35	1.45	160
9 7 - 2 D.A./Crop Area ha	.48	.53	.60	.63	131
10 Food Grain Prod. MMT	170	185	214	245	145
11 Food Grain Prod. Ratio	100	109	120	145	--
12 Yld/ha Kg/ha	1,430	1,517	1,665	1,801	126
13 Population Mid Crop Yr.	578	637	754	869	--
14 Population Ratio	100	110	130	150	--
15 13 - 1 Pop./Cult. Area	5.3	5.7	6.8	7.8	145
16 13 - 6 Pop./AU Ratio	5.6	5.7	5.2	5.3	100
17 Gross Chemical Fert. Avail. MMT	0.2	0.9	12.5	23-25	--
18 Chemical Fertilizer					
19 Food Crop ha kg/ha	--	1.1	17	32	--
20 Crop Nutrients					
21 Food Grain - Net Imports	1,000 MT	--	5,000	5,000	--
22 Net Exports					
23 Farm Labor Force Mil.	--	263	301	346	--
24 Animal Labor Force Mil.	67	90	97	107	--
25 Tractors 000	--	25	150	300	--
26 Irrigated Area Mh	30	38	39	45	150

[a] Mh = Million hectares.

[b] Official estimate (see Table 1).

[c] Our estimate (see Table 2).

[d] Animal Unit = 1 large animal, 5 pigs, 7 sheep, 100 chickens.

development in industry is needed to support agriculture and to improve the general economy.

Comments on Table 14 follow by principal items:

1-3. Cultivated area is based on official reports and calculations on reclamation (see Chapter 4). Crop area follows, but is at a higher ratio because of the rising crop index. Increase in crop index seems reasonable in view of a significant increase in multiple cropping on a moderately increased cultivated area as explained in Chapter 4.

5. Food grain area is projected at an increase of 12 per cent, yield increase at 23 per cent, and production by 50 per cent. The ratio to crop area remains high at 80. The increased trend is explained in Chapter 10. The increase in production estimated at 245 MMT is explained in Chapter 7.

6. Our estimated animal units for 1975/76 based on the trend in numbers at 163 million would be a large increase of 60 per cent over 1952/53, but seems supportable based on feed supply and government promotion. The increase is proportionally more in meat animals for food consumption than draft animals, which show a little less than the population increase.

7. The relation of animal units to cultivated area is +60 per cent and compares with food grain production at +45 per cent.

8. Draft animals at 107 million are estimated to increase by 45 per cent--only 36 per cent compared to crop area, but at the same ratio as food grain production, which seems logical. The basis of the estimate is explained in Chapters 8 and 9. The chief factors affecting the increase estimated were: (1) demand for farm work to fill a usual shortage, (2) available feed, (3) better breeding and care, (4) government promotion of breeding centers, and (5) provincial reports for 1963-67.

Admittedly, our estimate is optimistic, but the ratio to crop area is only .63 compared to about the same ratio in Taiwan, where more mechanical power is used.

9. Projected food grain production, increased at 50 per cent over 1952-53, is still somewhat below the population increase of 56.7 per cent, based on Aird's Model IV C. Our estimate of population in 1975/76 at 883 million seems conservative; it may well reach over 900 million, in which case required food grain production will be higher but attainable. Part of the requirement can be made up by imports, and, with a better-balanced diet and more efficient use of food supplies, the standard of nutrition can be moderately raised; but may still remain near the minimum adequate caloric level per capita of 2,150, which we assume.

13. Population to cultivated area increase is projected at 45 per cent but to animal units remains at 5.4 compared to 8.5 in Taiwan.

15. Gross chemical fertilizer requirement is placed at 23 million tons, as explained in Chapter 7. This represents a large increase over 12.5 MMT estimated for 1966-67, but is equivalent to only 32 kg of crop nutrients per hectare compared with Taiwan at 190. A large potential increase is evident by expanded use of chemical fertilizer. Our estimate for 1975-76 may be conservative, and a range of 23-25 MMT is shown in the table.

NOTES

1. Dr. Miller of the Shanghai Seventh-Day Adventist Hospital to the writer in Hong Kong, 1966.

2. Jen-Min Jih-Pao, People's Daily, Peking (Dec. 19, 1963).

APPENDIX

ESTIMATED RICE ACREAGE AND PRODUCTION
IN 1967

Rice is the mainstay of China's food resources.
Its annual acreage usually occupies 25 to 28 per
cent of the nation's grain sown area and its annual
output usually occupies 42 to 47 per cent of its
grain production. Under favorable conditions of
climate, soil, and water supply, China's rice paddies
have extended widely over the Mainland, with approximately 35 per cent distributed among the southern
provinces of Kwangtung, Kwangsi, Fukien, Yünnan, and
Kweichow, 60 per cent among the central provinces of
Kiangsu, Chekiang, Anhwei, Kiangsi, Hupeh, Hunan,
and Szechwan, and only 5 per cent among the provinces
of northern, northwestern, and northeastern China.

Since the advent of the first Five-Year Plan,
the Communists have put special emphasis upon the
promotion of rice production because (1) it is the
highest yielding food crop on a unit basis, (2) it
is the staple food for a majority of the population,
and (3) it is adaptable to most parts of southern
and central China, and also adaptable to certain
parts of northern China and the border provinces.

The National Conference on Rice Production Techniques held in 1955 resolved to increase China's
agricultural potential and its rice acreage to 50
million hectares by 1967. Although this ambitious
plan was not realized on account of various obstacles,
the Peking regime managed to "raise the nation's rice
acreage [sown area] from 29,000,000 hectares in 1955
to about 34,000,000 hectares in 1956. But this
dropped to 32,200,000 hectares in 1957, and slightly increased to 32,700,000 hectares in 1958."[1]

As shown in the October, 1967, Progress Report,
our estimates of rice acreage for 1964, 1965, and
1966 are respectively 32,400,000 hectares, 32,570,000
hectares, and 32,800,000 hectares, which are quite
close to the Communist figures for 1957-58. On the
principle of "gradual increase," we have conservatively set forth 33 million hectares as China's rice

acreage for 1967, which still is smaller than the
1956 Communist claim. This resumed upward trend is
considered as a continuation of the trend of development that started under favorable influences since
early 1960s and has gained momentum in recent years.

Classification of Rice Areas

1. Rice-producing areas are divided into
three classes, primarily according to the following
criteria:

a. Combined magnitude of acreage, yield,
and production, as revealed in "normal" years, with
reference to prewar data as well as to that of the
pre-"Leap" Communist period.

b. Recent tendencies in population concen-
tration and livestock increment that have contributed to the volume of labor power and manure.

c. Latest application of technical factors
such as soil improvement, water conservation, fertilizer use, and the spread of improved seeds, etc.

Distinctive Features of the
Classified Rice Areas

1. Class A embraces six major rice-producing
provinces, all ranking first in the aforesaid criteria and exhibiting outstanding advancement in
recent years:

a. Kwangtung is endowed with two productive "rice nurseries," one on the Pearl River delta
around Canton and the other on the Han-Chiang delta
around Swatow, both noted for their record-breaking
unit-yields of rice. Recent outstanding achievements in conservation works, in phosphate plants,
and in green manure extension have greatly helped
in raising this province to the top position among
China's rice producers.

b. Szechwan possesses the famous "Red

basin," with its ideal soil and climate for rice
growing. Its rice centers are scattered on the
Chengtu plain, along the Yangtze banks, and spread
over the lower reaches of To-Chiang, Peichiang, and
Kialing Chiang rivers. Slope terracing and high-
land irrigation have extended its rice area; hog
raising and green manure planting have enhanced its
rice yield; and its "double-rice" acreage has continued to expand along the southern fringe in recent
years.

        c. Hunan has its "rice basket" situated
around Tung-ting Lake, which has been amply enlarged
and enriched by a recent conservation project (1964-
66), with its network of electrical pumping stations,
involving 1,580 drainage and irrigation projects all
over the region. Besides, the terraced rice paddies
of this province, owing to its well-managed "mountain pond" system, have never failed to get plenty
of water in the growing seasons of rice.

        d. Kiangsi is similar to Hunan as a rice
producer, both in natural environment and in technical advancement, either on mountain terraces or
on the plain regions. The province has recently
augmented its rice-producing capacity through development of the Po-Yang Lake area and the Kan River
basin, over which a vast network of irrigation and
drainage has been built.

        e. Chekiang's rich paddy fields around
Tai-hu Lake and Hang-Chow Bay are famous for their
high yield and stable productivity. With the ample
aid of pumping facilities, drawing on the power
from nearby Hsin-Aun Chiang station, the rice output of this province has recently jumped up to match
that of the neighboring provinces of Kiangsi and
Kiangsu, in spite of the much smaller size of its
cultivated areas.

        f. Kiangsu has been regarded as the "rice
bowl" of eastern China. Its expansive Yangtze delta
is thickly studded with farm hamlets and closely
meshed with an interwoven network of rivulets and

irrigation canals. Recent development of electrical
pumping stations and chemical fertilizer plants have
greatly enhanced rice yield on the delta, and reclamation projects have extended its paddy fields along
the coast as well as on the old Hwai basin in the
northern part of the province.

These six Class A provinces in the Yangtze Valley and the Pearl River basin have jointly consti-
tuted 63.58 per cent of China's rice acreage and
65.14 per cent of its rice output according to our
estimate for 1967. It should be noted that the Communist grain policy since the period of "adjustment"
(1961-63) has decidedly shifted from the "equalitarian principle" to the "selective principle," under which both state investments and popular efforts
should be concentrated upon the nation's most promising lands, so that vast areas of stable, high-
yielding grain fields could be quickly built and
permanently maintained to guarantee its ever-
increasing requirement of food supplies. This is
why the Pearl River delta and Han Chiang delta of
Kwangtung, the Yangtze delta of Kiangsu, the Tai-hu
basin of Chekiang, the Po Yantze basin of Kiangsi,
the Tung-Ting basin of Hunan, and the Chengtu plain
of Szechwan have been marked out as the rice lands
with best prospects and are granted first priority
of input factors, either from state, local, or communal sources. This is also why the six provinces
embracing these rice centers have come to dominate
the nation's grain position with a combined magnitude of almost two thirds in its rice acreage as
well as rice production.[2]

2. Class B comprises also six rice provinces
of China, located in the eastern, central, southern,
and southwestern regions, and constituting 27.12
per cent of its rice acreage and 26.88 per cent of
its rice output. While all are adopting rice as
the major crop in terms of cultivated areas, most
of these areas are limited in varied degrees by
physical conditions, technical facilities, or power
or labor supply. Hupeh has not yet solved the Han
River's flooding problem, which has frequently

threatened rice fields on the Chiang-Han plain.
Anhwei is still plagued by waterlogging in broad
areas around Hung-tze Lake, and its Huai-Pei fields
are not yet entirely free from the attack of occasional droughts. Fukien's rice fields usually afford high yields, but paddy areas are limited on
account of its rugged terrain, and rice plants are
often subjected to typhoon blight in the growing
seasons. Kwangsi (now Kwangsi-Chuang Autonomous
Region), Yünnan, and Kweichow are favored by a warm
climate and plenty of rainfall, but the weather is
unstable, the soil is poor, and the paddy areas are
highly limited in all three. Compared with the
"Big Six" in Class A, rice production of this secondary group has often dragged behind in "normal"
years, in spite of special efforts to improve on
input factors.

3. The ten provinces of Class C are all situated north of China's 750 MM isohyet line along Chin-
ling Range and the Huai River, which is taken as the
demarcation line between the "wheat region" in the
north and the "rice region" in the south. These
northern provinces have adopted rice only as a minor
crop, wherever it is permitted by growing season and
water supply, usually with the purpose of utilizing
marshy lands along river banks, in the lake basins,
or on coastal plains that are too wet for ordinary
types of "dry-land crops."

The Communist "Northward Movement of Rice" was
started in the early 1950s, together with the conservation projects on the Huai River "to turn dry
lands into water fields." After a brief disruption
under the "Great Leap," the same movement was revived with double efforts, to be pushed onward with
a number of irrigation and drainage projects carried
out on the coastal plains of Shantung, Hopei, and
Liaoning, and also along the lower reaches of Yellow
River in Honan, along the Sungari River in Heilungkiang, and along the Manas River in northern Sinkiang.

In spite of energetic human efforts, however,
rice growing is not much adapted to these northern

regions. The growing season is short; the soil is
poor and arid in most places; and owing to low density of population and livestock in Manchuria and
Sinkiang, labor power and manure are often found
short of the requirement of rice fields. Under
these circumstances our 1967 estimates for these
Class C provinces have resulted in a combined figure
of only 9.30 per cent in rice acreage and 7.98 per
cent in rice production.

Differential Scale of Yield Increase
for the Three Classes

In the <u>Progress Report</u> of October, 1967, we
have assumed for recent years a gradual increase of
rice yield over the 1957 average of 2,700 kg/ha,
which ranges respectively 5 per cent for 1964, 6
per cent for 1965, and 7 per cent for 1966. In
view of the excellent weather conditions in 1967,
and the accumulated effects of various productive
factors, as revealed by up-to-date reports, the
rice yield for this year could easily reach up to
9 or 10 per cent over that of 1957.

In consideration of the slight setback from
the Cultural Revolution, however, we have conservatively set forth a differential scale of yield increase for three of the classes of rice-producing
areas, with an expected rough average of 8 per cent
over 1957. Thus a 9 per cent increase is assigned
to Class A provinces, which are most favored by
natural elements as well as human endeavors for the
year under study; 8 per cent of increase is assigned
to Class B provinces, which are only moderately fos-
tered by ecological conditions on the balance of
positive and negative influences; and 7 per cent of
increase is assigned to Class C provinces, which are
least accommodated under existing circumstances in
comparison with other groups.[3]

Process of Estimation on Acreage,
Yield, and Production

1. Rice Acreage of 1967:

Following the process of acreage assessment

for 1964-66, we take as "guiding points" two former
estimates made by the U.S. Consulate General at Hong
Kong and the Defense Research Institute at Taipei
and modify their data for each province either upward or downward according to the latest developing
trends as indicated in the reports of Agricultural
Notes (Hong Kong), the 1967 Yearbook on Chinese Communism (Taipei), Issues and Studies (Taipei), the
China Monthly (Hong Kong), and other up-to-date
materials available. In cases of wide discrepancies
occasionally occurring between different sources, we
have had to exercise our judgment with reference to
such background data of the prewar period as given
in Buck's Land Utilization Surveys and the NARB
crop reports of the 1930s.

China's rice acreage has experienced conspicu-
ous expansion in recent years, following the pre-
"Leap" differential scheme of grain promotion and
pushing onward mainly along two directions:

A. Extension of paddy areas by means of:

a. Opening new fields for rice grow-
ing through terracing low hill slopes, as is being
done in Szechwan, Yünnan, Kweichow, Hunan, Kiangsi,
Kwangtung, and Kwangsi.

b. Draining waterlogged depressions
to make paddy fields, as is being done in the basin
areas of Tung-ting Lake in Hunan, Po-Yang Lake in
Kiangsi, and Hung-Tze Lake in Anhwei, together with
other lake and lagoon regions along the Yangtze
Valley.

c. Converting salty marsh lands into
rice fields through drainage and dealkalinization,
as is being done on the coastal plains of northern
Kiangsu, eastern Shantung, and the southern borders
of Hopeh and Liaoning; also on the interior lowlands
of eastern Honan and western Anhwei, on the southern
prairies of Inner Mongolia, and in the northern
swamps of Heilungkiang. (Sources: Agricultural
Notes, 1967 Yearbook on Chinese Communism, Issues
and Studies, China Monthly.)

B.   Extension of the double-rice crop system by means of:

a.   Effective flood control and extensive drainage, as indicated by achievements in Ouh-Chiang and Chien-Tang basin of Chekiang; in Chiu-hung and Min Chiang of Fukien; and in the Pearl River (including Si-Chiang, Pei-Chiang, and Tung Chiang) and Han-Chiang valleys of Kwangtung.

b.   Consolidation and improvement in irrigation and drainage systems, as is being achieved in southern Kiangsi, southeastern Hunan, in the central basin of Yünnan, central plain of Kwangsi, and the southwestern borders of Szechwan.

c.   In certain parts of Leichow and the Hainan Island of Kwangtung, attempts have been made to change the existing double-rice system into a triple-rice system, wherever fertilizer and manpower are adequate to warrant its successful operation.   (Sources: Agricultural Notes, 1967 Yearbook on Chinese Communism, Issues and Studies.)

2.   Rice Yield of 1967:

The 1967 rice yields are derived from the 1957 yield rates for different provinces by multiplying the latter with a differential scale of percentages; 9 per cent for the Class A provinces, 8 per cent for Class B, and 7 per cent for Class C, resulting in a rough average of 8 per cent increase for the nation as a whole.   The standards for classification and percentage assignment have already been fully explained earlier in these notes.

The 1957 yield rates are mostly drawn from the Economic Geography of China (Peking, 1958-60), with necessary adjustments and comparable supplements. As these geographical volumes were published during the "Great Leap" years, the contents of their provincial yields data were heavily colored with the "Leap Forward Fever," as indicated by numerous instances of exorbitant records.   For such cases, we

have to exercise drastic adjustments on the basis
of prewar normal yields as reported in Buck's Land
Utilization Survey findings or the NARB publications,
allowing a reasonable amount of increase during the
twenty years between 1937 and 1957. Again, as the
Economic Geography volumes for North China and the
northwestern provinces are not available in the
U.S., the missing data for those regions have to be
supplemented with comparable estimates based upon
indirect information or prewar yield figures.

Besides natural factors such as temperature,
rainfall, growing season, soil productivity, etc.,
there are three technical factors that constantly
exercise controlling influences over the unit-
yields of rice, either separately or in various degrees of combination. These are (a) water supply,
(b) fertilizer application, and (c) adoption of improved seeds that are most adaptable to physical
conditions of specific regions as may be determined
by variety experimentation and soil surveys.

Regulation of Water Supply

1. According to rice expert Dr. Ting Yin,
China's rice-producing areas may be divided into
three belts in regard to "plant requirement" of
water. The amount of water required by each rice
cropping throughout its growing season is estimated
for the three belts as:

a. North of Chin-ling Range and the Huai
River basin: 533-1,533 m^3 per mow.

b. South of Chin-ling and Huai River and
north of the Yangtze and Chien-Tang rivers: 33-666
m^3 per mow.

c. South of the Yangtze and Chien-Tang
rivers: 200-466 m^3 per mow.

As China's precipitation and surface flow are
bountiful in the southern and central provinces and
fairly adequate in rice areas of the northern

provinces, the essential problem for the Yangtze
Valley and Pearl River basin is flood control and
drainage and that for North China and border provinces is flood control and irrigation.[4]

2. With the completion of Sanmen Gorge Dam in
1960, no serious flooding has been reported on the
Yellow River; the Huai River also has claimed a
capacity to withstand floods of fifty-year frequen-
cies, after completing ten reservoirs on its upper
and middle courses in 1959, Kwangtung again has
proved the effectiveness of its conservation projects in 1964 when "unprecedented" flood threatened
to engulf the rice fields of its lowland. Operation
of the main irrigation canal of North Kiangsu has
benefited more than 20 million mow of paddy fields
in the Huai basin. The flood-diversion projects on
the Han River and the irrigation and drainage projects around Tung-ting and Po-Yang lakes in recent
years have again contributed to raising rice output
in the three central Yangtze provinces of Hupeh,
Hunan, and Kiangsi. The irrigation system of Tu-
Chiang Weir on the Chengtu plain has been expanded
and improved up to 1962.

Szechwan rice acreage and production have closely followed that of Kwangtung, with an even higher
yield of 3,360 kg/ha for 1967.

3. But the most effective means in the promotion of water utilization among rice-producing
provinces is perhaps the wide range and efficient
application of power pumps for irrigation and drainage. It was reported in 1964 that 90 per cent of
China's 2,000-odd counties were already equipped
with either electrical or mechanical water pumps,
and that over 6 million H.P. was provided in that
year for pumping and other farm operations. Judging
from its speedy increase in recent years, the total
power supply must have reached 8 to 9 million H.P.
by 1967. It is estimated that one horse power of
mechanical or electrical power installation could
meet the minimum requirement of water operation
(irrigation or drainage) for about 2.6 hectares of

cultivated land. China's estimated 28 million hectares (420 million mow) of rice paddies would require at least 10,500,000 H.P. of technical installations, if all water operations were to be mechanized
(People's Daily, June 20, 1963).

Assuming 70 per cent of the 1967 power equipment is used on the rice fields, a supply of
5,600,000 H.P. would then be available for the operation on 224 million mow (15 million hectares) of
paddies, which is more than 50 per cent of the nation's total rice lands. This means that more than
half of the man-hours formerly spent on manual pumping operations can now be released for other farm
performances. Hence the benefits of power pumps
are twofold:

a. Swift, timely service in irrigation
and drainage could save threatened rice crops from
possible damage in sudden change of weather or
other factors.

b. Labor power (human or animal) thus released from water operations could be utilized in
fertilizer collection, soil improvement, more intensive cultivation, or the construction of more
conservation works.

Application of Fertilizers

As explained in our Progress Report of April,
1968, chemical fertilizers are rather costly in comparison with hog manure or other organic fertilizers.

Realizing the great importance of green manure
as a "natural food" for rice crops, China's southern
and central provinces have in recent years launched
a great campaign for its extensive cultivation.
Wherever other winter crops can be spared, green
manure takes their place as the "predecessor" of
early rice, to be plowed under in the original
field in early spring or to be distributed among
adjacent fields for the same purpose.

   According to NCNA (June 1, 1965), China's
green manure acreage had annually increased by
1,500,000 mow from 1952 until 1963; the 1964 increase was 10 million mow; the 1965 increase was
close to 20 million mow. The same agency again reported (December 30, 1965) that the nation's total
green manure acreage had reached 8 million hectares
(or 120 million mow) by the end of 1965. The following table shows its acreage distribution among
China's major producing areas of rice (figures in
brackets are estimated). This increase seems optimistic. The green manure acreage (in mows) in
rice-producing provinces of China from 1964 to 1967
were:

	1964-65	1965-66	1966-67
Kwangtung	6,000,000	10,700,000	[12,000,000]
Kwangsi	4,000,000	8,000,000	8,485,000
Fukien	[1,000,000]	2,000,000	8,150,000
Chekiang	[12,000,000]	[13,000,000]	[15,000,000]
Kiangsu	6,500,000	[8,000,000]	[9,000,000]
Anhwei	4,680,000	6,128,000	[8,000,000]
Hupeh	10,000,000	[12,000,000]	[15,000,000]
Hunan	15,000,000	[20,000,000]	[22,000,000]
Kiangsi	11,000,000	16,000,000	[20,000,000]
Yünnan	[8,000,000]	[10,000,000]	1,750,000

   Sources: Agricultural Notes, 1964-67.

                Extension of Improved Seeds

   The Communists, besides inheriting a great number of improved rice strains from the legacy of preceding administrations, have also developed a few
new varieties of their own, mainly through selection at local fields or breeding at experimental
stations. (See Chapter 6.) Notably among their
successful results are:

   "Kwangtung Station" No. 7 and No. 13
   "Chekiang Station" No. 3 and No. 9
   "Single String Red" (Nanking)
   "Continental Gem" (Szechwan)

"Silver Pagoda" (Hunan)
"Southern Yangtze 1224" (Kiangsi)
"Victory Indica" (Kiangsi)

These improved varieties, brought up during
the first Five-Year Plan period, have all claimed
to possess the superior qualities of high yield,
disease resistance, great adaptability to climate
and soil, etc. Energetic campaigns have been
launched for extension of these new strains in the
late 1950s. But their promising destiny is short-
lived as a result of the "Great Leap" failures.
Good seeds must have been left to decay and degenerate during the "disaster years." This is why the
People's Daily and other Communist papers urgently
called for "Regeneration of Improved Seeds" in the
early 1960s.

Seed breeding or regeneration is a slow and
complicated process that will take many years of
station experiments under controlled conditions.
Extension of good seeds again proves to be a difficult undertaking, often subject to chances of trial
and error, because no adopted fields can provide
identical surroundings as those of original seed-
bed areas. In spite of the Communist great urge
for new strains, Mainland China's paddy fields are
still covered mostly by the prewar improved varieties, which have been maintained and popularized
throughout the years of Communist rule. Double-
rice cropping is implemented not only by good seed
but also by the shorter growing season. A brief
list of these varieties may be presented as follows.

Name	Characteristics	Area of Best Suitability
1. "Top of Hat" (Central University)	Early ripening, high yielding, drought resistant, great adaptabil- ity, medium- quality rice	Yangtze delta areas of Kiangsu and Anhwei; Southern Yangtze bank areas of Kiangsi and Honan

Name	Characteristics	Area of Best Suitability
2. "Bamboo Indica No. 1"	Early ripening, strong stem, drought resistant, adaptable to soil, good-quality rice, high yielding	Pearl River Valley areas of Kwangtung and Kwangsi; mostly suitable to sandy loam soils
3. "Chekiang Station No. 9"	Late ripening, disease resistant, high adaptability, medium-quality rice, wind resistant	Most parts of Chekiang, eastern Kiangsi, southern Anhwei
4. "Southern Special" (Kiangsi)	Early ripening, high yielding, strong stem, drought resistant, great adaptability, good for single-cropping or double-cropping	Widely adopted in Kiangsi, Fukien, Kwangtung, Hunan, Hupeh, Chekiang, Szechwan
5. "Wanli Indica" (Hunan)	Intermediate ripening, high yielding, high-quality rice, suitable for plain fields and warm climate	Western Hunan, Kwangsi, Yünnan, Kweichow
6. "Golden Indica"	Intermediate ripening, drought resistant, disease and pest resistant, high yielding	Northern Hunan, Kweichow, and Yünnan
7. "Victory Indica"	Intermediate ripening, high yielding, drought and pest resistant, high-quality rice	Hunan, Kweichow, Kangsi, and Yünnan

	Name	Characteristics	Area of Best Suitability
8.	"Bamboo Twig"	High yielding, strong tillering, great adaptability, good-quality rice	West and south of Szechwan along the Min-Chiang Valley
9.	"Yun-Lien Indica"	High yielding, strong power of tillering, great adaptability	Most provinces along the Yangtze Valley
10.	"Central Station No. 4"	Early ripening, strong stem, pest resistant, good-quality rice	Eastern Szechwan, southern Kwangsi, and northern regions of Kiangsu
11.	"Nanking U. No. 1386"	High yielding, great adaptability, high-quality rice	Szechwan and Kiangsu, especially plain areas of Chengtu and Nanking
12.	"Wuli"	Strong stem, wind resistant, great capacity for tillering, high yielding	Eastern coastal areas of Fukien

Source: Yuen-chi Tang, ed., Roads of Production Enhancement in Chinese Agriculture (Taipei, 1953).

ESTIMATED WHEAT ACREAGE
AND PRODUCTION IN 1967

Wheat ranks second to rice as China's staple
food grain, with producing areas spreading all over
the country, but concentrating in ten provinces of
China proper. Wheat consists of two types of the
same crop, differentiated in respect to planting
seasons:

(a) Spring wheat, generally sown in April-May
and harvested in July-August, with a growing season
of about 120-150 days.

(b) Winter wheat, generally sown in September-
October and harvested in May-June of the next year
(excepting earlier harvest in southern China), with
a growing season of about 200-230 days.

The aggregated area of both types of wheat in
China usually occupies 20 to 22 per cent of the nation's grain area and approximately 11 to 13 per
cent of its total grain production. But the ratio
between the two types is rather uneven, with spring
wheat occupying only 11 per cent of the wheat area
and 13 per cent of the total annual output of wheat.

Producing areas of spring wheat are practically confined to Manchuria, Sinkiang, Chinghai, Kansu,
Inner Mongolia, and the northern tips of Shansi and
Hopeh provinces. It is found planted side by side
with winter wheat in many parts of Kansu and Sinkiang where the climate is suitable for both.

Winter wheat, with 89 per cent of sown wheat
area and 87 per cent of annual production in the
nation, has a much wider distribution among all
provinces in China proper. Its producing areas may
be divided into two broad belts: (a) the northern
winter wheat belt and (b) the southern winter wheat
belt.

(a) The northern winter wheat belt covers all
the producing areas south of the Great Wall, east

of Lu-Pan Mountain, and north of Chin-ling Range
and the Huai River basin. The sown area in this
region is estimated as usually 66 per cent of the
nation's wheat acreage.

(b) The southern winter wheat belt covers all
wheat fields in southern and central China, with
its producing areas occupying about 22 per cent of
the nation's total, and concentrated in the four
Yangtze provinces of Kiangsu, Anhwei, Hupeh, and
Szechwan.[5]

Classification of Wheat-producing Areas

1. The classification of wheat areas, as that
for rice, is also based upon three criteria according to their normal capacity and recent developments:

a. Combined magnitude of acreage, yield,
and production under normal conditions.

b. Recent growth of population and livestock as sources of labor power and organic fertilizers.

c. Latest advancement in technical factors
such as water conservation, power facilities, good
seeds, etc.

2. Distinctive features of the three classes
of wheat areas:

Class A embraces four provinces from the northern winter wheat belt (Hopeh, Shantung, Honan, and
Shensi) and four provinces from the southern winter
wheat belt (Kiangsu, Anhwei, Hupeh, and Szechwan).

a. The four provinces in the northern belt
are all situated in the Yellow River basin with a
frost-free season of 200-250 days and an annual precipitation of 400-600 MM. Being low-yielding but
high-valued, wheat is regarded as the most important
grain in this region and is given the best of soil
and water resources and the highest priority of fertilizer and other important factors. Wheat input

fields also enjoy the special treatment of summer fallow in the western section and winter fallow (every one or two years) in the eastern section of this northern belt.

       b. The four provinces in the southern belt are all situated in the Yangtze Valley, with a frost-free season of 300-325 days and an annual precipitation of 900-1,000 MM. Although regarded as a secondary grain in this region, wheat is important as a "rotation partner" with rice, cotton, or other summer crops. Thus:

       1. The double-cropping system of rice and wheat in the annual rotation. This system prevails along the Yangtze Valley south of Huau River, embracing the chief producing areas of Szechwan, southern parts of Honan, and northern parts of Anhwei and Kiangsu.

       2. The double-cropping system of cotton and wheat in annual rotation. This system prevails mostly on the northern bank of the Yangtze River wherever drainage facilities are adequate to guarantee the growth of cotton as a summer crop.

       3. The triple-cropping system of wheat, rice, and coarse grain (late variety). This system is usually adapted to warm, moist, fertile soils in parts of Szechwan, Hunan, Kiangsi, and other south bank provinces of Yangtze, where the intermediate rice is grown after the harvesting of wheat and before the sowing of certain types of quick-ripening coarse grains or potatoes.

       4. The triple-cropping system of double-rice and wheat. This system is usually adopted in subtropical or tropical regions where the frost-free season is over 300 days, as the southern parts of Kwangtung, Kwangsi, Fukien, and southern parts and borders of Chekiang, Kiangsi, and Honan.

Class B embraces six provinces (Shansi, Kansu, Sinkiang, Liaoning, Kirin, and Heilungkiang) from the north and four provinces (Chekiang, Hunan, Kweichow, and Yunnan) from the south.

a. The northern group of provinces is situated in the North China plain, Manchuria, and the northwestern plateau where spring wheat is raised alone or alongside winter wheat. Although regarded as an important crop, wheat is limited in growth by short growing season, poor quality of soil, and deficient water supply in the northwest and lingering waterlogging in the northeast, more often than not. Wheat growing in these regions is exposed to sharp land competition from potatoes and coarse grains, which are comparatively more high-yielding than wheat and cost much less on input factors.

b. The southern group of provinces is situated in Central and southern China where wheat is raised as a minor crop, partly to supplement local food requirements, partly to rotate with other autumn harvesting crops, and partly to utilize terraced hilly slopes that are too dry for rice planting. Labor, manure, and field attendance are given to wheat only when not required by rice or other high-yielding crops.

Class C consists of those provinces in the north (Ningsia, Chinghai, and Inner Mongolia) and those in the south (Kiangsi, Kwangtung, Kwangsi, and Fukien) where wheat growing is often handicapped either by climate and soil and water resources or by labor power, fertilizer, and other technical factors. The acreage is limited, the yield is low, and the output is unstable from year to year. While this group occupies 9.21 per cent of the nation's wheat acreage, its annual production contributes only 6.74 per cent to the national total.

3. Differential scale of yield increase for the three classes:

As in the case of rice grading, we have assigned
to Class A provinces 9 per cent of increase yield,
1967 over 1957; to Class B, 8 per cent of increase,
and to Class C, 7 per cent of increase, expecting a
rough average of 8 per cent on the whole. As it
turns out, the 1967 unit-yield is calculated as 926
kg/ha on the average, which is only slightly higher
than the result of 1957 rate, 855 kg/ha multiplied
by 8 per cent of increase: 923 kg/ha.

Process of Estimation on Acreage,
Yield, and Production of Wheat

The 1967 acreage of wheat:

1. For the assessment of wheat acreage, as in
the case of rice, we have taken former estimates as
guide posts, that is, the 1963-64 to 1965-66 wheat
estimates by the U.S. Consulate General Office in
Hong Kong, and the 1965 wheat estimate by the Defense Research Institute at Taipei. Besides, we
have also frequently referred to the 1957 acreage
data of different provinces as reported in various
volumes of the Economic Geography of China (Peking,
1958-60). As already explained in connection with
the rice assessment, supplements have to be made
wherever the original data are missing and adjustments have to be made in light of prewar normal
records, wherever the reported figures are found to
be too exorbitant, even under the changed conditions
of recent years.

2. Special attention is also paid to Peking's
shift in wheat policy since 1958. As shown by the
following figures, a steady push was given to wheat
acreage during the "Plan Period," but was suddenly
reduced to 26,620,000 hectares in 1958; no report
was made public since that date.

	Wheat sown area (1,000 Mow)	Wheat production (1,000 M.T.)
1952	371,700	18,100
1953	384,540	18,300
1954	404,510	23,350

	Wheat sown area (1,000 Mow)	Wheat production (1,000 M.T.)
1955	401,080	22,950
1956	409,080	24,800
1957	413,120	23,650
1958	399,350	28,950

Source: Official data from Ten Great Years, 1959.

Although this 1958 sharp drop in wheat acreage may be ascribed to statistical adjustment in that period, the fact remains that China's wheat status never recovered its 1957 level until the mid-1960s and still remains stationary in comparison with the swift advancement of rice, potatoes, and corn of the miscellaneous grains group. The reason for this shift may be stated briefly as follows:

3. The "Great Leap" failures, together with serious blunders in a great many conservation projects, inflicted special damage on the North China plain, which contributes over 60 per cent of the nation's annual wheat output. As wheat is low-yielding and highly exacting on productive factors, the Peking regime had to sacrifice part of its usual acreage in favor of such high-yielding grains as rice, corn, potatoes, and even certain types of the coarse grains. It also found it necessary to import an annual average amount of wheat in order to fill the gap in the nation's grain requirement. Since its initiation in 1960, China's wheat-importing policy has been held as "economical" and probably will be continued indefinitely until its "population-food balance" can be achieved at some future date. It seems also part of the policy to have buffer stocks available for industrial centers.

4. Peking's recent manifestations regarding this new wheat policy, as revealed in reports from the agricultural notes and other up-to-date materials, may be summarized in the following outline:

a.   Spring wheat acreage is to be expanded, wherever it offers no land competition against other high-yielding food grains or high-valued economic crops. This is especially emphasized in the border regions of Manchuria, Sinkiang, Chinghai, Kansu, and Inner Mongolia.

b.   Winter wheat acreage is to be constrained or curtailed as a rule, but with the following exceptions:

1.   Highlands or terraced slopes where soil structure, water supply, and general climate conditions are not fit for other high-yielding crops. This especially refers to the tablelands and hilly slopes of Szechwan, Yünnan, Kweichow, Hunan, Hupeh, Kiangsi, Kwangtung, and Kwangsi.

2.   Paddy fields converted from marshy lands in interior provinces, to be drained (after rice harvest) in autumn and planted with wheat where other winter crops are found to be less adaptable. This especially applies to the lake regions of Tung-ting, Po-Yang, and Hungtze, as well as the Yun-Meng basin of the Chiang-Han plain in Central China.

3.   Paddy fields reclaimed through de-alkalinization of the coastal plains have been found advantageous to the planting of wheat as a winter crop, because autumn and winter drainage helps to preserve mineral nutriments in the soil, and wheat cultivation always leaves the fields with ample amounts of residual fertilizers. This is generally practiced along the coastal areas of Kiangsu, Shantung, Hopeh, and Liaoning.[6]

5.   As a result of these considerations on land use efficiency, China's winter wheat has to follow a downward trend in its acreage allotment. The result is a comparative decline of wheat output since 1958, in spite of desperate efforts for yield promotion. With the general recovery of farm

economy in the mid-1960s, however, wheat acreage has
gradually regained its 1957 status, although it is
by far outdistanced by that of rice and the miscellaneous grains. The estimate on China's wheat
acreage is 408 million mow for 1964, 412 million
mow for 1965, and 418 million mow for 1966; for
1967, it is advanced to 419,400,000 mow, which is
even 1.5 per cent higher than the 1957 figure
(413,120,000 mow). This gradual recovery and improvement may be explained by two causes, among
others: (1) expansion of spring wheat area through
reclamation in the borderlands of Manchuria, Sinkiang, Chinghai, and Inner Mongolia; (2) practical
restitution of original winter wheat areas, mainly
in the northern belt and partially in the southern
belt, with slight increases of acreage in the reclaimed lands of the central and lower Yangtze
provinces.

China's Class A wheat provinces occupy about
68 per cent of its wheat acreage, with nearly 70 per
cent of its wheat production; Class B occupies about
22 per cent of acreage with 24 per cent of production; and Class C occupies 9 per cent of acreage
with nearly 7 per cent of production.

The 1967 unit-yield of wheat:

1. The 1967 unit-yields of wheat are derived
from the 1957 yield rates of different provinces by
multiplying the latter with a differential scale of
percentage increases. Thus for Class A, the 1967
yield is 9 per cent over that of 1957; for Class B,
8 per cent; and for Class C, 7 per cent.

2. The 1957 yield data for the provinces are
mostly drawn from the Economic Geography of China,
with adjustments based on normal yields of prewar
records and with supplements for missing data based
on the same sources.

3. Wheat is probably the most delicate and
most expensive among China's food grains, so far as
its demands on ecological factors are concerned.

We may briefly sketch its ecological requirements
as follows:

Water requirement:

      With the North China plain as an illustra-
tion, winter wheat in this area usually must take in
200-350 M3 per mow as its "life requirement" throughout the whole growing season. The soil moisture must
be kept at 16-20 per cent by means of frequent shallow sprinkling during the critical stages of its long
months of growth. The general practice of wheat irrigation in North China is "5 watering," "7 watering," or "11 to 15 watering," depending upon the
seasonal distribution of rainfall among different
regions. (People's Daily, July 7, 1957.)

Fertilizer requirement:

      a. Previous research[7] indicated 1 MT of
wheat required 53 kg of crop nutrients (N,P_2O_5, K_2O)
and 145 MT of organic fertilizer per MT of crop
nutrients. At this rate a yield of 900 kg/ha would
require 47.7 kg of N.P.K. and about 6.7 MT of organic fertilizer. (See Chapter 7.)

      b. While fertilizers may be applied as
many as eleven times during wheat growth, there are
three critical stages when the dosage and procedure
of application must be well adjusted to its actual
requirement at those particular periods:[8]

            1. Basic dressing. Ample amount of
      farm fertilizers to be applied to well-prepared
      fields at the time of sowing. The minimum
      amount is about 50 per cent of the crop's
      "life requirement" of fertilizers.

            2. Winter dressing. Adequate amount
      of farm fertilizers to be applied in midwinter,
      to foster lush tillering and early revival in
      the spring. The minimum dosage is at least 30
      per cent.

3.   Spring dressing. Proper amount of
high-quality fertilizers such as night soil,
oil-seed cakes, or a small portion of chemical
fertilizers, to be applied two or three times
in early spring, preceding the periods of heading and flowering. The dosage should be about
20 per cent of total requirement.

Unit-yields of wheat under "normal" conditions:

In spite of its high demands on productive factors, wheat has proved to be the lowest yielding
among China's food grains. Its unit-yield is about
one third that of rice, one half that of corn, and
even 30 to 40 per cent lower than kaoliang and millet.
Whatever wheat acreage is extended, the grain output
of that area would be pulled downward on account of
the low yield of this item. Take Hopeh province as
an illustration.

	Wheat Average (1,000 Mow)	Increase Over 1952 (1,000 Mow)	Total Wheat Output (1,000 M.T.)	Total Grain Output (1,000 M.T.)	Grain Decrease from 1952 (1,000 M.T.)
1952	27,676		1,300	9,084	
1953	28,145	+ 499	1,123	7,659	-1,452
1954	36,668	+ 8,992	1,908	7,509	-1,526
1955	34,872	+ 7,196	1,773	8,649	- 486
1956	31,869	+ 4,193	1,935	7,778	-1,306
1957	40,950	+13,274	1,950		

Source: Ma Chiu-wong: "Prospects of China's
Coarse Grain Output," Chinese Agricultural Journal,
Aug. 8, 1957.

The 1967 production of wheat:

1. The 1967 production figures are obtained
by multiplying the estimated acreage with the derived yield rates for that year. As the yield figures for the provinces are rounded out in each case,
there are found to be slight margins of error in

the lower digits of production figures. But the
class subtotals for both acreage and production will
check perfectly with the national totals on wheat.

2. The final results of our wheat estimates
show a total acreage of 419,400,000 mow for 1967,
with a "capacity" distribution of 68.31 per cent for
Class A, 22.48 per cent for Class B, and 8.21 per
cent for Class C.

Calculating on the basis of differential yield
increase, 1967 over 1957, we get 69.74 per cent of
production for Class A, 23.52 per cent for Class B,
and 6.74 per cent for Class C, resulting in a
national total output of 25,892,400 M.T. for 1967,
which is about 9.48 per cent higher than that of
1957.

THE 1967 SITUATION OF MISCELLANEOUS
GRAINS PRODUCTION

General Characteristics of the
Miscellaneous Grains

The category of miscellaneous grains embraces
three major crops--corn, kaoliang, millet--and a
number of minor crops, including barley, oats, buck-
wheat, rye, field peas, cowpeas, broad beans, string
beans, black beans, green beans, mud beans, etc.
(Soybeans have been classified as an oil crop since
1955.) The group as a whole occupies about 45 per
cent of the nation's total grain acreage and 28 per
cent of its total grain production (1957). The
1958 average yield of this group shows a low rate
of 139 catties per mow, even with inclusion of the
high-yielding corn varieties.

As most crop items in this category are endowed
with strong resistance against adverse environment
and are highly adaptable to diversified climate and
soil conditions, their sown areas have spread far
and wide in all parts of the country:

1.   In South and Central China, these grains are grown usually on high-level dry fields with deficient water and manure supply.

2.   On the Yellow and Huai River basins they are mostly scattered over low-lying depressions with poor irrigation and drainage.

3.   Over the prairie lands of Inner Mongolia and along the northern borders of Kansu, Shensi, Shansi, and Hopeh, they are scattered among patches of loess-sandy soils not infrequently blighted with snow storms or sand storms.

4.   Even on the "home grounds" of North China and on Manchuria's rolling plains, they are usually assigned to the second-grade lands with secondary shares of input factors.

But miscellaneous grains constitute the staple foods for China's northern lands. As a group they usually occupy 80 per cent of grain acreage in Manchuria; 50-60 per cent in the four "main source" provinces of Hopeh, Shantung, Honan, and Shansi; and a wide range of 10-40 per cent among the hilly regions and rugged plateaus in Central and South China, where they are grown as supplements for food and feed or for the purposes of land utilization in rotation with other crops.

Total acreage of this grain category has undergone a great deal of fluctuation under the Communist regime in the last seventeen years. It was 722 million mow in 1950, 756,600,000 mow in 1952, and 759,110,000 mow in 1957. The 1957 figure shows only a fractional increase of 0.31 per cent over that of 1952, which is in sharp contrast to the long-stride increases of 13.60 per cent for rice, 11.12 per cent for wheat, and 20.79 per cent for potatoes in the same period of five years. This was a stage when the Communists adopted a "differential scheme for grain promotion" under which the high-yielding grains (including low-yielding wheat) were invariably given the best chance for acreage extension

and the highest priority of production investments.
On the other hand, all miscellaneous grains (excepting high-yielding corn), because of their low-
yielding and space-consuming disadvantages, have
suffered a great setback on account of acreage con-
straint, labor curtailment, shortage of fertilizer
supply, negligence of conservation projects, and so
forth.

After the sharp drop of its acreage down to
684,750,000 mow in 1958, the category of miscellaneous grains was not able to regain its former
status of the mid-1950s until the sudden repeated
clamor of "restitution of the dry-land crops" in
1963 and 1964, which suggests a new turn in the Communist crop policy in favor of miscellaneous grains,
probably for the following reasons:

1. The "home grounds" of coarse grains in
North China and Manchuria, besides being free from
serious flooding for more than a decade, have recently witnessed considerable improvements in their
conservation mows as indicated by the Heilungkiang
and Tzeyoke projects of Hopeh, the Tukai and Machai
projects of Shantung, the "Red Banner irrigation
system" of Honan, the Tengkow electrical pumping
station of Inner Mongolia, and the drainage systems
on the Liaoho-Sungari plain of Manchuria.

2. The traditionally low-yielding kaoliang
and millet have recently achieved considerable success in the breeding and "popularizing" of certain
new strains with superior qualities of strong resistance, great adaptability, and above all, high-
yielding capacities far above that of ordinary
varieties. Notable among the new strains are:

      Kaoliang: "Kuantung Yellow" (from Manchuria)
                  "Fragrant Sorghum" (from Shantung)
      Millet: "Silver Torch" (from Shensi)
                  "Golden String" (from Honan)
                  "Borderland No. I" (from Inner
                    Mongolia)

Besides, according to NCNA (May 17, 1966), "A new
strain of kaoliang was successfully bred by a grain
expert, Dr. Kung Chi-tae of the Shen Yang Agricultural College, in collaboration with the peasants,
which is capable of yielding 50-100 per cent more
than the ordinary types, besides retaining its in-
nate qualities of drought resistance, moisture resistance, and pest resistance, as well as great
adaptability to poor lands including moderately
salinized or alkalinized soils. It is called
multiple-ear kaoliang, because whereas ordinary
types bear only one ear, this new strain is found
to bear four to a dozen ears."

   3.   The traditionally high-yielding corn again
enhanced its capacity through new types of hybrid
corn.   According to NCNA (November 15, 1965),
"starting with 1958, the Agricultural Research Department in China has evolved a large number of
double-cross hybrids of corn and have placed about
thirty items for extension. The unit-yield of these
new varieties has proved to be 30 to 50 per cent
higher than ordinary types of corn." It is reported
that sixteen provinces and regions in the country
have already achieved wide areas of extension for
adoption of these new varieties of double-cross
hybrid corn. The adopting areas in 1965 have tripled
that of 1964 and the movement is gaining momentum in
all directions. (Agricultural Notes, No. 18, May 6,
1966.)

   4.   Most miscellaneous grains, especially corn,
kaoliang, and millet, usually provide enormous
amounts of by-products (stalks, leaves, roots, cobs,
husks, linters, etc.) that may be used as feeds,
fertilizers, fuels, beddings, or even building materials for farm hamlets and raw materials for cottage industries. These supplies have been greatly
reduced along with the stagnation or decline in
magnitude of miscellaneous grains (except corn)
following the post-"Leap" years.

   With the recent revival of agriculture and
multiplication of livestock in North China and

Manchuria, the Communists have found it necessary
to increase the supply of these by-products through
"restitution of the dry-land crops," with corn,
kaoliang, and millet as the core targets. This, of
course, is found to be feasible as a result of frontier expansion through reclamation in the borderlands, as well as increase of cultivated areas
through improvement of irrigation, drainage, desalinization, and control of waterlogging in the
interior provinces.

The Changed Pattern of Distribution
Among the Miscellaneous Grains

Although China's northern provinces (North
China, Manchuria, and the Northwest Region) have
continued to occupy about two thirds of the total
acreage of miscellaneous grains, the "center of
gravity" of this group has gradually shifted from
North China toward Manchuria. The 1956 acreage
ratio between these two "domains" is 21.12 per cent
for the latter and 39.15 per cent for the former.
Their output ratio would roughly correspond to the
same pattern, because their acreage-yields rate was
closely comparable between these regions during
that period. That is, North China shared about 40
per cent of the nation's total output of miscellaneous grains while Manchuria's share was around 20
per cent in the late 1950s.

In our estimates of 1967 output of this grain
category, both Manchuria and North China have ac-
quired practically the same share in that year's
national total, namely 28.12 per cent for Manchuria
and 28.47 per cent for North China, showing an expansion of about 8 per cent for the former and a
shrinkage of about 11 per cent for the latter in
comparison with their relative positions ten years
before. Perhaps a slight amount of bias is involved
in the complicated process of estimation based upon
fragmentary data of recent years, but there is no
mistake about the general trend of relative changes
in the producing capacity between these two regions,
so far as miscellaneous grains are concerned. Main

reasons for this change may be traced to the following facts:

1. Manchuria offers a better climate with adequate rainfall and vast stretches of new fields with
higher productivity for the same types of coarse
grains that have been gradually crowded from the
North China plain under the "Differential Scheme for
Grain Promotion" during and after the first Five-
Year Plan period.

2. Manchuria suffered much less damage from
the "Great Leap" era, which seriously damaged North
China's producing capacity with its overskimmed
labor allotment, ill-conceived conservation projects,
irrational crop planning, and all sorts of wasteful
drives for rural construction. While these damaged
areas began weakly to struggle for revival in the
early 1960s, the northeastern provinces are well on
the way to full-scale advancement, as evidenced by
their grain output records for these years.

3. Manchuria is China's new frontier, with a
low population density (1957) of ninety persons per
square mile. North China is a saturated area with
a high density (1957) of 215 persons per square mile.
(Economic Geography of China.) Of China's reclaimed
new lands during the first Five-Year Plan period,
Heilungkiang alone tried to claim almost one third
as its share of annual contribution (29.1 per cent
in 1957). Our estimated area of reclamation for
China as a whole amounts to a figure of 17,500,000
mow from 1959 to 1963 and 12 million mow from 1964
to 1966 inclusive, with roughly 50 per cent in the
first period and 60 per cent in the second period
ascribed to all the borderlands, including Manchuria,
Sinkiang, Chinghai, and Inner Mongolia.

We may conservatively assume that the three
northeastern provinces as a group have contributed
one third of the accumulated reclamation of 29 million mow from 1959 to the end of 1966. This would
give Manchuria roughly 9,800,000 mow of new lands,
of which a major portion of the annual additions

must have been used for the purpose of grain production, either by state farms or by the rural communes.
With the combined aids of technical and power facilities, chemical and organic fertilizers, together with
the newly bred, high-yielding varieties of corn,
kaoliang, and millet (as recently claimed by the Communists), this northeastern frontier could have
easily added a few million tons of coarse grain to
the regional granary each year and thus raised its
annual share to match North China's 1967 percentage
of 28.47. North China, on the other hand, with all
its cultivatable lands almost exhausted long before
the Communists, could hardly have offered any effective competition in the line of producing space-
consuming grains of this miscellaneous group.

The only other important area for miscellaneous
grains is the southwestern region, embracing the
Szechwan Red basin and the Yünnan Kweichow plateau,
which have contributed almost 20 per cent (19.67 per
cent) to the 1967 total output of this category.
Here the rainfall is plentiful with a fairly even
distribution among all seasons. The soil is adequate but requires erosion control and frequent
manuring. The frost-free season is long so that
most miscellaneous grains could always find a suitable place in the double-harvesting or triple-
harvesting rotation systems.

Corn, being high-yielding, multifunctional,
and easily adaptable to most areas of this region,
plays a leading role among all coarse grains in the
following capacities:

1. As supplement food for the farm population.
Usually mixed with rice or beans in the form of
congie or steamed meals.

2. As raw materials for home brewing, starch-
making, sugar extraction, oil pressing, and a number of other household "industries."

3. Corn seeds as well as by-products (stalks,
leaves, cobs, husks, etc.) are used as feeds,

fertilizers, fuel, stable beddings, roof thatching, etc. (Seeds are used for seeds only.)

4. Corn and its by-products have also begun to enter the fields of food industries and plastics manufacturing in urban areas.

Kaoliang, millet, beans, peas, and other minor crops in the miscellaneous group are grown in this region primarily for two purposes:

1. To supplement food or feed, or to be used as raw materials for various types of handicrafts or cottage industries.

2. To utilize poor lands on hill tops and mountain wastes at the foothills around big plateaus.

The most baffling problem for this region, considering the rugged terrain and inaccessibility in many places, is how to get cheap power for farm work, such as earth moving, water running, and machine propelling, together with the requirements of processing mills, repair shops, local transports, etc. If the bountiful water-power resources of the southwestern provinces could be developed as a basis for rural electrification, accompanied by a comprehensive power system, connecting the power centers with numerous local stations to be established at key points for service, the developmental problem of this region may be regarded as being more than half solved, as illustrated by the miraculous advancement made through the adaptation of power pumps in farm areas of the south and the southwest.

Final Results of the 1967 Estimates for Miscellaneous Grains

1. The 1967 acreage of miscellaneous grains is estimated as <u>799,690,000 mow, with 5.34 per cent increase over 1957</u>.

2. The 1967 average yield is calculated as 149.01 catties per mow, with an increase of 7.20 per cent over 1957.

3. The total 1967 output of the miscellaneous grains is estimated as <u>59,577,350 M.T., with an increase of 13.16 per cent over 1957</u>.

THE 1967 PRODUCTION OF POTATOES

Special Qualities of Potatoes

The category of potatoes consists of all food tubers, including sweet potatoes, Irish potatoes, yams, taros, cassavas, etc., with the potato items dominant in acreage and output in most parts of China. Sweet potatoes, being multifunctional and most adaptable, usually afford a high-yielding rate of 1,500 to 5,000 catties per mow. Besides substituting for grain seeds as food at times of emergency, they are also frequently used as feeds, fertilizers, or raw materials for brewing, sugar-making, starch derivation, and a number of other industrial purposes. It is estimated that every 100 catties of sweet potato by-products can be converted into 85 catties of feed concentrates, and that every catty of potato vine possesses the feed value of one-half catty of coarse grains.

Because of its superior qualities and high-yielding rate, the Communists have since the early 1950s tried to extend the acreage of the potato group for the following purposes:

1. To replace or supplement low-yielding crops in China's grain-deficient areas such as the overcrowded plains in North China and the crop-scanty plateau of the northwest.

2. To utilize dry fields or hilly slopes or poor soils at valley bottoms as frequently found in Szechwan Red basin, in southwestern Yünnan Kweichow plateau, and in the mountainous regions of central Yangtze provinces.

3. To augment food acreage by squeezing into the double-cropping or double-rice system with some

of its quick ripening varieties, as is being practiced in most provinces of southern China and in
many parts of central and lower Yangtze reaches.[9]

4. To be planted as an emergency crop wherever
regular crops are threatened or actually damaged on
account of natural calamity or social disturbances.

According to the calculation of Communist experts, potatoes can always be planted with great ad-
vantage as a substitute for grain crops, thus:

1. Assuming a reduction of 32 million mow in
acreage of an ordinary type of grain, the loss of
output thereby would usually amount to 4 billion
catties (2 million M.T.).

2. If 10 million mow of potatoes are planted
in place of such a grain, it would give a bountiful
harvest of 15 billion catties to 20 billion catties
(10 million M.T.) because potato yields usually exceed 1,500 catties per mow.

3. When this potato harvest is counted as one
quarter the quantity of ordinary grains, it is still
equivalent to 3 million to 4 million M.T., which is
quite adequate to offset the original loss of 2 million M.T. of grain.

4. Besides, only 10 million mow of cropland
are taken up for the planting of potatoes. There
still remain unused 20 million mow (reduction from
the original 30 million mow) to be utilized by other
grain or mow grain crops as a "net gain."

It is because of these and other exceptionally
economical qualities that potatoes as a group have
been upheld as an all-time "life-saver" in China's
farm economy. Following the traditional pattern of
distribution, the Communists have redoubled their
efforts for potato promotion. The nation's potato
acreage has increased 20 per cent from 1949 to 1959.
For the same period of ten years, while China's
total grain output has increased only onefold,

that for potatoes has increased fourfold. After a
brief disruption during the post-"Leap" years, this
policy of "galloping advancement" began to gain
momentum after the early 1960s, with a cumulative
result of 27.6 per cent increase in acreage and
36.20 per cent increase in output between 1957 and
1967.

General Pattern of Potato Distribution

The Communist policy for potato distribution
seems to confirm the truth of a simple Chinese adage
that "Potatoes will always go where they are needed
by the hungry man and will stay where they are
needed by the hungry land." As shown by the regional figures, there are in China three big "potato
domains" jointly contributing over 60 per cent of
the nation's annual output, with a share of 28 per
cent from North China, and about 16 per cent each
from the northwestern and southwestern regions.

North China represents the nation's most dense-
ly populated, highly food-deficient, and heavily
calamity-ridden areas where low-yielding wheat,
kaoliang, millet, and other coarse grains (corn being the only high-yielding grain of this group)
have failed to support its 180 million people and
120 million livestock even in "normal" years. Here
the potatoes have to step in to save the "hungry
man" year after year in various proportions, as illustrated by the 1967 output figures of the four
major producers: 25 million M.T. in Honan; 23 million M.T. in Hopeh; 19 million M.T. in Shantung;
and 13 million M.T. in Shansi.

With Irish potatoes prevailing in the northwest and sweet potatoes prevailing in the southwest,
these two regions are endowed with vast tracts of
"hungry lands" in the forms of wind-swept loess
gullies, sun-scorched sandy basins, debris-covered
piedmonts, weed-swallowed stony fields, or erosive
hilly slopes with thin soil and poor irrigation.
With a little spade retouch and manure reconditioning, these "unwanted" nooks and strips could be and

often have been converted into "comfortable homes"
for the potato family. Similarly, this "scavenging"
principle of land utilization is also applied to
other farm regions with 7 to 12 per cent of output
in 1967 (Manchuria and Central China), where potatoes have never failed to flourish on "leftover"
lands with meager investments of labor and other
inputs.

   This is the reason why potatoes have for the
last fifteen years continued to expand in sown area
in a steady or accelerating rate in accordance to
needs of the time. The percentage share in the nation's total grain acreage tends to ride on an
ascending scale, as 6.17 per cent in 1952, 8.68 per
cent in 1957, and 10.42 per cent (based on our estimate) in 1967, in contrast with the descending
scale of the miscellaneous grains, which is 44.92
per cent in 1952, 41.86 per cent in 1957, and 41.50
per cent in 1967 (based on Dawson's and Tung's estimate).

Final Results of the 1967
Potato Estimates

   1.   The 1967 acreage of potatoes is estimated
as 200,870,000 mow, with 27.61 per cent increase
over 1957. (The 1967 Yearbook on Chinese Communism
gives a rough estimate of 200 million mow for "recent years.")

   2.   The 1967 average yield is calculated as
296.99 catties per mow, with an increase of 6.04
per cent over 1957.

   3.   The total potato output for 1967 is estimated as 29,828,950 M.T., with an increase of 36.20
per cent over 1957.

PRODUCTION AND TRADE OF SELECTED CROPS

   Data on the production of and trade in selected
crops in Mainland China are presented and discussed

in this section.* In general, available data on
these crops are scanty; estimates made by other
organizations usually differ considerably and, in
the absence of information on the estimating procedures used, it is difficult to assess the reliability of such estimates. For estimates made by
Asia Science Research Associates (ASRA), the methods
of estimation are also presented. In cases where no
estimates can be made because of the lack of relevant data, the trends in production and trade are
indicated, wherever it is possible to do so, based
on our analysis of other related information.

Soybeans

Generally speaking, soybeans consist of yellow
soybeans, green soybeans, and black soybeans. They
constitute an important element both in the Chinese
diet and in China's foreign trade. Before World
War II, China produced more than two thirds of world
soybean output and dominated the export market. Its
average annual production was 10.36 million M.T. in
the period 1931-37, and the average annual export
was 2.5 million M.T. 1934-37.[10] Because of the
prevalence of unrecorded land in prewar China, and
consequently the probable underestimation of soybean
acreage, it is believed that the prewar estimates of
production are understated.

The main producing areas for soybeans are northeastern China (Manchuria) and the Huang-huai plain
(including Shantung, Kiangsu, Anhwei, and Honan).
Due to its favorable climate and the nature of its
soils, northeastern China is the largest single producing area in the country, accounting for about
one quarter of the total soybean acreage and about
40 per cent of the total national output.[11] Production is heavily concentrated in the Sung-liao plain
(Sungari plain). The Huang-huai plain, on the other
hand, accounts for one third of the national acreage.

---

*Prepared by Asia Science Research Associates.

Production of soybeans declined after the war. In 1949 it totaled only 5.10 million M.T., but jumped to 9.5 million M.T. in 1952, and was further increased to 10.05 million M.T. and 10.50 million M.T. in 1957 and 1958 respectively.[12] In other words, it had regained the reported prewar level. However, in view of the underestimation of prewar output, it appears likely that the actual prewar production level has never been reached in the post-war period. Since the "Great Leap Forward," both acreage and production of soybeans have been drastically reduced. As with other crops, its output declined sharply in the three consecutive years 1959-61. Since 1960, official reports on national soybean production have not been available. Our estimates of production for selected provinces are presented in Table 1 in the Appendix.

The Chinese economy began to recover in 1962 from the setbacks of the "Great Leap Forward." The production of most crops has increased since then. In general, the harvest in 1962 was better than that of 1961. But the production of soybeans had not improved as much as that of other crops. In an effort to suggest improvement, one source reported in late 1962 that despite the unsatisfactory soybean yield in northeastern China, it was still about one third higher than the average yield in other parts of the country.[13] This unsatisfactory state was further confirmed by another report in late 1965 that the yield of soybeans in northeastern China had not increased so rapidly as the yield of other crops in the area.[14] Farmers were treating it as a low-yield crop and were reluctant to increase its acreage. Soybean yield in the Sung-liao plain is reported as 150 catties per mow (equivalent to 1,124 kg/ha).[15] The yield was as high as 1,164 kg/ha even in China proper (twenty-two provinces) for the period 1931-37.[16] Since the yield per hectare outside the Sung-liao plain can be assumed to be three fourths of 1,124 kg, and since the soybean acreage in the Sung-liao plain is about 90 per cent of the total acreage in northeastern China, which constitutes one quarter of the national acreage,

TABLE 1

Soybean Production in Selected Provinces

Province	1963		1964		1965	
	Acreage (ha.)[a]	Estimated Output (1,000 M.T.)	Acreage (ha.)	Estimated Output (1,000 M.T.)	Acreage (ha.)	Estimated Output (1,000 M.T.)
Fukien (843 kg/ha)	33,350 (CNS May 24/63)	28.11	29,348 (CNS Apr. 27/64)	24.74	38,019 (Radio Foochow Aug. 7/65)	32.05
Heilungkiang[b] (1,124 kg/ha)	1,200,600 (NCNA Oct. 5/63)	1,349.47	...		1,300,000 (Radio Peking May 31/65)	1,461.20
Inner Mongolia (843 kg/ha)	104,052 (Radio Huhehot June 27/64)	88.72	142,071 (Radio Huhehot June 27/64)	119.77	...	
Kiangsu (843 kg/ha)	...		409,538 (Radio Nanking June 30/64)	345.24	...	
Shantung (843 kg/ha)	...		1,334,000 (NCNA Aug. 24/64)	1,124.56	...	

[a] Ha. = hectare.

[b] As was mentioned in the text, the yield in northeastern China is higher than that of other areas. Therefore, we use 1,124 kg per ha for Heilungkiang and 843 kg per ha for other areas.

Note: "..." indicates "no data available."
"---" indicates "nil."

256

the national weighted average yield is about 916
kg/ha. This figure is much lower than that of 1931-
37. These two sources combined give the picture
that since 1960 both the acreage and the output of
soybeans have not improved to any significant degree
and have probably been still below the 1957 level.

Two alternative methods are used in estimating
national soybean production since 1960. Our estimates as well as those by the FAO and the USDA are
shown in Table 2 in the Appendix.

Our first approach is to use the ratio of soybean export in 1955-59 to soybean production in
1954-58. In this case, we assume that the export
in a certain year (t) is drawn from the production
of the previous year; therefore, it is the amount
of export in (t+1) that is relevant to estimating
production in year t. The soybean production in
1954-58 amounted to 49.60 million M.T. at an average
of 9.92 million M.T. per year,[17] while the total exports in 1955-59 were 5.10 million M.T. at an average of 1.02 million M.T. annually (FAO Series). The
ratio of soybeans exported to total production in
this period was 10.3 per cent. Because of the lack
of recovery in soybean production indicated above
and the necessary increasing demand inside China,
the same ratio cannot be maintained in the period
after 1960, particularly in 1960-61. On the other
hand, we know exports have continued. It seems
reasonable to assume that the ratio is in the range
of 6-7 per cent for the whole 1960-67 period. More
specifically, we use 6 per cent for 1960-62, 6.5
per cent for 1963, and 7 per cent for 1964-67.

The second method is based on sample data of
exports in 1955-59 and of production in 1954-58.
Since we wish to estimate the quantity of production
corresponding to a given quantity of export, the procedure is to estimate the quantity of production from
a least squares line that fits the sample data. This
line is the regression line of production on exports.
Production is taken as the dependent variable while
export is the independent variable. Although

TABLE 2

Soybean Production, 1957-67
(million M.T.)

	Our Estimates Method 1[1]	Method 2[a]	FAO[2] Estimates	USDA[3] Estimates
1957	10.05[4]	10.05[4]	10.00	
1958	10.50[4]	10.50[4]	10.50	
1959	11.50[5]	11.50[5]	11.50	9.36 (1955-59 average)
1960	5.6	8.58	10.16	...
1961	5.6	8.59	10.36	7.89
1962	5.6	8.57	10.21	7.70
1963	7.6	8.89	10.41	7.07
1964	8.1	9.03	11.18	6.94
1965	8.1[b]	9.03[b]	11.18	6.80
1966	8.1[b]	9.03[b]	...	...
1967	8.1[b]	9.03[b]	...	...

[a]Year	X_t (Soybean Exports) (1,000 M.T.)	Y_{t-1} (Soybean Production)
1954		9.68
1955	920.2	9.12
1956	940.3	10.25
1957	971.7	10.05
1958	928.3	10.50
1959	1,343.2	

$$Y_{t-1} = 7.95 + 0.0019X_t$$

[b]Assumed to be at the 1964 level.

Sources:

1. The export figures are based on FAO series. See also text.

2. For 1957 figure, see FAO, 1958 Production Yearbook (1959), p. 109; 1958-60, FAO, 1961 Production Yearbook (1962), p. 116; 1961-65, FAO, 1966 Production Yearbook (1967), p. 208.

3. USDA, Foreign Agriculture Circular (Oct., 1966), p. 9. Original data are in thousand bushels.

4. Wei-ta ti Shih-nien (Ten Great Years), p. 109.

5. Peking Review, Vol. 43, No. 4 (Peking, Jan. 26, 1960), pp. 9-13.

logically export should be considered to be dependent on production and the demand for the commodity,
we have reversed the relationship here. This seems
to be justifiable on account of the positive correla-
tion between exports and production. The results of
our estimate are very close to those made by the FAO
and the USDA.

In view of the constant ratio of export to output employed in the first method, the results obtained from the second method are probably more reliable. For the years 1965, 1966, and 1967, our
estimated outputs are likely to be minimal esti-
mates--actual outputs are probably higher. The estimates for 1960, 1961, and 1962 by the FAO and the
USDA seem to be much too high because the implied
ratio of export to production would be too low in
view of the known strenuous efforts made to sustain
export at the expense of domestic consumption and
the probable exportation from stock.

Our estimate for production in 1967 was at the
same level as 1964. Although Communist China's reports stated that a considerable increase was registered for soybeans in 1967,[18] there was no percentage
figure given.

Table 3 in the Appendix shows China's soybean
and soybean oil exports in 1956-65. Soybean export
showed an upward trend in 1956-59, with the exception of 1958, and a downward trend since 1960. Export in 1963 was the lowest, but it started to increase slightly from 1964 on. For 1956-59, there
are large discrepancies between the series on exports of soybean oil published by the FAO and that
published by the USDA. It is not known which series
is more accurate.

Other Oil-bearing Crops

According to the crop classification system
adopted in China, the oil-bearing crops (excluding
soybean) consist of peanuts, rapeseed, sesame, seed
of bowstring hemp, linseed, sunflower seed, perilla,
castor bean, and other minor items.[19]

TABLE 3

Soybean and Soybean Oil Exports, 1956-65
(thousand M.T.)

Year	FAO Estimates		USDA Estimates	
	Soybean	Soybean Oil	Soybean	Soybean Oil
1956	970.4	1.08	970.4	51.7
1957	971.7	1.28	972.1	23.6
1958	928.3	4.44	944.0	45.4
1959	1,343.2	0.50	1,279.9	45.4
1960	995.9	24.39	1,011.6	...
1961	335.4	1.02	400.0	0.9
1962	338.9	1.02	361.9	1.0
1963	328.0	2.54	381.0	2.5
1964	494.9	2.50	552.4	2.5
1965	570.3	2.00	598.6	2.5
1966	...	...	...	...
1967	...	...	...	...

Sources:

1. For 1956-59, see FAO, 1961 Trade Yearbook (1962), pp. 196, 236; for 1960-65, see FAO, 1966 Trade Yearbook (1967), pp. 262, 308.

2. 1956-60 data are from Trends and Developments in Communist China's World Trade in Farm Products 1955-60 (Sept., 1962), pp. 28, 30. 1961-65 are from Foreign Agriculture Circular (Oct., 1966), pp. 30-31. Original data for 1961-65 are in thousand bushels for soybean exports and in short tons for soybean oil.

Peanuts

China is second only to India in the production
of peanuts. Chinese peanut production in 1931-37
was at an average of 2.85 million M.T. annually.[20]
The main producing areas are Shantung, Honan, Hopeh,
Kwangtung, Kiangsu, and Liaoning. According to a
Communist Chinese estimate,[21] the percentage distribution of the total acreage used for peanuts among
the several provinces is as follows:

	Per Cent
Shantung	25
Honan	over 10
Hopeh	less than 10
Kwangtung	less than 10
Kiangsu	7-8
Liaoning	6-7
Anhwei	5
Szechwan	5
Fukien	3
Hupeh	2.5
Kiangsi	1.5

This information serves as the basis for estimating
production for several years in the 1960-67 period.
Our estimates of production in 1960-67 and estimates
by the FAO and the USDA are shown in Table 4 in the
Appendix.

For the year 1959, we have used FAO's estimate.
In 1960, large areas of Hopeh, Honan, and Shantung
were hit by drought while the coastal provinces of
Kwangtung and Liaoning were seriously damaged by
typhoon. Therefore, peanut production dropped sharply. Since there is no basis for estimating the extent of the decline, we have used the FAO estimate
of 2.27 million M.T., which is the same as the FAO
estimate for 1959, as a maximum output estimate in
Table 4.

In 1961, there were again drought in the north
and some flooding in the south. In the light of
these circumstances, our judgment is that the 1961

TABLE 4

Peanut Production (in Shell), 1957-67
(million M.T.)

Year	Our Estimates[1]	FAO Estimates[2]	USDA Estimates[3]
1957	2.57[4]	2.63	...
1958	2.80[4]	2.80	...
1959	2.27	2.27	2.78 (1955-59 average)
1960	2.27	2.27	...
1961	1.70	1.70	1.68
1962	1.98	1.63	1.63
1963	2.18	1.90	1.90
1964	2.75	2.29	2.29
1965	2.80	2.30	2.26
1966	2.86	...	...
1967	2.92	...	...

Note: "..." indicates "no data available."
        "---" indicates "nil."

Sources:

1. See text for 1960-67.

2. FAO, 1958 Production Yearbook, 1959, p. 110; FAO, 1961 Production Yearbook, 1962, p. 117; FAO, 1966 Production Yearbook, 1967, p. 211.

3. USDA, Foreign Agriculture Circular, October, 1966, p. 8.

4. Wei-ta ti Shih-nien (Ten Great Years) (Peking, 1959), p. 109.

harvest could not be better than that of 1960.
Since there was a general decline in agricultural
production during this period, we have used the FAO
figure of 1.70 million M.T., which is about 75 per
cent of the 1960 FAO production estimate, as a minimum estimate of output in 1961.

There were no serious natural calamities during the middle and the latter parts of the growing
season in 1962. The harvest can therefore be expected to have been much better than in 1960. Both
the FAO and the USDA estimates, however, show a decline in output from 1961. This figure appears to
be too conservative. In the absence of other information, we have therefore used the average of the
1960 and 1961 figures as the estimated output for
1962.

The harvest in 1963 was reported to be better
than that of 1962. Output in Shantung was claimed
to be 20 to 30 per cent higher,[22] while that in
Anhwei was reported to be 60 per cent above the
1962 level.[23] Fukien, one of the major peanut production areas, was hit by severe drought throughout
the peanut sowing season; however, it was reported
that its 1963 production was still 10 per cent above
that of 1962.[24] We have therefore estimated 1963
output on the basis of a 10 per cent increase over
1962. This result appears to be reasonable when
checked against the following alternative estimate
based on published acreage data.

In 1963, peanut acreage was reported for four
provinces. The figures in hectares are: Shantung,
390,000;[25] Kwangtung, 211,439;[26] Liaoning, 86,710;[27]
and Fukien, 60,000.[28] Since these four provinces
account for approximately 45 per cent of the national
peanut acreage, we could estimate that the total
national acreage of peanuts in 1963 was about 1.66
million hectares [(390,000 + 211,439 + 86,710 +
60,000) ÷ 45%]. Assuming that the yield of peanuts
is about 1,200 kg/ha (FAO estimate was about 1,140
kg/ha for 1961-65), total output would be around
2 million M.T. in 1963.

In 1964, it was officially reported that production was 26 per cent greater than in 1963.[29] Peanut
acreage data were also available for some provinces
for 1964. A check of our estimate was also made on
the basis of this information.

Peanut acreage in hectares in Shantung was reported at 470,000 in 1964;[30] Kwangtung, 220,777;[31]
and Fukien, 56,028.[32] These three provinces account
for about 38 per cent of the total acreage for peanuts. On the assumption of a 1,200 kg/ha yield,
production in 1964 would be 2.36 million M.T. for
the country as a whole.

No reports on national production of peanuts
were available for 1965-66. Except for Shantung
and Kwangtung, there were also no reports on provincial outputs. 1965 production in Shantung was reported to be 11 per cent higher than that of 1964,[33]
while output in Kwangtung was said to be as high as
29 per cent more than 1964.[34] Since in recent years
there has been competition in land utilization between food grains and peanut production, it seems
reasonable to assume that neither peanut acreage
nor its production had reached the 1955-56 level.
Outputs for 1965 and 1966 were estimated by applying
the annual growth rate of 2.1 per cent, which prevailed during 1952 to 1957.

In 1965, Shantung was reported to have 455,900
hectares (less than that reported for 1964) under
cultivation for peanuts.[35] Since this is the only
available report on acreage, and Shantung accounts
for roughly 25 per cent of the national acreage,
total acreage for the country would be 1.87 million
hectares. Production can be estimated as 2.24 million M.T. in 1965 based on our previous yield assumption. This is somewhat less than the 2.80 M.T.
shown in Table 4.

For 1967, a considerable increase in the production of peanuts was reported,[36] but the percentage increase was not given. Therefore we continue to use the 2.1 per cent growth rate in deriv-
ing the 1967 estimate.

China's exports of peanuts and peanut oil are shown in Tables 5 and 6. There was a downward trend in the export of both commodities in 1956-62, which reached an all-time low in 1961-63. The average annual exports of these products for 1956-65 were estimated by the FAO to be 92.4 thousand M.T. of peanuts and 12.4 thousand M.T. of peanut oil.

TABLE 5

Peanut Exports (in Shell), 1956-65
(thousand M.T.)

Year	FAO Estimates[1]	USDA Estimates[2]
1956	376.0	376.0
1957	250.4	250.5
1958	95.2	92.3
1959	71.0	63.0
1960	27.7	24.7
1961	5.1	7.3
1962	5.1	7.3
1963	8.1	11.8
1964	36.0	50.8
1965	49.0	68.0

Sources:

1. For 1956-60, see FAO, 1961 Trade Yearbook (1962), p. 280; for 1961-65, see FAO, 1966 Trade Yearbook (1967), p. 252.

2. For 1956-60, see USDA, Trends and Developments in Communist China's World Trade in Farm Products, 1955-60 (Sept., 1962), p. 30; for 1961-65, see USDA, Foreign Agriculture Circular (Oct., 1966), p. 28; the original figures for 1961-65 are in short tons.

TABLE 6

Peanut Oil Exports, 1956-65
(thousand M.T.)

Year	FAO Estimates[1]	USDA Estimates[2]
1956	11.1	40.8
1957	24.5	23.6
1958	17.5	38.1
1959	17.0	17.5
1960	31.5	...
1961	4.6	4.5
1962	3.1	2.7
1963	2.5	2.7
1964	6.0	6.4
1965	6.0	7.3

Sources:
1. For 1956, see FAO, 1960 Trade Yearbook (1961), p. 74; for 1957-59, see FAO, 1961 Trade Yearbook (1962), p. 240; data for 1960-65 are from FAO, 1966 Trade Yearbook (1967), p. 314.

2. 1956-59 data are from USDA, Trends and Developments in Communist China's World Trade in Farm Products, 1955-60 (Sept., 1962), p. 30; 1961-65 data are from USDA, Foreign Agriculture Circular (1966), p. 28; the original figures are in short tons.

Rapeseed

Rapeseed is one of the major oil-yielding crops in China. Its total output is second only to that of peanuts. The seeds are pressed for edible oil and the residue is used as a high-grade fertilizer.

Rapeseed is grown in most parts of China except the northeastern provinces. The leading producing area is Szechwan. Classified by the seasons in which the seed is planted, there are autumn rapeseed and spring rapeseed. The provinces in which autumn rapeseed is grown are Szechwan, Hunan, Hupeh, Kiangsi, Anhwei, Chekiang, Fukien, Kwangtung, Kwangsi, Kweichow, Yünnan, and Shensi. The acreage of autumn rapeseed accounts for more than 90 per cent of the total acreage under rapeseed. Inner Mongolia, Sinkiang, Kansu, Tsinghai, Shansi, and Hopeh, on the other hand, are spring rapeseed areas; acreage there is roughly 7 per cent of the total.[37]

In 1931-37, the output of rapeseed produced in China proper (twenty-two provinces) was 2.47 million M.T. per year.[38] After the war, the highest production attained was 3.48 million M.T. in 1947.[39] However, according to official statistics, production dropped after 1949 to a level much less than that of the pre-Communist period.[40]

Our estimates of rapeseed production as well as those by the FAO and the USDA are shown in Table 7.

Agricultural production as a whole was at the lowest level in 1960-61. Since there is no information on which to make an independent estimate, we have used the FAO estimate of 1.00 million M.T. and .85 million M.T. for 1960 and 1961.

In 1962, the harvest was in general better than 1961. But the production of oil-bearing crops did not improve to the same extent. The FAO estimate for that year is also used in Table 7.

TABLE 7

Rapeseed Production, 1957-67
(million M.T.)

Year	Our Estimates[1]	FAO Estimates[2]	USDA Estimates[3]
1957	0.89[4]	...	
1958	1.10[4]	1.10	
1959	1.10	1.10	0.96 (1955-59 average)
1960	1.00[5]	1.00	...
1961	0.85[5]	0.85	0.59
1962	0.96[5]	0.96	0.52
1963	1.01	1.04	0.57
1964	1.74	1.12	0.66
1965	1.91	1.12	0.70
1966	1.91	...	...
1967	2.10	...	...

Sources:
1. See text.

2. For 1958-60, see FAO, 1961 Production Yearbook (1962), p. 123; for 1961-65, see FAO, 1966 Production Yearbook (1967), p. 225.

3. USDA, Foreign Agriculture Circular (Oct., 1966), p. 11; the original figures are in short tons.

4. Wei-ta ti Shih-nien (Ten Great Years), p. 109.

5. FAO estimate.

The total acreage of rapeseed in 1963 was claimed to be 10 per cent greater than that of 1962, but the harvest did not increase proportionally.[41] Drought was reported in some parts of southern and southwestern China after the seeds were sown in the autumn, while the Yangtze River basin had too much rain in the spring.[42] In addition, parts of Yünnan and Chekiang were also affected at first by drought and then by too much rainfall. On the other hand, reports from Szechwan, Hunan, and Kweichow indicated better harvest than in 1962.[43] Output in Szechwan was said to have increased 10 per cent over 1962; the increase in Hunan and Kweichow was, however, small. It appears then that 10 per cent will be the upper limit to the increase in production. The actual increase is probably less. In Table 7, the production of 1963 was estimated to be 5 per cent higher than that of 1962.

1964 was a bumper year for rapeseed according to Communist Chinese reports. The acreage of rape-seed was said to have increased by 10 per cent over 1963, while production was said to be 72 per cent above the previous year.[44] The increase in produc-tion would appear to have been exaggerated. How-ever, it is still below the prewar figure and is used in our estimate of 1964 output in Table 7.

For 1965, the rapeseed harvest in the Yangtze River basin was reported to be better than that of 1964.[45] The same source reported a 20 per cent in-crease in rapeseed production in Szechwan, a 10 per cent increase in Kweichow, and a 10 to 15 per cent increase in Yünnan. Increased output was also claimed for Kiangsu and Hupeh.[46] It appears that a 10 per cent increase in national output would be a reasonable approximation. This assumption is used in Table 7 for estimating 1965 production.

No official report for 1966 was released. To be conservative, we have assumed in Table 7 that there was no increase over 1965.

In 1967, increased output ranging from 10 to 20 per cent above the 1966 level was reported in

Hupeh, Kiangsi, Szechwan, and Hunan.[47] Total output
for the whole country was claimed to be 10 per cent
higher than that of 1966.[48] The estimate of 1967
output was based on this reported percentage increase.

China's exports of rapeseed and rapeseed oil
are shown in Table 8. The export of these commodities reached a peak in 1960, then dropped sharply
in 1961 and remained at a low level until 1964. Exports of both rapeseed and rapeseed oil began to increase in 1965. The reason for the considerable decline in 1960-64 exports must be due to the reduced
production as well as keen competition from other
exporting countries (e.g., Canada, France, and Sweden).

TABLE 8

Rapeseed and Rapeseed Oil Exports, 1956-65
(thousand M.T.)

Year	FAO[1] Rapeseed	FAO[1] Rapeseed Oil	USDA[2] Rapeseed	USDA[2] Rapeseed Oil
1956			9.2	2.0
1957	13.4	2.1	1.5	---
1958	6.5	4.4	3.8	3.5
1959	20.4	18.0	---	---
1960	27.3	16.5	...	...
1961	0.8	1.9	0.8	1.9
1962	0.9	0.03	---	---
1963	0.2	---	---	---
1964	---	---	---	---
1965	5.8	3.8	---	---

Note: "..." indicates "no data available."
         "---" indicates "nil."

Sources:
    1. Data for 1957-59 are from FAO, 1961 Trade
Yearbook (1962), pp. 204, 251; those for 1960-65 are
from FAO, 1966 Trade Yearbook (1967), pp. 270, 322.
FAO's figures include mustard seed and oil.

    2. 1956-59 data are from USDA, Trends and De-
velopments in Communist China's World Trade in Farm
Products, 1955-60 (Sept., 1962), p. 30; for 1960-65,
see USDA, Foreign Agriculture Circular (Oct., 1966),
p. 34. The original figures for 1960-65 are in
short tons.

Sesame

China is the second largest sesame-seed producing country in the world. Sesame oil is an important edible oil in China.

The major producing provinces are Honan, Hopeh, Shantung, Kiangsu, and Hupeh. In 1931-37, the annual average output of sesame was 851,000 M.T. in China proper.[49] It increased to 867,000 M.T. and 776,000 M.T. respectively in 1946 and 1947.[50] No Communist report on sesame production has been available since 1949. Output was estimated to be 520,000 M.T. in 1952, 320,000 M.T. in 1956, 330,000 M.T. in 1957, and 280,000 M.T. in 1958.[51]

A Taiwan source estimates output in 1960 to be as high as 900,000 M.T.[52] However, estimates by both the FAO and the USDA are much lower. FAO's estimate is about 349,000 M.T. annually in 1961-65, while that by the USDA is about 290,000 M.T. in the same period. The Far Eastern Economic Review puts the output for 1963 and 1964 at 240,000 and 310,000 M.T. respectively.[53]

Table 9 shows estimated sesame production by the FAO and the USDA.

TABLE 9

Sesame Seed Production, 1961-65
(thousand M.T.)

	FAO Estimates[1]	USDA Estimates[2]
1961	325	308
1962	340	299
1963	340	299
1964	370	272
1965	370	272

Sources:
1. FAO, 1966 Production Yearbook (1967), p. 227.

2. USDA, Foreign Agriculture Circular (Oct., 1966), p. 12.

In addition to domestic consumption, China also exports sesame to other countries. Table 10 shows estimates of sesame seed exports by the FAO and the USDA. These two estimates, however, differ considerably.

TABLE 10

Sesame Seed Exports, 1956-65
(thousand M.T.)

	FAO Estimates[1]	USDA Estimates[2]
1956	13.1	8.3
1957	4.5	3.6
1958	11.1	5.4
1959	10.3	5.4
1960	9.0	9.0
1961	2.2	2.2
1962	0.9	2.0
1963	1.6	2.0
1964	0.6	...
1965	8.2	...

Sources:
    1. For 1956-59, see FAO, 1961 Trade Yearbook (1962), pp. 205, 282; for 1960-65, see FAO, 1966 Trade Yearbook (1967), p. 272.

    2. For 1956-59, see USDA, Trends and Developments in Communist China's World Trade in Farm Products, 1955-60 (Sept., 1962), p. 30; for 1960-65, see USDA, Foreign Agriculture Circular (Oct., 1966), p. 36.

According to the FAO series, China's sesame production in 1957-58 averaged about 305,000 M.T. while its average export was 7,800 M.T. in the same period. The percentage of exports to production in 1957-58 was, therefore, 7.8 per cent. Using this percentage, we estimate that corresponding to

an export of 8,200 M.T. in 1965, sesame production
was about 320,000 M.T.

Castor Bean

Castor bean is mainly a tropical and subtropical plant. However, in China it is also grown in
northern China and northeastern China. Its oil has
multiple usages. It can be used as a raw material
in medicine and the chemical industry and as a
lubrication agent.

The prewar output of castor bean was 25,000 to
30,000 M.T. in northeastern China.[54] There were no
output estimates for other areas.

According to FAO's estimates, the yearly production of castor bean was 40,000 M.T. in the
1952-56 period and about 35,000 M.T. in 1961-62.[55]

Table 11 shows the export of castor bean and
castor oil. As can be seen from the table, the FAO
and the USDA estimates are quite different, especially for 1957-58. The FAO estimate of exports was at
an average of 11,300 M.T. annually in 1956-65, while
the USDA estimate was at 13,200 M.T. yearly for
1956-59 and 1961-65.

No other information is readily available.

Tea Seed Oil

Tea seed oil is used as an edible oil or as a
raw material for industrial products (e.g., lubri-
cating oil, rust inhibiting oil, ignition oil).
The residue from the processing of tea seed oil can
be used as a fertilizer or detergent.

The prewar estimated output was about 25,000
M.T. in 1937.[56] The annual export in 1935-39 was
6,100 M.T.[57] No national production figure was
available for the years immediately following World
War II.

TABLE 11

Castor Bean and Castor Bean Oil
Exports, 1956-65
(thousand M.T.)

| | FAO Estimates[1] | | USDA Estimates[2] | |
	Castor Beans	Castor Oil	Castor Beans	Castor Oil
1956	34.9	1	22.7	...
1957	8.7	---	24.0	...
1958	8.3	0.5	22.6	...
1959	11.2	---	19.3	...
1960	16.0	0.4	...	...
1961	1.1	0.1	0.9	...
1962	1.9	0.05	1.8	...
1963	5.3	0.3	9.1	...
1964	10.7	0.03	9.1	...
1965	14.6	0.1	9.1	...

Note: "---" indicates "nil."
        "..." indicates "no data available."

Sources:
    1. For 1956-59, see FAO, 1961 Trade Yearbook
(1962), pp. 281, 286; for 1960-65, see FAO, 1966
Trade Yearbook (1967), pp. 268, 335.

    2. For 1956-59, see USDA, Trends and Developments in Communist China's World Trade in Farm
Products, 1955-60 (Sept., 1962), p. 30; for 1960-
65, see USDA, Foreign Agriculture Circular (Oct.,
1966), p. 45.

The major producing provinces of tea seed oil are Hunan, Kiangsi, and Kwangsi. These three provinces account for 60-70 per cent of the total output,[58] with the remaining 30 to 40 per cent produced in Fukien, Kweichow, Yünnan, Szechwan, Hupeh, Anhwei, Chekiang, and Kwangtung.[59] Hunan alone accounts for one half of the national output.[60] Its production was 35,000 M.T. before 1949.[61]

A Japanese source placed the 1958 output at about 100,000 M.T. According to a Chinese Communist source, Hunan produced about 47,000 M.T. of tea seed oil in 1957.[62] Since Hunan's output is about one half the total output, the national output could be estimated at 94,000 M.T. in 1957. Thus the Japanese estimate would seem to be quite plausible.

No official or Western reports on tea seed oil production after 1958 were available. Since agricultural production in recent years has generally been higher than the 1957-58 level, it seems reasonable to assume that output of tea seed oil for the same period has also risen above 100,000 M.T.

Sunflower Seed

According to FAO's estimates, the annual output of sunflower seed in recent years is about 66,000 M.T. Table 12 shows its estimated production in 1961-65.

TABLE 12

Sunflower Seed Production, 1961-65
(thousand M.T.)

1961	61
1962	66
1963	66
1964	66
1965	66

Source: FAO, 1966 Production Yearbook (1967), p. 231.

In addition to domestic use, China also exports
sunflower seed and sunflower seed oil to other countries. Table 13 shows China's sunflower seed and
sunflower seed oil exports. There is again a large
discrepancy between the FAO series and the USDA series. The reason for this difference is not known.
According to the FAO series, sunflower seed exports
show a downward trend since 1961.

TABLE 13

Sunflower Seed and Sunflower Seed Oil
Exports, 1956-65 (thousand M.T.)

	Sunflower Seed		Sunflower Seed Oil	
	FAO Estimates[1]	USDA Estimates[2]	FAO Estimates[1]	USDA Estimates
1956	33.0	21.7	---	...
1957	18.2	5.3	---	...
1958	16.7	5.5	0.2	...
1959	21.9	4.3	2.4	...
1960	11.7	...	0.3	...
1961	3.1	3.1	---	...
1962	5.8	3.1	---	...
1963	2.9	3.2	---	...
1964	1.3	...	---	...
1965	4.6	...	---	...

Sources:
    1. For 1956-59 figures, see FAO, 1961 Trade
Yearbook (1962), pp. 252, 282; for 1960-65, see
FAO, 1966 Trade Yearbook (1967), pp. 274, 320.

    2. USDA, Trends and Developments in Communist
China's World Trade in Farm Products, 1955-60 (Sept.,
1962), p. 30.

    No official reports were available for the
production of either sunflower seed or sunflower
seed oil.

Perilla

Perilla is harvested once a year. The leading
producing area is northeastern China. For 1934-37,
annual output of perilla in the northeast was 128,000
M.T.[63] It is reported that output has declined sharply since World War II.[64] According to an estimate
made by the Northeastern Economic Commission at
Mukden in 1944, total output in northeastern China
was about 38,090 M.T.[65] No other reports on production were available either for the period before
1949 or that after the establishment of the Communist
regime.

Tung Oil

Tung oil is an important raw material for the
manufacture of paints and varnishes and a large number of other industrial products. Its by-products
(including the leaves and the pressed residue) are
used as fertilizer because of their high nitrogen
and phosphorus contents. Before the Sino-Japanese
War, China was the sole supplier of tung oil in the
world market. In the period 1935 to 1937, it was
the most important agricultural export of China.
The average annual export was 83,000 M.T., valued
at U.S. $25 million.[66]

No official production data were available before the war. Production was, however, estimated
on the basis of the quantity exported. Of the total
production of tung oil, about 30 to 40 per cent was
estimated to be used domestically; the balance was
exported.[67] The Central Planning Board of the
Chinese Nationalist Government estimated that pre-
World War II production was around 159,700 M.T. per
year. Estimates made by the Agricultural Attaché
of the American Consulate General in Shanghai placed
the annual output at 120,000 M.T. for 1931-37, of
which 83,000 M.T. were for export and 37,000 M.T.
were for domestic use.[68]

Since World War II, China's production of tung
oil has fallen. But there were no estimated

TABLE 14

Tung Oil Exports in 1956-65 (in metric tons)

Year	FAO[1]	USDA[2]
1956	45,886	45,240
1957	46,089	46,086
1958	48,416	47,938
1959	37,841	37,833
1960	32,191	31,031
1961	15,565	15,420
1962	16,481	16,082
1963	12,375	12,149
1964	17,125	16,275
1965	18,884	17,875

Sources:

1. For 1956-59, see FAO, 1961 Trade Yearbook (1962), p. 286; data for 1960-65 are from FAO, 1966 Trade Yearbook (1967), p. 338.

2. 1956-60 data are from USDA, Trends and Developments in Communist China's World Trade in Farm Products, 1955-60 (Sept., 1962), p. 31; those for 1961-65 are from USDA, Foreign Agriculture Circular (Oct., 1966), p. 47. The original figures are in short tons.

production figures. For the period after 1949, output data are also not available. One Japanese source estimated output per year to be as high as 180,000 to 200,000 M.T.[69] Another Japanese source estimated production in recent years at 140,000 to 150,000 M.T.[70] Estimates by the FAO are much lower. For 1961-65, the FAO estimate of annual output was less than 75,000 M.T.[71] The USDA also estimated annual production for 1961-65 at less than 75,000 M.T.[72] According to Communist Chinese sources, the planting of tung trees was doubled between 1949 and 1963.[73] However, it is not likely that production could increase in the same proportion. Our judgment is that the Japanese estimates are probably too high; they are more probably estimates of potential production capacity rather than annual output. Our estimate is that annual output of tung oil is about 100,000 to 120,000 M.T.

TABLE 15

Major Countries Exporting Tung Oil

Year	China	Argen-tina	Para-guay	U.S.	Rhodesia	Total of Four Countries	World Total
1960	45.7	27.5	4.7	14.1	1.4	47.7	100.0
1961	29.7	31.2	8.7	17.1	2.2	59.2	100.0
1962	35.2	35.1	11.1	8.3	2.7	57.2	100.0
1963	30.6	39.6	11.0	0.7	3.1	54.4	100.0
1964	36.5	39.8	12.5	0.9	---	53.2	100.0
1965	46.2	28.5	11.1	0.8	---	40.4	100.0

Source: Derived from FAO, 1966 Trade Yearbook (1967),
          p. 338.

China's exports of tung oil in metric tons for the 1956-65 period are shown in Table 14. In the last decade, the physical volume of its export has shown a downward trend and reached an all-time low in 1963. In 1964-65 there was a slight increase. The average quantity of export per year for 1956-65 was 29,085 M.T.,[74] while the average value of the annual exports for the same period was about U.S. $9,129,000.[75] The decline of China's exports is due to the increase in tung oil production and export by several major producing countries, including the United States, Argentina, Paraguay, and Rhodesia. The relative share of each of these major exporting countries in total world tung oil exports for 1960-65 is shown in Table 15.

Flue-cured Tobacco

The leading producing provinces of flue-cured tobacco are Anhwei, Honan, and Shantung. Yünnan and Kweichow also produce some flue-cured tobacco. In 1937 production was 87,606 M.T. for China proper,[76] but declined after the war to 43,000 M.T. in 1949.[77] However, China's output increased greatly to 221,500 M.T. in 1952, 256,000 M.T. in 1957, and 380,000 M.T. in 1958.[78]

It was reported that 1959 production increased by 11 per cent over that of the previous year, i.e., 421,800 M.T.[79]

For 1960-63, no official report for national production was available. The only provincial figures for this period were: For 1963, output in Yünnan was 20 per cent above that of 1962;[80] production in Kwangtung for 1963 increased by 35.8 over that for 1962;[81] and Kiangsi was reported to have a bigger harvest in 1963 than the previous year.[82]

In 1964, one report claimed that national output of flue-cured tobacco was 28 per cent higher than that of 1963.[83] At the First Session of the Third National People's Congress held December 21-22, 1964, Chou En-lai reported that flue-cured tobacco

production in 1964 exceeded the 1957 level. Therefore, 1964 production was at least around 256,000
M.T. In the same year, output in Honan was reported
to have increased substantially over that of 1963.[84]

Tobacco production in 1965 was said to have surpassed its historical peak of 421,800 M.T. in 1959.[85]
For the provinces, output in Hupeh increased 30 to
50 per cent over that of 1964, while Kweichow was
reported to have a large increase in production over
the previous year.[86]

1966 was reported to be a bumper year for flue-
cured tobacco, and output was above that of 1965.[87]

Our estimates of flue-cured tobacco production
in 1963-67 are presented in Table 16.

TABLE 16

Estimated Production of Flue-cured
Tobacco, 1963-67

1963	200,000 M.T.[1]
1964	256,000 M.T.[2]
1965	421,800 M.T.[2]
1966	434,032 M.T.[3]
1967	446,619 M.T.[3]

Notes:
1. Derived from 1964 report that production
in 1964 was 28 per cent above 1963.

2. Production in 1957 and 1959 used as estimates of minimal production for 1964 and 1965 respectively.

3. 1966 and 1967 outputs are estimated on the
basis of the 1952-57 annual growth rate of 2.9 per
cent.

Table 17 shows China's tobacco exports and imports in 1956-64. Average export was 27,700 M.T. annually in 1956-64, while average import was 5,100 M.T. in the same period, with net export at 22,600 M.T. Net export reached its peak in 1957. After 1958, the amount of net exports fluctuates greatly from year to year.

TABLE 17

Tobacco (Unmanufactured) Exports and
Imports, 1956-65
(thousand M.T.)

	Exports	Imports	Net Exports
1956	45.4	14.9	30.5
1957	53.8	4.5	49.3
1958	50.6	17.8	32.8
1959	43.5	---	43.5
1960	23.3	1.5	21.8
1961	10.3	---	10.3
1962	3.8	---	3.8
1963	14.1	3.3	10.8
1964	4.5	3.6	0.9
1965	...	...	...

Note: "---" indicates "nil."
        "..." indicates "no data available."

Sources: For 1956-60, see FAO, 1961 Trade Yearbook
           (1962), pp. 187, 280; for 1961-65, see
           FAO, 1966 Trade Yearbook (1967), pp. 246,
           248.

Sugar Refining Industry

Sugar is not only an important supplementary
foodstuff but also a raw material for the food
processing, pharmaceutical, and certain organic
chemical industries. Its by-products also have
valuable uses. (For example, it is claimed that one
ton of sugar cane refuse could yield 250 kilograms
of paper or 15 kilograms of synthetic fiber or one
cubic-meter of synthetic timber; the stalks, leaves,
and green roots could be used as feed.)[88]

Cane sugar's production average in 1947-48 was
362,800 M.T.[89] Its import in 1931-37 averaged
246,000 M.T.[90] Immediately after the establishment
of the Communist regime, annual production of sugar
dropped to 199,000 tons.[91] It was not until 1952
that production began to rise and exceed the 1947-48
level. Since 1952, production has increased greatly.
It reached 900,000 M.T. in 1958 and 1,130,000 M.T.
in 1959.[92] Parallel to the decline in sugar cane
and sugar beets production since 1960, sugar production also decreased drastically but began to increase in 1963. In 1952, the ratio of sugar production to that of sugar crops was 5.9 per cent; it
was increased to 7.2 per cent in 1957, but fell to
5.5 per cent in 1967. Communist sources have revealed that the average ratio of sugar production
to sugar crops production is about 7 per cent.[93]
Our estimates of sugar production from 1960 to 1967
in Table 18 are based on our estimated sugar cane
(Sugar Cane section in Appendix Table 21, series I)
and sugar beets (Sugar Beets section, Table 24)
production by applying the conversion ratio of 7
per cent.

China's sugar refining season normally extends
from November to May.[94] Kwangtung is the leading
sugar producing province in China, with an output
amounting to more than two thirds of the cane sugar
produced in the country[95] and 60 per cent of the
total sugar production in China. Heilungkiang,
utilizing its sugar beets crop, is the second major
sugar producing province in China; it accounts for
13.2 per cent of the total output of sugar.[96]

China's sugar production is insufficient for domestic consumption and must therefore depend on imports to meet the deficiency. The production and consumption of sugar in 1949, 1952, and 1957 are shown below.[97]

	1949	1952	1957
Consumption	190,000 tons	516,000 tons	958,000 tons
Production	199,000 tons	451,000 tons	864,000 tons

TABLE 18

Sugar Production,[1] 1952-67
(thousand M.T.)

	Our Estimates[2]	Taiwan's Estimates[3]
1952	451	451
1953	638	638
1954	693	693
1955	717	717
1956	807	807
1957	864	864
1958	900	900
1959	1,130	1,130
1960	965	900
1961	697	800
1962	740	900
1963	839	950
1964	1,173	1,130
1965	1,245	1,360
1966	1,348	1,200
1967	1,549	

Sources:

1.   1952-58 figures are from Wei-ta ti Shih-nien (Ten Great Years, Peking, 1959), p. 89.

2.   1960-67 figures are calculated at 7 per cent of sugar cane plus sugar beets production for each year.

3.   1960-66 data are from Fei-ching Yueh-pao (Studies on Chinese Communism), Vol. 1, No. 9 (Taipei, Sept., 1967), pp. 96-109.

A Communist source revealed that during this
period about 100,000 tons of sugar were imported
annually to supplement the inadequate domestic supply.[98] It was also reported that in 1957 annual
consumption of sugar was at only 1.5 kilograms per
person.[99]

Although China imports sugar from other countries, it also exports sugar to Ceylon, Hong Kong,
Malaysia, etc. China's exports and imports of sugar
are shown in Table 19 and her imports from Cuba are
presented in Table 20. Since the total imports for
1964 and 1965 shown in Table 19 are less than the
imports from Cuba in these years, it is probable
that the FAO series does not include imports from
Cuba for 1963-65.

TABLE 19

Sugar Exports and Imports, 1956-67
(thousand M.T.)

	Exports	Imports	Net Imports
1956	0.8	105.9	105.1
1957	5.7	68.1	62.4
1958	114.3	221.4	107.1
1959	37.0	5.1	-32.8
1960	15.6	476.5	460.9
1961	126.8	1,534.4	1,407.6
1962	273.9	937.9	664.0
1963	207.8	511.4	303.6
1964	344.5	403.7	59.2
1965	362.3	398.2	35.9

Sources: For 1956-59, see FAO, 1961 Trade Yearbook
           (1962), p. 278; for 1960-65, see FAO, 1966
           Trade Yearbook (1967), pp. 175, 177.

TABLE 20

Sugar Imports from Cuba, 1961-66 (M.T.)

1961	1,000,000[1]
	(Agreement signed by China, Feb. 2, 1961. Probably delivered in 1961-62)
1962	...
1963	500,000[2]
1964	500,000[2]
1965	800,000[2]
1966	600,000[2]

Sources:

1. China Trade & Economic Newsletter (London, Feb., 1961), p. 5.

2. China Trade Report (Hong Kong, Jan., 1966), pp. 7-8.

In 1965, China's sugar production was estimated to be 1,245,000 M.T., while its net imports were 835,900 M.T. (net imports in Table 19 plus imports from Cuba). Therefore, total domestic consumption was about 2,081,000 M.T. Population in the year was estimated to be 728 million.[100] Therefore, per capita sugar consumption in 1965 was 2.86 kg. per year. This figure is much lower than the 10.03 kg annual per capita sugar consumption in Taiwan for the same year.[101] For comparison, we might mention that the per capita consumption in the United States in 1965 was 44 kg ,[102] while the per capita consumption in Japan for the same year was 25.7 kg.

Sugar Cane

Sugar cane and sugar beets are the two principal raw materials for China's sugar refining industry; of the two, sugar cane is by far the more important. The major producing provinces of sugar
cane are Kwangtung, Kwangsi, Szechwan, Fukien,
Yünnan, and Chekiang. Kwangtung alone accounts for
one half of the total sugar cane acreaage in China.[103]

Before 1949 the highest annual output of sugar
cane was 5.65 million M.T. in 1940, but production
declined sharply after that year.[104] Under the Communist regime, a concentrated effort was made to increase the acreage of both sugar cane and sugar
beets in order to develop the sugar industry. The
acreage of sugar cane was increased from 108.25
thousand hectares in 1949 to 182.6 thousand in 1952
and 266.73 thousand in 1957.[105] As a result, output
increased from 2.64 million M.T. in 1949 to 7.12
million M.T. in 1952, 10.39 million M.T. in 1957,
and 13.53 million M.T. in 1958,[106] an increase of
412.5 per cent between 1949 and 1958. The average
yield also rose from 24.4 M.T. per hectare in 1949
to 39.0 M.T. per hectare in 1952. Between 1952 and
1957 yield remained fairly constant.

Our estimates of sugar cane production as well
as those of the FAO are shown in Table 21.

The acreage for sugar cane production has been
reduced substantially since the "Great Leap." For
1961, acreage was reported as only 200,000 hectares,
or 21 per cent below that of 1957.[107] If yield per
hectare had not changed from the 1952-57 level (i.e.,
39 M.T. per hectare), production in 1961 would be
only 7.8 million M.T. This is used as our estimate
in Table 21.

The average growth rate of sugar cane output
was 7.8 per cent per annum for the 1952-57 period.
The estimated output for 1962 and 1963 was calculated on the basis of this growth rate. Alterna-
tively, the average annual growth rate of 39.2 per

TABLE 21

Sugar Cane Production, 1957-67
(million M.T.)

	Our Estimates[a]		FAO Estimates[1]
	I	II[b]	
1957	10.39[2]		10.21
1958	13.53[2]		13.53
1959	13.93[3]		13.93
1960	10.87[c]		...
1961	7.80		14.00[d]
1962	8.41	5.67	15.00[d]
1963	9.07	8.43	20.00[d]
1964	13.33	12.49	22.00[d]
1965	14.37	16.02	23.00[d]
1966	15.49	18.37	...
1967	17.81		...

[a]See text.

[b]See text and Table 19.

[c]Average of 1959 and 1961.

[d]From March of the year to February of the
following year.

Sources:
1. The figure for 1957 is from FAO, 1958 Production Yearbook, p. 66; data for 1958 and 1959 are
from FAO, 1961 Production Yearbook, p. 69; for 1961-
65, see FAO, 1966 Production Yearbook, p. 86.

2. Wei-ta ti Shih-nien (Ten Great Years,
Peking, 1959), p. 109.

3. Chung-kuo Hsin-wen (China News Service,
Jan. 24, 1960).

cent in 1949-52, which is much higher than that in
1952-57, could be used. Our judgment is that the
recovery in agriculture production in 1962-63 does
not seem to justify the use of the 1949-52 rate.

The estimated production for 1964 is computed
on the basis of a reported 47 per cent increase in
output over 1963.[108] For 1965 and 1966, the growth
rate of 7.8 per cent is used in calculating estimated production. Production in 1967 was reported
to be 15 per cent more than that of 1966.[109] The
reported increase is used in estimating output for
1967.

An alternative series of estimated production
is shown in Table 22 based on reported acreage and
production in Kwangtung. As mentioned above, Kwangtung is the largest sugar cane producing province.
Its acreage of sugar cane is one half of the national
total, and its sugar cane production accounts for 60
per cent of the national output. In 1957, acreage
and production in Kwangtung were 117,446 hectares
and 5 million M.T. (48.1 per cent of the national
total) respectively.[110] The yield in 1957 was 42.6
M.T. per hectare, a little higher than the national
average in 1952-57. The trend of production and
acreage planted in Kwangtung followed the national
pattern. Acreage declined sharply after 1960 and
did not return to the 1957 level until 1964.

A comparison of our estimates and the FAO production estimates indicates that the FAO series is
far too high, probably a result of not noting the
decline in acreage in 1960-61. Besides Kwangtung,
Szechwan and Fukien are also important sugar cane
producing areas. The reported acreage for certain
years and estimated production for these two provinces are shown in Table 23.

TABLE 22

Alternative Estimates of Sugar Cane Production

	Acreage (ha.)			Production (million M.T.)		
	Kwangtung	Estimated Other Areas[a] (excluding Kwangtung)	Estimated National	Kwangtung	Estimated Other Areas[b] (excluding Kwangtung)	Estimated National
1962	69,368[1]	69,368	138,736	2.96[c]	2.71	5.67
1963	76,038[2]	76,038	152,076	5.46[3]	2.97	8.43
1964	142,017[4]	142,017	284,034	6.95[5]	5.54	12.49
1965	180,757[6]	180,757	361,514	8.97[7]	7.05	16.02
1966	189,795[8]	189,795	379,590	10.97[9]	7.40	18.37

[a]Kwangtung accounts for half of the total acreage.
[b]The yield is assumed to be 39 M.T./ha--the national average yield in 1952-57.
[c]The yield is assumed to be 42.6 M.T./ha--the 1957 Kwangtung yield.

Sources:

1. Yang-ch'eng Wan-pao (Canton, Oct. 3, 1963).
2. Ibid.
3. Chung-kuo Hsin-wen (China News Service, Sept. 18, 1964) and Economic Geography of South China (1959).
4. CNS (Jan. 14, 1965).
5. Ta-kung Pao (Hong Kong, Jan. 20, 1965).
6. NCNA (Aug. 23, 1965).
7. Nan-fang Jih-pao (Canton, Dec. 21, 1965).
8. Wen-hui Pao (Hong Kong, April 23, 1966).
9. Nan-fang Jih-pao (Canton, Dec. 21, 1965).

TABLE 23

Estimated Production of Sugar Cane
in Fukien and Szechwan

	Acreage (ha.)		Production (million M.T.)	
	Fukien	Szechwan	Fukien[a]	Szechwan[1]
1957	$24,812^2$	$41,354^3$	0.97	1.72^4
1960	$29,348^5$	...	1.14	...
1963	$13,340^6$	$12,740^7$	0.52	0.53
1964	$20,010^8$	$26,000^9$	0.78	1.08
1965	...	$32,500^{10}$	...	1.35

[a]Assume the yield was 39 M.T./ha--the national average yield in 1952-57.

Sources:

1. Estimates based on the 1957 Szechwan yield of 41.6 M.T./ha.

2. Economic Geography of South China (1959).

3. Economic Geography of Southwestern China (1960).

4. Ibid.

5. People's Daily (May 19, 1959).

6. China News Service (May 24, 1963).

7. Radio Chengtu, April 17, 1964: It was reported that the acreage was 51 per cent less than 1964.

8. China News Service (Aug. 19, 1964).

9. NCNA (Dec. 16, 1964).

10. Radio Chengtu (Sept. 19, 1965)--25 per cent over 1964 acreage.

Sugar Beets

The main producing areas of sugar beets are northeastern China (Manchuria), North China, and northwestern China. Heilungkiang, Kirin, and Inner Mongolia are the leading producing provinces.

Before the Communist regime, the highest annual output was 0.33 million M.T. in 1939.[111] In 1949 output fell to 0.19 million M.T. with a total acreage of 15,941 hectares.[112] Both acreage and output increased substantially after 1949. Total acreage increased from 35,084 hectares in 1952 to 159,413 hectares in 1957, while production increased from 478,525 M.T. to 1.5 million M.T. in the same period.[113] Despite the increase in acreage and production, however, its yield in 1957 was below that of 1949 and 1952. The yield in 1949 was 11.9 M.T. per hectare, 13.6 M.T. in 1952, but only 9.4 M.T. in 1957.

Prior to 1959, Heilungkiang, Kirin, and Inner Mongolia accounted for 99.49 per cent of the national acreage of sugar beets and 99.47 per cent of its total production.[114] In 1961, the total sown acreage in five provinces--Heilungkiang, Inner Mongolia, Kirin, Sinkiang, and Shansi--was said to be more than 180,000 hectares.[115] This figure should be very close to the national acreage in that year. Assuming that the yield per hectare is 12 M.T. (the mean yield of 1949, 1952, and 1957), the output in 1961 would be 2.16 M.T.[116] This is shown in Table 24.

No reports on acreage and production were available for 1962 and 1963. In Table 24, 1962 output is assumed to be the same as that in 1961. The production figure for 1963 is the FAO's estimate. For 1964, the China Monthly of Hong Kong reported an increase of 17 per cent over 1963; the FAO series also reflects an increase of 17 per cent.[117] Therefore we have also used the 17 per cent increase in calculating 1964 output.

TABLE 24

Sugar Beets Production, 1957-67
(million M.T.)

	Our Estimates[a]	FAO Estimates[1]
1957	1.50[2]	1.84
1958	2.90[2]	3.68[b]
1959	3.68[3]	...
1960	2.92[b]	...
1961	2.16	2.50[b]
1962	2.16	2.92[b]
1963	2.92	3.50[b]
1964	3.42	3.83[b]
1965	3.42	4.00[b]
1966	3.76	...
1967	4.32	...

[a]See text.

[b]Average of 1959 and 1961. From March of the year to February of the following year.

Sources:

1. For 1957, see FAO, 1967 Production Yearbook, Vol. 12 (1958), p. 68; for 1958, see FAO, 1960 Production Yearbook, Vol. 15 (1961), p. 70. Data for 1961-65 are from FAO, 1965 Production Yearbook, Vol. 20 (1966), p. 91.

2. Ten Great Years (Peking, 1959), p. 109.

3. Tsu Kuo (China Weekly, Hong Kong, March, 1960), p. 13.

In 1965, Inner Mongolia was affected by drought, and output of sugar beets was said to be equal to that of 1964. The total output in Heilungkiang and Kirin was reported to be better than that of 1964. However, no national or provincial output figure was available for 1965. The only exception is Heilung-kiang, where the sown acreage was reported at 73,370 hectares.[118] Apparently not much progress was made in 1965; we therefore assume that output was the same as 1964.

The 1966 output in Heilungkiang was reported to be 10 per cent above that of 1965.[119] This percentage increase is the basis for estimating 1966 output.

For 1967, it was reported that production increased 15 per cent over 1966.[120] Our estimate in Table 24 is based on this reported increase.

Ramie

The main ramie-producing provinces are Hupeh, Hunan, Szechwan, and Kiangsi along the Yangtze River. More than one half of the ramie grown in China comes from these four provinces, and among these Hupeh is the leading producer.[121] Three crops of ramie can be grown in a year.

Before World War II, China was the leading ramie-producing nation in the world. The prewar average output was 45,000 M.T. per year.[122] About one half of the annual output was used domestically, while the other half was exported to Japan, the United Kingdom, France, and the United States. In 1936 total export was 19,747 M.T.

Total output of ramie was 51,350 M.T. in 1947. Production declined sharply in 1949 and it was not until 1955 that the output and acreage of ramie regained prewar levels.[123] For the period 1953 to 1955, average annual output was 52,681 M.T.,[124] of which Hupeh accounted for 27.6 per cent and Hunan and Szechwan accounted for 19 per cent each. These three provinces produced nearly two thirds of the

nation's total output. Since Hupeh and Hunan accounted for 46.6 per cent of China's production in
1953, the output in these two provinces is used in
estimating total national output in Table 25. Our
estimates show that output in recent years was in
the range of 50,000-70,000 M.T. per year. A Japanese source, however, reports that Chinese production of ramie is about 80,000 M.T. per year, accounting for approximately 80 per cent of the world's
total.[125] It was reported by the same source that
annual export by China is about 20,000 M.T.

The only data on ramie exports are those published by the FAO, which are shown in Table 26.
The FAO series, however, only extends to 1961. It
is possible that export of ramie from China has been
insignificant since 1962. Average export was about
5,700 M.T. per year for the 1956-61 period. Before
1957, the U.S.S.R. was the main ramie importing
country. China's export to the U.S.S.R. was 5,500
M.T. in 1957, or 77.5 per cent of the total exported.
Since 1958 the U.S.S.R. has not imported any ramie
at all.[126] This may be one of the major reasons for
the decline in exports. Japan also imported ramie
from China; the amount of import was 1,500 M.T. in
1958, 1,700 M.T. in 1959, 1,400 M.T. in 1960, and
500 M.T. in 1961. France imported 1,100 M.T. in
1961 from China.[127]

Hemp

The main producing areas of hemp are northeastern China (Manchuria), east China, and some
parts of Szechwan. Production is for domestic use
and exports to such countries as Japan, the United
Kingdom, and Germany.[128]

Before World War II, hemp production was reported to be 63,637 M.T. annually, and its acreage
at 127,595 hectares in northeastern China; for
North China, production was said to be 26,000 M.T.
per year.[129] But no data were available for total
national output. Since 1949 there have been neither
official reports nor Western estimates of national

TABLE 25

Acreage and Production of Ramie in Hupeh and
Hunan and National Production Estimates

	Acreage (ha.)		Production (M.T.)		Estimated National Production
	Hupeh	Hunan	Hupeh	Hunan	
1953[1]	11,313	...[a]	14,556	10,000	52,695[2]
1964	...	6,670[3]	...	8,584[4]	45,179[b]
1965	12,006[5]	9,338[3]	15,452[5]	12,018[4]	58,948[c]
1966	14,407[6]	...	18,542[6]	...	67,181[d]

[a] "..." indicates "no data are available."

[b] Hunan accounted for 19 per cent of the total output in 1953.

[c] Hupeh accounted for 27.6 per cent and Hunan, 19 per cent of the total output, respectively.

[d] Hupen produced 27.6 per cent of the total output.

Sources:

1. Liu Hung-chu, Wo-kuo ti Ma (China's Hard Fibres, Peking, 1956), p. 49.

2. Ibid., pp. 49-54.

3. NCNA (Jan. 8, 1966).

4. According to China's Hard Fibres, the yield in Hupeh in 1953 was 1,287 kg/ha. We assume that the yield in Hunan is the same as that in Hupeh.

5. NCNA (April 20, 1965). The yield is assumed to remain at the 1953 level, i.e., 1,287 kg/ha.

6. NCNA (Aug. 9, 1966). The yield is also assumed to be 1,287 kg/ha.

TABLE 26

Ramie Exports, 1956-61
(thousand M.T.)

	Exports
1956	14.9
1957	7.1
1958	3.7
1959	3.2
1960	2.6
1961	2.9

Sources: For 1956-60, see FAO, 1961 Trade Yearbook
           (1962), p. 284; for 1961, see FAO, 1962
           Trade Yearbook (1963), p. 281.

output.   Information on provincial production and
acreage is also fragmentary.   According to Liu, annual production for the country as a whole was
about 108,600 M.T. during 1950-55, with Anhwei accounting for 9.2 per cent of the total, Shansi 13.8
per cent, and Shantung 12.4 per cent in 1953.[130]

    One source revealed that in 1965 the yield of
hemp ranged between 2,249 kg/ha and 3,748 kg/ha,
with an average yield of about 3,000 kg/ha.[131]   For
1963 to 1965, acreage figures are available for
Anhwei and Shantung.   The estimated provincial and
national output for this period is shown in Table
27.

    China's exports of hemp are shown in Table 28.
There has been a drastic decline in exports since
1956.

TABLE 27

Estimates of Selected Provincial Output
and National Output of Hemp

	1963			1964			1965		
	Acreage (ha.)	Provincial Output[a] (M.T.)	National Output (M.T.)	Acreage (ha.)	Provincial Output[a] (M.T.)	National Output (M.T.)	Acreage (ha.)	Provincial Output[a] (M.T.)	National Output (M.T.)
Shansi	11,206[1]	33,618	235,237	5,336[2]	16,008	222,333	5,603[3]	16,809	244,569
Shantung	9,338[4]	28,014 61,632		10,672[5]	32,016 48,024		12,006[6]	36,018 52,827	

[a]Provincial output is estimated on the basis of the 1965 average yield of 3,000 kg/ha. Total output for the country as a whole is estimated from the 1953 relative shares of the national output produced by the following provinces: Anhwei, 9.2 per cent of total output; Shansi, 13.8 per cent; Shantung, 12.4 per cent.

Sources:

1. Ta-kung Pao (Peking, Sept. 30, 1963).

2. NCNA (Peking, Aug. 14, 1964).

3. Radio Hofei (Aug. 30, 1965).

4. PF (Jan. 2, 1964).

5. NCNA (Peking, Oct. 22, 1965).

6. NCNA (Peking, Oct. 1965).

TABLE 28

Hemp Exports,[a] 1956-65
(thousand M.T.)

Year	Exports
1956	12.5
1957	2.4
1958	3.0
1959	3.6
1960	3.8
1961	2.3
1962	0.9
1963	0.4
1964	0.3
1965	0.6

[a]Hemp tow and waste.

Sources: 1956-60 figures are from FAO, 1961 Trade
          Yearbook (1962), p. 226; 1961-65 figures
          are from FAO, 1966 Trade Yearbook (1967),
          p. 268.

Jute

China is a net importer of jute, although next
to India she is the second largest jute producing
country in the world. The main producing areas are
Chekiang, Kwangtung, Kiangsi, Hunan, and Kiangsu.
According to a 1965 report, production in these
five provinces accounts for 95 per cent of the

total national output; of the five provinces,
Chekiang alone produces one half of the total.[132]

The outputs in 1957 and 1958 were said to be
307,750 tons and 309,000 tons respectively.[133] From
1950 to 1959, production of jute increased by 200
per cent, but subsequently declined considerably
during 1960-62. However, the level of output was
reported to have recovered since 1963.[134]

Several divergent estimates of jute output are
available. A Japanese source estimated production
in recent years at 300,000 M.T.[135] Estimates made
by the FAO for 1957-65 are shown in Table 29. It
averaged about 353,000 M.T. per year, a little higher than the Japanese estimate. The Far Eastern Economic Review estimated that output of jute and
kenaf was about 450,000 tons in recent years.[136]

In February, 1966, a National Jute Production
Conference was held in Peking for the purpose of
continuing the effort to increase both acreage and
yield. It was reported at the conference that
Chekiang, Kwangtung, Fukien, and Kiangsu had a relatively good harvest in 1965, while Kiangsi and Hunan
had also begun to move toward higher production.
But total output was said to be still insufficient
to meet domestic demand. The conference then
called for increased production by enlarging the
acreage for jute in areas suitable for its cultivation.[137] It may be inferred from reports on the
conference that production has not been entirely
satisfactory. The recent output of jute may still
be at the 1957-58 level, i.e., around 300,000 M.T.
The FAO's estimates may therefore be somewhat too
high.

China's exports and imports of jute are shown
in Table 30. The data show that her net imports
of jute have increased substantially since 1960.

TABLE 29

Jute Production, 1957-65
(thousand M.T.)

	FAO Estimates
1957	305
1958	309
1959	...[a]
1960	...
1961	296
1962	300
1963	350
1964	390
1965	430
1966[b]	460
1967[b]	480

[a]"..." indicates "no data available."

[b]Includes kenaf and arbitilon.

Sources: 1957 figure is from FAO, 1958 Production Yearbook (1959), p. 136; 1958 figure is from FAO, 1961 Production Yearbook (1962), p. 143; 1961-65 figures are from FAO, 1966 Production Yearbook (1967), p. 270.

TABLE 30

Jute Trade in 1956-65
(thousand M.T.)

	FAO Estimates		
	Exports	Imports	Net Imports
1956	24.8	31.0	6.2
1957	8.7	13.8	5.1
1958	3.6	7.4	3.8
1959	2.5	12.6	10.1
1960	1.0	14.5	13.5
1961	0.4	14.6	14.2
1962	...	13.0	...
1963	0.5	22.9	22.4
1964	...	56.7	...
1965	...	60.6	...

Sources: 1956-60 figures are from FAO, 1961 Trade Yearbook (1962), pp. 221-83; 1961-65 figures are from FAO, 1966 Trade Yearbook (1967), p. 292.

Raw Silk

The leading producing provinces of raw silk are Chekiang, Kiangsu, Kwangsi, and Kwangtung. Maximum annual production during the pre-Sino-Japanese War period was estimated at not less than 12,335 M.T.[138] As a result of the war, production fell to 3,720 M.T. in 1946.[139] After 1949, however, production was encouraged by the Communist government and rose from 3,548 M.T. in 1952 to 6,191 M.T. in 1956, 6,563 M.T. in 1957, and 7,548 M.T. in 1958.[140]

A Japanese sericulture mission sent to China by the Central Raw Silk Association of Japan in April, 1967, reported upon its return that China's raw silk production had increased at an annual growth rate of 15 per cent during the preceding several years and that growth was likely to continue. For 1965 the mission estimated Chinese raw silk output at 9,600-10,200 M.T.[141] On the basis of the 15 per cent annual growth rate, we could estimate the production in 1966 to be between 11,000 and 11,700 M.T. and that of 1967 at 12,700 to 13,500 M.T. In other words, by 1967 production had regained the prewar level.

China's export of silk and silk fabrics has been growing in importance, especially in recent years. The United Kingdom, the Soviet Union, Poland, Italy, and France have been among the large importers of silk and silk fabrics from China. Even Japan, an exporter of raw silk until recently, imported 732 M.T. of raw silk from China in 1966, which amounted to 60 per cent of Japan's total silk imports in that year.[142] During the same year France imported 583 M.T. of silk from China and only 24 M.T. from Japan.[143] The low price of Chinese silk has begun to pose a threat to Japanese raw silk producers. During its visit to China in 1967, the Japanese mission informed China of the wish of the Japanese raw silk industry to have China join the International Silk Association and to adopt the Japanese standard export price of U.S. $15 per kg as a reference point for pricing.[144] Peking, however, maintained silence on this point.[145]

Table 31 presents China's raw silk exports in 1956-65. Reflecting the decrease in production, Chinese silk export contracted during 1958-62 and reached its lowest point in the latter year. Exports started to increase in 1963 and reached the 1957 level in 1965.

TABLE 31

Silk Exports, 1956-65 (M.T.)

1956	3,847
1957	3,424
1958	2,674
1959	3,019
1960	2,344
1961	1,832
1962	1,088
1963	1,232
1964	1,816
1965	3,282

Sources: For 1956-59, see FAO, 1961 Trade Yearbook (1962), pp. 209, 282; for 1960-65, see FAO, 1966 Trade Yearbook (1967), p. 279.

Concluding Remarks

The detailed data on the production and trade in selected crops have been presented in the preceding sections. Our findings are summarized in Table 32, where our estimates of production in recent years are placed against the background of the prewar and the pre-"Great Leap" data.

The following observations may be made. Comparing the production of these crops under the Communist regime with that of the prewar period, of the eight vegetable oil seeds, output has exceeded the unadjusted prewar level only in the case of soybean, peanut, tea seed, and possibly castor bean. Production of rapeseed and sesame never reached the prewar level. For sunflower seed and perilla, no information is readily available for such a comparison. The output levels of tung oil and raw silk are about equal to the prewar figures in recent years. For the other crops, outputs of both sugar cane and sugar beets, ramie, tobacco, and probably hemp have surpassed the prewar levels. No information is available for jute.

If the adjusted prewar production figures are used (see Note a, Table 32), then only the outputs of two oil seeds (castor bean and tea seed) would exceed the prewar levels.

The "Great Leap Forward" brought about declines in the outputs of all crops for which information is available. These include soybeans, peanuts, rapeseed, sugar cane, sugar beets, jute, and tobacco. The production of castor beans and ramie has probably also decreased. In the case of sesame, tea seed, sunflower seed, perilla, silk, and tung oil, no information is available for comparing the pre-"Great Leap" output with that of the post-"Great Leap" period. For hemp alone no decline may have occurred. The earliest year in which recovery from the decline was reported is 1962 (peanuts); for the other crops, recovery was said to have set in over the years 1963-65. The degree of recovery from the "Great Leap" setback is also not uniform. The

TABLE 32

Production of Selected Crops (Summary)
(unit: million M.T. except as otherwise noted)

Crops	1931-37 (Unadjusted)	(Adjusted)[a]	1952	1957	1958	1959	1960
Soybeans	10.36	13.81	9.50	10.05	10.50	11.50	5.6-8.71
Peanuts	2.85	3.80	2.32	2.57	2.80	2.27	2.27
Rapeseed	2.47	3.67	0.93	0.89	1.10	1.10	1.00
Sesame	0.85[b]	1.13	0.52	0.33	0.28	...	...
Tea Seed Oil (M.T.)	25,000 (1937)		...	94,000	100,000	...	...
Castor Bean (M.T.)	25,000 - 30,000[d]		40,000[c] (1952-56)	...	...	...	...
Sunflower Seed (M.T.)	...		...	...	...	...	...
Perilla (M.T.)	128,000 (1934-37)[d]		...	...	...	...	...
Tung Oil	0.12		...	...	...	...	...
Ramie (M.T.)	45,000		52,695 (1953)	...	...	...	...
Jute (M.T.)	...		...	307,750	309,000	...	...
Hemp (M.T.)	63,637[d] 26,000[e]		108,600 (1950-55)	...	...	...	...
Sugar Cane	5.65 (1940)		7.12	10.39	13.53	13.93	10.87
Sugar Beets	0.33 (1939)		0.48	1.50	2.90	3.68	2.92
Silk (M.T.)	...		3,548	6,563	7,548	...	...
Flue-cured Tobacco	.09[b] (1937)		0.22	0.26	0.38	0.42	...

[a]The adjusted amounts are 1-1/3 of the unadjusted figures. The adjustment is made to correct the underestimation of prewar output due to the large amount of unrecorded land in China. The adjustment factor of 1-1/3 is supplied by O. L. Dawson.

961	1962	1963	1964	1965	1966	1967
6-8.71	5.6-8.69	7.6-8.99	8.1-9.12	8.1-9.12	8.1-9.12	8.1-9.12
1.70	1.98	2.18	2.75	2.80	2.86	2.92
0.85	0.96	1.01	1.74	1.91	1.91	2.10
0.33[c]	0.34[c]	0.34[c]	0.37[c]	0.32	...	...
...	...	...	...	...	...	...
5,000[c] (961-62)		...	...	...	...	...
1,000[c]	66,000[c]	66,000[c]	66,000[c]	66,000[c]	...	...
...	...	...	...	...	...	...
...	...	0.10-0.12 (1963-67)				
...	...	...	45,179	58,948	67,181	
,000[c]	300,000[c]	350,000[c]	390,000[c]	430,000[c]	...	
...	...	235,237	222,333	244,569	...	
.80	5.67-8.41	8.43-9.07	12.49-13.33	14.37-16.02	15.49-18.37	17.81
.16	2.16	2.92	3.42	3.42	3.76	4.32
..	...	...	...	9,600-10,200	11,000-11,700	12,769-13,500
..	...	0.20	0.26	0.42	0.43	0.45

[b]China proper--twenty-two provinces only.
[c]FAO estimates.
[d]Northeastern China.
[e]North China.

pre-"Great Leap" height in output has not been
reached for soybeans as late as 1967; the same conclusion probably holds true for castor beans. For
peanuts, production reached the pre-"Great Leap"
maximum by 1965. The production of the following
crops, on the other hand, has exceeded their highest pre-"Great Leap" level: jute (1963), rapeseed
(1964), tobacco (1965), ramie (1965), sugar cane
(1965), and sugar beets (1966).

The following conclusions seem to be warranted.
First, there is a general decline during the "Great
Leap" period in the outputs of the crops included
in this report. The decrease in production set in
as early as 1959 but mostly in 1960. Second, the
earliest year in which recovery from the aftermath
of the "Great Leap" occurred is 1962; but the production of most crops recovered in 1963 and, in
some cases, recovery did not take place until 1965.
Third, the oil crops as a group seem to lag behind
in recovering from the disastrous results of the
"Great Leap Forward," while the sugar crops and
fibers appear to have performed much better. We
might conjecture that the difference in performance
between the oil crops and the others is due to several reasons: (1) The heavy emphasis on food grain
production in the post-"Great Leap" period may have
required reductions in the acreage of some oil-
yielding crops such as soybeans in Manchuria, thereby limiting the extent of recovery that could be
attained; (2) divergent developments in the world
market for these crops may be another factor; (3)
the decline in Soviet trade with China could also
have an adverse effect on the production of the oil
seeds.

If the relatively liberal economic policy of
the post-"Great Leap" period is continued--which
depends on the outcome of the Cultural Revolution--
one could expect continued expansion of the output
of these crops in the future. On the other hand,
the above-mentioned factors may militate against
any rapid recovery and development of oil-seed production. The world demand for oil seeds may be

inelastic, thus precluding the development of new
outlets for Chinese products. Under such circumstances, if production does increase continuously,
the increased output would flow into the domestic
market. One would then expect domestic consumption
to rise. Also, the limiting factor to increased
production does not lie in land utilization alone.
Much of future increase will depend on the production and allocation of fertilizers. Thus if the
present emphasis on food grain production is maintained, the possibility of rapid expansion of oil-
seed output will necessarily be limited.

Forestry

As noted in the prewar review, China's vast
forest area had been gradually denuded. Mountain
ranges were deforested and due to heavy overcutting
serious soil erosion had resulted, especially in
the watersheds of the Yellow and Yangtze rivers.
As a result China was short of timber and forced to
make heavy imports to meet essential needs.

The Communists were early aware of the critical need of conserving and increasing forestry production. The development and increased efficiency
of irrigation depended on water conservation. The
principal projects in the first Five-Year Plan were
designed to regulate river flow onto the North China
plain.[146] Projects included forty-six large dams in
the upper reaches of the Yellow River and other
major projects. To be successful, these ambitious
projects required vast catchment-afforestation
schemes and shelter-belt establishment.

If the total cultivated area amounts to some
11 per cent of the land area of China, about 10 per
cent of the remainder is under forest. This may
reach near 100 M hectares, although much of it is
inaccessible. Ambitious plans for protection of
forestry were sketched out involving some 100 million hectares of "wasteland and desert." The
Minister of Forestry said this was only a start:
To plant trees on 100 M hectares in twelve years

was only a beginning and there were still 70 to 100 million hectares of barren mountains to afforest. Great shelter belts were planned, and it was even thought a large part of the cultivated area of China could be planted to trees.

The great needs of China were for timber for expanding railways and for fuel wood and paper. Educational needs and propaganda campaigns demanded geometrically increased supplies of paper. This latter need could be to some extent met by other sources of pulp. Many forestry plantations established since the Communist take-over may eventually contribute to the pulp wood resources, which make up 30 per cent of the requirement, but there is now a patent dearth of all kinds of forest products in China, particularly for construction purposes, according to S. D. Richardson.[147]

There is a variety of estimates relating to industrial wood production in China during 1957-58. Richardson accepts 28 M^3 for 1957 and 35 M^3 for 1958 for industrial wood (i.e., excluding fuel) removals. FAO estimated 39 M^3 for 1960. There was a decline from 1960 based on end-use categories. Richardson puts timber production in 1962 at 29 M, or about a recovery to the 1957 level. The drop in production was due to the general retrenchment in heavy industry. Until such time as the Chinese publish formal statistics, the estimates from various sources must be treated with reserve.

With recovery in the developing economy since 1963, great demands are being made on timber output for construction purposes and for pulp or fiber. According to the People's Daily (Jan. 24, 1958), the deficit by 1972 might reach 38.5 M^3.[148] This could partly be made up by produce from afforestation schemes. But since there is widespread evidence of failure in these plantations--and it is realized they cannot be relied on to supplement production from the natural forests in the near future-- Chinese foresters have been made uncomfortably aware of the dangers of overcutting their limited resources.

Legislation was made in 1963 to conserve forests
and timber and to use timber substitutes where possible. This also seems reflected in gradual tem-
porary reduction output.[149]

In connection with over-all requirements for
timber, not sufficient consideration has been made
for fuel wood. No forest areas are maintained specifically for this purpose. The bulk of the requirement is filled by loppings of branches, dead
trees, and debris from the forest floor. Peasants
have been allowed to remove trees and prune dead
branches at two-year intervals. These practices
have promoted an interest in early mortality of
trees and also the disfigurement of trees by reck-
less pruning. A more satisfactory program for meeting fuel wood requirements is much needed.

According to Richardson, the estimated future
requirements of wood for forest products in 1975
for Mainland China will be 150 M^3, and supply only
107 M^3, showing a deficit of 43 M^3.[150] He also be-
lieves that forest resources will last only about
thirty years. It is difficult to forecast to what
extent afforestation projects will contribute to
the national timber requirement.[151] At the rate of
annual consumption in 1962, it would equal some
.05 ca M compared to 1.88 in the United States.

Many visitors to China in recent years have
been amazed at the vast scale on which afforestation has been attempted, and claims of the Chinese
have been startling. But the failure of plantations
has been widespread and, according to Richardson,
"over vast areas particularly in the hilly country
plantations now provide ground cover of less than
50 per cent. In many instances survival in terms
of number of stems is less than 10 per cent."[152]
Chinese claims are higher, but their method of calculation is not realistic. Chinese labor in afforestation has been prodigious, but much of the effort
has been nullified by poor maintenance. Since 1960,
regulations designed to ensure proper care and
adequate protection have been issued, and it is

hoped that in a few years a self-sufficient forestry
program will be under way.

Fisheries

China has one of the largest fishing areas of
the world, but the catch estimated by FAO at some
5 million tons for 1959 was only some 14 per cent
of the world catch of 35 million.

The pressing demand for increased sources of
food quantitatively and especially qualitatively
due to deficient sources of protein in the Chinese
diet has impressed the Communist authorities, and
active measures were taken to expand the fishing industry. Besides, a large number of aquatic products
are important in the export trade.

Prior to the Communist take-over, about two
thirds of the fish catch was from marine sources
close to the coast. Owing to transportation and
marketing problems, the major part of the marine
catch was concentrated near the coast; as a result,
the large mass of the population in the interior
had a very sparse access to fishing, with the result
that the average consumption of fish per capita for
all China was and still is lamentably low.

Since the Communist take-over, the freshwater
fishing industry has taken great strides to a more
important place in the total fishery output, providing more needed supplies from rivers, lakes, ponds,
and rice paddies for interior consumption. A table
of production by provinces would be impressive but
cannot be included in this brief review.

In 1953 an estimate of inland fishery production was given as only 1-1/2 million tons, which in
1959 had increased to some 2-1/2 million tons, or
nearly 50 per cent of the total catch compared with
about one third prewar.

Figures on available freshwater area of China
are imposing if acceptable. According to Mr.

Solecki, the total area of fresh water in China
(excluding paddy fields) has been estimated at 20
million hectares (Saburenkov 1961, Joint Publications Research Service [JPRS], U.S. Department of
Commerce 11475), of which one third could be used
for fish culture.[153] In addition, it was estimated
another 1.5 million tons could be produced in paddy
fields. There are also reservoirs and other potential areas, although of small total capacity.

Marine Fisheries Resources

Mainland China faces the sea over a distance
of 14,000 kilometers. In addition there are along
the coast approximately 5,000 islands that bring
the length of the coastline to between 20,000 and
21,000 kilometers (Saburenkov 1961, JPRS 11475).
Along this coast the area within twenty miles of
the shore line amounts to 150 million hectares, comprising 23.7 per cent of the total fishing grounds
of the world. The area of the sea shelf suitable
for fish culture amounts to 1 million hectares.
Chinese territorial waters consequently extend over
both temperate and tropical zones of marine resources.

Estimates of landings from the Chinese fishing
grounds have varied greatly in recent years, running
around 4.5 million tons from marine fisheries.

The total possible catch including freshwater
landings was estimated at 7.4 million tons.[154] In
weight this was stated to be equal to 20 million
head of cattle, 70 million pigs, or 300 million
sheep. The comparison on the basis of weight is
useful for illustrative purposes if correct, but
from the standpoint of comparative use is limited.

Solecki goes on to state that at the end of
1962 only one eighth of the freshwater areas and
one tenth of the coastal ports and bays were said
to be utilized, and that the middle and surface
layers of the East China and Yellow seas have been
poorly exploited.

According to the statement of the Ministry of
Aquatic Producers, by the end of the second Five-
Year Plan (1958-62) the annual output of the fishing industry was to have reached 20 million tons.
This enormous increase was to have been achieved by
shifting emphasis from marine to freshwater culture.
One of the most persistent notes in the government
statements has been that the fishing resources of
the country are not sufficiently utilized. Other
statements indicate progress has been made within
limits of available resources.

Fish Culture in Marine Waters

At the conference of fish-culture experts held
in Kwantung Province in March, 1959, the special advantages of fish rearing in the sea were set forth.
Sea water is rich in available food, plankton, in
fish-rearing areas, and oxygen is constantly re-
plenished by the tides.

At the beginning of the present decade the
total fish culture production accounted for 32 to
36 per cent of the total output, with over 55 per
cent being obtained from the seas.[155] Total marine
areas suitable for culture were estimated at 450,000
hectares. However, Chang (1959) gave the total salt-
water area suitable for culture as 900,000 hectares,
with only 90,000 being utilized. The higher yield
of fish from culture areas is striking. It is possible to obtain 35 kg of fish from .06 ha by
rearing, and only 5 kg without rearing. Yet in
1961 only 14 per cent of the water areas suitable
for rearing were being utilized.

Other Marine Products
of Importance

These include sea weed, kelp, and different
forms of algae which grow in abundance and are increasing. Other products include mussels, sea
cucumbers, prawns, shrimp, and abalone, besides
crabs, clams, and scallops. The total production
of these products is not given, but they are a

large and important food source in addition to fish
and provide many products for export.

The whaling industry has become important in
recent years and the catch during the first half of
1962 was 104, which was more than the whole catch
for 1961 and at the present time (1967) must have
grown considerably.

Other Freshwater Products

In plans for fisheries development, freshwater
area can be profitably used for growing a number of
valuable plants such as lotus or water caltrap,
reed and rushes and other plants used for paper or
malting, and lotus water roots. It was stated one
mow could produce enough to feed three hogs, as reported to Mr. Solecki.[156] This seems too high, or
else it would be a phenomenal source of hog feed.
Water chestnuts are widely raised, and production
in some provinces very large, as in Kiangsi. There
are numbers of other items too numerous to list but
important for food and industry.

Processing, Marketing, and Foreign Trade

Dried and salted fish, canned fish, fish sau-
sage, and frozen fish, as well as fresh fish, are
produced and consumed by the Chinese people. The
government has provided several fish-marketing centers and facilities, including freezing plants.
The price of fishery products produced and sold in-
ternally is fixed by the government.

In the northern part of the country 70 to 75
per cent of the catch is sold in live, fresh or
frozen form. In subtropical regions 70 per cent
is deep-salted or dried. Recently there has been
a significant expansion in freezing facilities. In
the spring of 1957 the refrigerating capacity of
meat-packing and cold-storage houses was said to
have increased over 4-1/2 times the 1949 level, but
not all of it was available to the fishing industry.
However, since 1959 it has been adequate.

In 1964, China imported 15,300 metric tons of fishery products from Japan, valued at U.S. $13.9 million.[157]   Imports included live fish; fresh, frozen, salted and dried, and canned fish; and such nonedible fishery products as agar and seashells. Up to 1960, when trade declined to a very small volume, the U.S.S.R. was one of the most important buyers of Chinese fish.

Communist China in 1964 exported U.S. $37.7 million of edible fishery products to Free World countries, surpassing even the Soviet Union (whose comparable exports amounted to U.S. $23.7 million).[158]   The 1964 export figure represented a large increase in value over 1963, when Communist China exported U.S. $21 million worth of edible fishery products to Free World countries.

Policies and Outlook

The post-World War II development of Communist Chinese fisheries has been characterized by the two Five-Year Development Plans (1953-57 and 1958-62). These plans, for the most part, have emphasized the development of inland and coastal fisheries, including extensive fish culture of freshwater and marine species, through collective effort. A "Walking on Two Legs" policy was applied to fisheries development, and in fisheries terms meant the simultaneous development of the ocean fishing industry and the inland fishing industry, including emphasis on intensifying fishing effort and on the propagation of various species through fish culture.

Cooperative associations, people's communes, state-owned companies, and provincial government-managed enterprises all contribute to fishery production. Cooperative associations and people's communes (people-operated fisheries), however, have contributed by far the greatest share of the catch, and have consistently out-produced state-operated fisheries enterprises. State-owned enterprises have only recently emerged as a dominant factor in the development of the distant-water phase of

China's fishing operations; the high cost of developing high-seas fishing capability is undoubtedly
the reason for this. The rate at which Communist
China will develop its distant-water fisheries will
depend much upon the capital that can be diverted
to the procurement of high-seas fishing and support
vessels, trained manpower, and mechanized equipment.
Fish culture in both marine and inland areas is being intensively developed and has good future prospects.

Organization and Administration

As with other Communist countries, notably the
Soviet Union, the state (central government) directs
all fisheries policy and planning. The fishing industry of Communist China is under the Ministry of
Fisheries, which was officially established in 1956.
At the provincial level, either a Fisheries Department or Fisheries Bureau has been established, depending upon the particular province involved. A
Fisheries Department is administered by the Provincial People's Council as distinguished from a Fisheries Bureau, which can be administered by either
the Provincial People's Council or the Agriculture
Bureau.

Conclusions

There is no doubt that the fishing industry of
China has experienced a rapid increase in the last
fifteen years but now experiences some problems in
obtaining equipment to expand in deep-sea areas
where the good prospects lie. Another area where
much expansion can take place is through freshwater
culture of aquatic products. But development is
hampered by shortage of trained manpower, capital,
and technical knowledge. A number of fishery institutes have been set up for training of technicians.

In spite of the increase in production over the
recent years, the per capita output of aquatic products is only some 20 pounds compared with Japan's
120 pounds. To double or triple it by 1975-76 to
meet food and industry needs will require strong
government support.

NOTES

1. <u>1967 Yearbook on Chinese Communism</u> (Taipei,
Taiwan, 1967), p. 980.

2. "Provincial Reviews," <u>Agricultural Notes</u>
(U.S. Consulate General, Hong Kong, 1964-67).

3. <u>Ibid</u>.

4. Ting Yin, <u>Techniques for Rice Cropping in
China</u> (Peking, 1952).

5. Shen Yu-Ching, "A Discussion on the Position and Prospect of Wheat Among China's Food
Grains," <u>Chinese Agriculture Journal</u> (June 23, 1957).

6. <u>Ibid</u>.

7. John Lossing Buck, Owen L. Dawson, and
Yuan-li Wu, <u>Food and Agriculture in Communist China</u>
Published for the Hoover Institution on War, Revo-
lution and Peace, Stanford University (New York and
London: Frederick A. Praeger, 1966).

8. National Conference on Wheat Research Work,
"The Key to High Yields of Wheat in Common Fields,"
<u>Agricultural Science Bulletin</u> (Sept. 6, 1958).

9. Tseng-ling, "Food and Feed Functions of
Sweet Potatoes," <u>Economic Research</u> (May, 1958).

10. Shen Tsung-han, <u>Chung-kuo Nung-yeh Tzu-yüan</u>
(<u>Agricultural Resources in China</u>, Taipei, Taiwan,
1953), pp. 169-74.

11. <u>Ta-kung-pao</u> (Peking, Dec. 18, 1962).

12. <u>Wei-ta ti Shih-nien</u> (<u>Ten Great Years</u>,
Peking, 1959), p. 109.

13. <u>Ta-kung-pao</u>, <u>op. cit</u>.

14. <u>Jen-min Jih-pao</u> (<u>People's Daily</u>, Sept. 15,
1965).

15. Ta-kung-pao, op. cit.

16. Shen Tsung-han, op. cit., pp. 170-71.

17. State Statistical Bureau Communique in People's Daily (Sept. 25, 1958; Jan. 3, 1959).

18. NCNA (Nov. 3, 1967).

19. Nung-yeh T'ung-chi King-tso Shou-tse (Handbook for Agricultural Statistical Work, Peking, 1956), pp. 15-16, 40.

20. Shen Tsung-han, op. cit., p. 191.

21. Hua-sheng Tsai-p'ei (The Cultivation of Peanuts, Shanghai, 1963).

22. NCNA (Peking, Nov. 9 and 22, 1963).

23. NCNA (Peking, Oct. 18, 1963).

24. Ibid.

25. NCNA (Tsinam, Nov. 21, 1964).

26. Chung-kuo Esing-wen (China News Service [CNS], Canton, Sept. 7, 1963).

27. CNS (Oct. 11, 1963).

28. NCNA (Peking, Oct. 18, 1963).

29. CNS (Dec. 25, 1964).

30. NCNA (Tsinan, Nov. 21, 1964).

31. NCNA (Peking, Aug. 31, 1964).

32. CNS (Aug. 10, 1964).

33. NCNA (Peking, Nov. 9, 1965).

34. Nan-fang Jih-pao (Dec. 21, 1965).

35. NCNA (Peking, Nov. 7, 1965).

36. NCNA (Peking, Nov. 3, 1967).

37. Jen-min Jih-pao (People's Daily, June 15, 1957).

38. Shen Tsung-han, op. cit., p. 189.

39. Ibid.

40. Wei-ta ti Shih-nien (Ten Great Years), p. 109.

41. Ta-kung-pao (July 10, 1963).

42. NCNA (Peking, June 1, 1963).

43. Ibid.

44. CNS (Dec. 25, 1964).

45. NCNA (Peking, June 13, 1965).

46. Ibid.

47. NCNA (Peking, July 18, 1967).

48. NCNA (Peking, July 6, 1967).

49. Shen Tsung-han, op. cit., p. 193.

50. Ibid., p. 170.

51. Yuan-li Wu and others, The Economic Potential of Communist China, Vol. II (Stanford Research Institute, Menlo Park, Calif., 1963), p. 59.

52. Fei-ching Yueh-pao (Monthly Report on Communist China, June, 1960), p. 51.

53. 1966 Far Eastern Economic Review Yearbook (Hong Kong), pp. 132, 134.

54. Shen Tsung-han, op. cit., p. 198.

55. FAO, <u>1966 Production Yearbook</u> (1967),
p. 234.

56. Shen Tsung-han, <u>loc. cit</u>.

57. <u>Ibid</u>., p. 199.

58. <u>Chūgoku Kenkyū Geppō</u> (<u>Monthly Research on China</u>, May, 1964), pp. 33-34.

59. <u>Ibid</u>.

60. <u>Ta-kung Pao</u> (Peking, Aug. 9, 1962).

61. <u>Ibid</u>.

62. <u>Ibid</u>.

63. Shen Tsung-han, <u>op. cit</u>., p. 196.

64. <u>Ibid</u>.

65. <u>Ibid</u>.

66. <u>Ibid</u>., p. 175.

67. <u>Ibid</u>.

68. <u>Ibid</u>.

69. <u>Ajia Keizai Jumpō</u> (<u>Asian Economic Tri-monthly</u>, Oct., 1963), p. 2.

70. <u>Ibid</u>., p. 3.

71. FAO, <u>1966 Production Yearbook</u> (1967), p. 237.

72. USDA, <u>Foreign Agriculture Circular</u> (Oct., 1966), p. 21.

73. NCNA (Peking, April 22, 1964).

74. FAO, <u>1961 Trade Yearbook</u>, p. 286; <u>1966 Trade Yearbook</u>, p. 338.

75. _Ibid_.

76. Shen Tsung-han, _op. cit._, Vol. III, p. 13.

77. _Wei-ta ti Shih-nien_, _op. cit._, p. 109.

78. _Ibid_.

79. CNS (Jan. 24, 1960).

80. NCNA (Peking, Nov. 23, 1963).

81. CNS (July 23, 1964).

82. Radio Nanchang (Oct. 1, 1963).

83. CNS (Dec. 25, 1966).

84. NCNA (Peking, Sept. 23, 1966).

85. CNS (Sept. 28, 1965).

86. NCNA (Peking, Sept. 11, 1965); Radio Kweiyang (Nov. 2, 1965).

87. CNS (Sept. 29, 1966).

88. _Selections from China Mainland Magazines_ (SCMM), p. 25.

89. Shen Tsung-han, _op. cit._, p. 147.

90. _Ibid_.

91. _Wei-ta ti Shih-nien_, _op. cit._, p. 89.

92. _Ibid_.; _Peking Review_ (Jan. 26, 1960).

93. SCMM, _op. cit._, p. 27.

94. NCNA (Peking, May 1, 1966).

95. NCNA (Canton, April 25, 1963).

96.   SCMM, op. cit., p. 22.

97.   Ibid., p. 27.

98.   Ibid.

99.   Ibid.

100.   Edwin F. Jones, "The Emerging Pattern of China's Economic Revolution," An Economic Profile of Mainland China, Vol. I, Joint Economic Committee (Feb., 1967), p. 93.

101.   Chang Yen-tien, Population Growth and Food Production and Consumption in Taiwan (Taipei, 1967), p. 82.

102.   Statistical Abstract of the United States (1967), p. 88.

103.   NCNA (Peking, Nov. 12, 1963).

104.   SCMM, No. 194 (Jan. 4, 1960), p. 17.

105.   Ibid.

106.   Wei-ta ti Shih-nien, op. cit., p. 109.

107.   NCNA (Peking, June 7, 1961).

108.   CNS (Canton, Dec. 25, 1964), p. 10.

109.   Ta-kung Pao (Hong Kong, Oct. 27, 1967).

110.   Economic Geography of South China (1959).

111.   SCMM, No. 194 (Jan., 1960), p. 17.

112.   Ibid.

113.   Ibid.

114.   Ibid., p. 22.

115.   NCNA (Peking, June 7, 1961).

116. Inner Mongolia and Sinkiang were reported to have a yield per ha. of 22.5 M.T. (see SCMM, No. 194 [Jan., 1960], p. 23; NCNA [Urumchi, April 3, 1960]). The yield in Kirin was said to be 12 M.T. per ha. (see SCMM, op. cit., p. 23).

117. Another report claimed that sugar beets production increased by 107 per cent over 1963 (see CNS [Dec. 25, 1964], p. 10). Since this increase is much too high to be credible, it is possible that the figure given in the original news dispatch is the result of a typographical error.

118. Chinese Communism Yearbook, 1967, p. 987.

119. Jen-min Jih-pao (Peking, Oct. 12, 1966).

120. Ta-kung Pao (Hong Kong, Oct. 27, 1967).

121. NCNA (Peking, July 8, 1965).

122. Liu Hung-chou, Wo-kuo ti Ma (China's Hard Fibres, Peking, 1956), p. 48.

123. Ibid.

124. Ibid., pp. 49-54.

125. Ajia Keizai Jumpō (Asian Economic Tri-monthly, Jan., 1962), p. 5.

126. FAO, 1962 Trade Yearbook (1962), p. 281.

127. Ibid.

128. Liu Hung-chou, op. cit., p. 54.

129. Shen Tsung-han, op. cit., p. 60.

130. Liu Hung-chou, op. cit., pp. 54-59.

131. NCNA (Peking, Feb. 1, 1966).

132. NCNA (Hangchow, May 24, 1965).

133. The 1957 figure was reported by Po I-po in his speech at the National People's Congress on Feb. 3, 1958. The 1958 figure was reported in the State Statistical Bureau Communiqué of August 26, 1959.

134. Far Eastern Economic Review (Sept. 22, 1966), p. 572.

135. Ajia Keizai Jumpō (Jan., 1962), p. 9.

136. Far Eastern Economic Review (Sept. 22, 1966), p. 572.

137. NCNA (Peking, Feb. 1, 1966).

138. Shen Tsung-han, op. cit., p. 63.

139. Ibid.

140. Chūgoku Nenkan 1959 (China Yearbook 1959, Tokyo, 1960), p. 219.

141. China Trade Report (Hong Kong, May, 1967), p. 9.

142. Ibid.

143. Ibid.

144. According to the FAO, China exported its silk at U.S. $4.40 per kg in 1960-65 (see FAO, 1966 Trade Yearbook [1967], p. 279).

145. China Trade Report (May, 1967), p. 9.

146. Stanley D. Richardson, Forestry in Communist China (Baltimore: Johns Hopkins Press, 1966).

147. Ibid.

148. Ibid.

149. Ibid.

150. Ibid., Table A-7, p. 172.

151. Ibid., p. 173.

152. Ibid., p. 63.

153. Jan J. Solecki, Economic Aspects of the
Fishing Industry in Mainland China (Vancouver, B.C.:
Institute of Fisheries, University of British Colum-
bia, 1967).

154. Ibid.

155. Ibid.

156. Ibid.

157. Fishery Products Trade Statistics
(Tokyo: Fisheries Agencies, Japanese Government,
1964).

158. U.S. Department of Commerce.

ABOUT THE AUTHOR

Owen L. Dawson spent seventeen years in prewar China as United States Agricultural Attaché. With Dr. T. H. Shen, Director of the National Agricultural Research Bureau, he originated the Sino-American Agricultural Mission in 1948 and served as adviser on a fundamental program of agricultural reconstruction in China--a prelude to the first Five-Year Plan in Taiwan. From 1949-52, he was Economic Counselor to the U.S. Embassies in Korea and Taiwan and the ambassadors' representative on their Economic Stabilization Committees.

After retiring from the State Department in 1952, Mr. Dawson joined the Food and Agriculture Organization of the U.N. as Economist for South East Asia. He has also worked with an American engineering company as an agricultural adviser on planning crop programs in Iraq and is currently a consultant to the U.S. Department of Agriculture.

Mr. Dawson co-authored FOOD AND AGRICULTURE IN COMMUNIST CHINA and has published articles about China's agricultural situation in several journals. He received his B.S.A. from the College of Agriculture, University of Illinois and did graduate work at South Dakota State College and the U.S. Department of Agriculture's graduate school.